In memory of Tony Binns
(1943–1999)

CONTENTS

PROLOGUE

The black and white newspaper page from the early 1980s provides the haziest representation of the goal which delivered one of Liverpool Football Club's most improbable victories and how it came to pass.

There is the outline of a white-shirted footballer, the tight black shorts of his day barely covering the thighs, the arms outstretched as he, Ray Kennedy, holds his balance having struck the ball with his left foot. It is grainy, with none of the cropped-in, telephoto focus to which we have become accustomed, and which could shout down through the years the story of *that* goal, in Bayern Munich's Olympic Stadium.

And way down beneath, so small as to be barely legible, tucked away in near six-point type, are the briefest reflections of the Liverpool manager, which today, when every comment on football is pored over, deconstructed and analysed, would command the back page headline of every paper in the land. 'This was our 113th European match and I believe it was our best performance in all these years,' said Bob Paisley, after Kennedy's studiously delivered shot had brought him the goal which sent Liverpool forward into the final of the 1981 European Cup: a match which they would win, amid scenes of wild acclaim in Paris.

It was in an April clear-out that I stumbled across this clipping and more like it, cut out from the newspapers of early teenage years and later stuffed into a cardboard box. The fragments had been first read and collected at our home in North Wales, where the foggy impression of the Kennedy goal belonged to the beautiful mystique those football nights held back then. There were BBC radio commentaries of matches from distant lands, too, but it was the newspapers' breathless dispatches and corny headlines we really devoured. One for that Munich night, on which Liverpool's defence was beseiged, carried the headline: 'Back to the Blitz.'

Eight years after that match, I began my own career as a reporter on the *Liverpool Daily Post* – then still one of the great daily regional newspapers – in a city 50 miles away. In time, a circuitous path would lead me, late, into the world of sports reporting, for the *Independent,* then still one of the great daily national newspapers. By that point the monochrome world had long gone, replaced by a digital appetite for football information so relentless that the managers' words were the talk of the land within minutes of a post-match press conference. Nowadays their observations are dissected so relentlessly that they generally avoid giving out any superlatives for fear of generating hyperbole. Those words from Paisley in Munich – 'our best performance of all these years' – would be gold-dust now, republished thousands of times above an image of the manager.

It was the new world which, amid the smudged and faded clippings, provoked a thought about the old one: 'Where is Paisley?' How could he possibly be absent from this narrative? His tactical imagination against the Germans that night had certainly been just as significant as Kennedy's goal. His star forward, Kenny Dalglish, had been injured and withdrawn inside ten minutes. Paisley replaced him with Howard Gayle, a rookie substitute who became the game's outstanding player. He then substituted the substitute and, having done so, saw Liverpool's critical goal arrive. His defence was so injury-wracked that two of its constituent parts had a handful of games' experience between them. He had repositioned Kennedy, a midfielder, to the place where the centre-forward should be, when he scored. And yet Paisley barely emerged from the newspaper margins. He was the six-point leader, you might say.

Today we are hurtling through the age of the box-office football manager, in which the most ordinary of that number assume the significance of international statesmen, the best are considered divinely gifted, and someone as undemonstrative as Bob Paisley, with his propensity for flat caps, Brylcreem and cardigans, is considered an anachronism. Sir Alex Ferguson won the European Cup twice at the helm of Manchester United and in retirement has become the subject of Harvard theses, speaking tours and management manuals. Paisley won the European Cup three times. He became a freeman of the City of Liverpool.

Ferguson delivered 28 trophies in 27 years; Clough 11 trophies in 18 years. Paisley won 14 in nine years, adding six league titles to the European Cups. If success in football management is judged – as it well might be – by the ratio of trophies to seasons, then Paisley stands head and shoulders above them all: 1.5 to Clough's 0.61 and Ferguson's 1.03. And yet that Munich match report was a metaphor for his abiding obscurity. Why?

There is a clue on the cover of the definitive encyclopaedia of Liverpool FC, written by the club's celebrated Icelandic historians Arnie Baldursson and Gudmundur Magnusson. It carries a montage of those who have made Liverpool one of the most famous football teams in the world and on the right flank – the margins – is Paisley in flared grey suit and vivid, patterned tie, grinning. Centre stage, arms outstretched as if to say, 'This is what

I bequeathed you,' is the legendary Bill Shankly, Paisley's predecessor. Shankly was the man who took the club up to football's First Division, secured a first title in 17 years, and with his charisma and vaulting self-belief established himself in perpetuity as the man who made Liverpool great. Shankly *did* make Liverpool great. And Paisley made Liverpool very much greater.

Within three years of succeeding Shankly, he had delivered Liverpool's first European Cup, having introduced a new style of football. By the time he bowed out, he had won that trophy for a third time with an entirely reconstructed team. Shankly's Liverpool won the English title three times in 15 years. Only twice in eight years, after his own first season of acclimatisation, did any team *but* Paisley's Liverpool win that title.

Noisy, demonstrative, extrovert managers were becoming all the rage when, at the age of 55, Paisley succeeded Bill Shankly. Brian Clough, Malcolm Allison and Don Revie were the alpha-male leaders, running the alpha-male players who were living life large and basking in the new trappings of celebrity status.

Those managerial protagonists seem more attractive than ever now. We are transfixed as they leap to their feet from the dugout, ripping up the plan, ruling with a rod of iron, wheeling and dealing in the transfer market as football's carousel spins faster and faster. We like their sound and fury because anything less than noise is viewed with scepticism in football's widening gyre. The extrovert managers, with their jokes and aphorisms, controversies and stunts, make the writers' jobs so easy, too. They construct the narrative and write their own headlines.

Not so the introvert. Paisley's jokes were often lame, his County Durham accent was sometimes impenetrable and the idea of self-promotion embarrassed him. The only vivid aspect of Bob Paisley was the colour and pattern of his very wide ties.

Only in the past five years has quietness been shown to have a value in life, work and management. Susan Cain's analysis, in her book *Quiet*, reveals a group who 'listen more than they talk, think before they speak'. Some of the characteristics Cain describes – such as an aversion to personal conflict – do fit Paisley. Some, including a predisposition to deep conversations, do not. Invaluable though Cain's work was, in society at large and sport most particularly, there is still no recognition of quietness having, say, an equal value to extrovert behaviour.

But Paisley showed there was another way. The quiet man broke a football management mould by adhering to the principles and working practices that his predecessor, Bill Shankly, had put in place and resisting the temptation to rip it all up and create a team in his image. Then, undemonstratively and assuredly, he made changes to personnel and the playing system which took the team on to far greater heights.

With an innate distrust of grandstanding and the grandiose, Paisley worked in the finer details and built a route to success through the accretion of small improvements, decades before Dave Brailsford, as performance director of British Cycling, articulated the theory of marginal gains. 'There are no big things, only a logical accumulation of little things done at a very high standard of performance,' the late John Wooden, US basketball coach and leadership guru once said. Paisley left behind no such pearls of spoken wisdom, though these words pretty much encapsulate what he brought. Equally integral to his success was the capacity, identified by Cain as the crucial component of the quiet man's armoury, to empower others and to embrace their input.

To take failing teams to greatness – as Ferguson and Clough did – was an almighty challenge. To succeed a managerial legend and make a great club even greater was unprecedented. Twice in the past half-century, Manchester United have demonstrated the near impossibility of doing so. Cain's book was published in 2012, the year before Ferguson's departure from United presaged a chronic disintegration at Old Trafford, which reacquainted the club's faithful with an appreciation of what it takes to replace an individual who has become the heartbeat of a club. Ferguson's successors are still ripping it up and starting again.

Appreciation of Paisley did not seem to be tumbling out of that box of artefacts I found. There was an 'Official Annual' series that Liverpool produced for a number of years. He didn't even make it onto the cover of the 1983 edition, even though it was to be his final year at the helm. 'There's been a lot of talk about my retirement,' he says in the ghosted preface. 'As this is written, I can say that I've not made any decision yet. I'm still on a contract. I feel well, I have a few minor things to sort out about my pension but the main thing is that I'm not being forced into anything . . .'

How extraordinary to read Paisley – who had already delivered Liverpool 14 trophies in eight years by then – expressing gratitude that he was not being pushed out of the door.

It was in 1999, 13 years after he stepped down from the managerial seat and three years after his death, that his contribution was physically acknowledged in a set of black, wrought-iron gates erected outside the Liverpool FC stadium on Anfield Road. They were the product of the club's realisation that it might have done more to mark the achievement of its most successful manager. The ironwork included the words 'Paisley Gateway' – though with Liverpool's modern souvenir shop set ten metres behind them the gates did not lead anywhere. They were a 'gateway' to a redbrick wall. The accompanying tile depicting Paisley's face, set into brickwork beneath, is generally overlooked because the fans who pass by don't tend to stop and stare. They are absorbed by a different, more obvious landmark: the 7-foot-tall bronze statue of Bill Shankly, a few metres away.

As the club's search to rediscover the success Paisley brought them in the 1970s and 1980s goes on, the thirst quickens for an understanding of why he delivered so much. When one of the journalists who reported day to day on his managerial career, the *Daily Express's* John Keith, decided to stage a series of evening events in which some of Paisley's former players shared their memories, he found that they were quickly selling out. The response, on one of those evenings, when someone suggested that there should be a statue to Paisley too, was spontaneous and unscripted: 150 people rose to their feet in unanimous applause.

Beyond Liverpool, there is less talk, though. The 25th anniversary of Liverpool's last title – secured by Paisley's successor Kenny Dalglish with a squad including most of Paisley's team – came and went. Yet in the past two years, Paisley's body of work has warranted barely a hundred mentions in the quality national press, a fifth of the number claimed by Brian Clough.

How could it have been that an individual so lacking in the egotism which has been a prerequisite of elite football could come to command a dressing-room of stars? How did he manage to assemble the greatest side of the late 1970s and 1980s when he lacked the powers of oration and was so palpably undemonstrative? How did he accomplish the feat of becoming Bill Shankly's successor when football is littered with stories of failure after the second in command has stepped up to fill such huge boots? How did he keep winning, year after year? What did he really feel about the fact that the Shankly legend overshadowed him back then, as it still does now?

There was not a single image in the newspapers of Paisley from that spring evening in Munich, though the photographic archive did turn one up. It reveals the Liverpool 'dugout' in the Olympic Stadium to have been a makeshift bench, carried over the stadium running track to the side of the pitch. Paisley leaves the seats to others. The camera captures him in his overcoat, on his feet, eyes intently fixed on the pitch, his coaching team clustered behind him. To stare at this image is to be struck by what the most unobtrusive and unaffected leader can bring out in others. 'Who was Paisley?' After all of these years, it seemed like a good time to find out.

1

ON BANK

The war was over and the land of the free called for a young man with the world at his feet. The *Queen Mary* passenger liner would sail from Southampton at 1 p.m. on Saturday 4 May, and he would be on it.

At the other end of the Atlantic Ocean lay an itinerary including the film premieres of Rita Hayworth and Lucille Ball, air travel, the jazz sound, baseball and heavyweight boxing at Madison Square Garden in New York City. There were to be two weeks of it, because the United States awaited the pleasure of young stars of Liverpool Football Club. It was a place for them to escape the bleak British post-war reality of factory closures and bread rations, to feel alive and to feel for the first time how it was to be famous. A group of GI brides would be setting sail with the Liverpool team, destined for their own new worlds. It was a voyage of discovery, for sure, and anticipation filled the air.

Yet even as they sailed, he longed for the day they would be back. He carried a small, blue gilt-edged diary in which he would measure out the days, chronicling how he had filled each one in small black capital letters, six square inches for each entry. In the future, when this diary was one of the very few written testaments to the workings of his interior mind, it would reveal that the celebrity sound didn't suit him all that well. The quietness of his own front room was what he actually liked best. The diary reveals the kaleidoscope of experiences those 22 days brought: deck tennis and quoits on board the *Queen Mary*; travel on an aeroplane, from New York to St Louis, with a refuel at Daytona – 'Lie down as usual while plane is in motion. Find it much the best,' he wrote; watching LA Dodgers beat San Francisco Giants 5–4 in beautiful California sunshine – 'Nothing to arouse our spirits'; and discovering that there were no tickets to watch European heavyweight champion Bruce Woodcock fight – 'Disappointment.'

The letters he received were where the joy resided: 11 on a single day in the second week away, and all of them from home, restoring him to the quotidian preoccupations of life back there – which is to say, love and a promise to bring home some stockings. His girl was called Jessie and he had told her he would fetch some.

'Two letters from Jess and one from mother. Letters always help the moral [sic], especially from Jessie,' he writes one day. 'Two more letters from Jess, I think she loves me now,' he reports on another. 'Arrive hotel about 9. Lovely surprise 11 letters, eight from my darling,' he relates. 'More letters today. I have only got to see wether [sic] she keeps her word.'

They set sail again for home and the days of sunshine faded to cloud, though that was a good thing. 'Today is more like our own weather. Still, it shows we are getting nearer,' he writes as the ship neared port. And then the purgatory was over. The diary was no longer needed. Bob Paisley was home.

Hetton-le-Hole sounds like a place that puts you down in the earth, with a distance to climb if you want to reach for the stars. That much is true. It was built on a coal seam, reached via a 6-foot-square-cage lift which sent a workforce 100 feet below the surface.

It was Bob Paisley's place, though – the town south of Sunderland in England's industrial north-east where he was born and to which he would look for any chance to drop in, down the years. He was 27 years old when he made his pre-season trip to the United States with Liverpool Football Club in 1946, but Hetton was still home to him, even then. It was the place that he carefully wrote on the address page of the diary he briefly kept during that trip: 'Mr R. Paisley, 31 Downs Lane, Hetton-le-Hole, Co Durham.'

That was the Paisleys' fourth house in the village. There had been Front Street, where he was born on 23 January 1919, then a rented place on The Avenue, followed by a Hetton Lyon's Colliery house at Nicholas Street and, finally, the redbrick terrace on Downs Lane. The frequent house moves reflected the struggle to find somewhere big enough for a growing family of four sons.

The coal seam was becoming exhausted when he arrived as the second child of Samuel and Emily Paisley (née Downs). The miners pushed their luck to extract what was left of the raw material. Paisley's father suffered a serious arm injury and insisted that his sons would not go underground as he had. Paisley was subsequently assigned a role sorting coal from stone in an area at the top of the pithead known as 'On Bank'. The mine closed three months after Samuel sustained the injury. There was an air of grim resignation about that.

Some 200 miles away on the Ayrshire coalfield, the family of Bill Shankly railed against the same diminishing natural resource and working-class impoverishment. Shankly's father, John, breathed socialist hellfire. But Samuel Paisley was a quiet, more passive soul. He would not have minded admitting that horse racing absorbed him more than socialism and he did not see himself as an organiser. In the only remaining image of him and

Emily, taken on the doorstep of Downs Lane, it is she who stands in the foreground, hands clasped, exuding warmth, with the unmistakable air of a woman who got things done. Samuel stands in the semi shadow, the tie, waistcoat and jacket just visible.

It was Emily who decorated the house every year – papering over the previous year's soot-caked wallpaper – and produced Yorkshire puddings baked in the kiln oven on the wall. The ceremonial fetching down of the tin bath from its hook on the wall, when the pit-shaft cage brought Samuel back to the surface, was her job.

It was Emily, with her round face and inclination to grin, who Paisley most resembled, though it was Samuel whose character he took: taciturn, sometimes brusque, 'not given to emotions', as someone once said of Paisley Snr. And yet doggedly determined to prevail, as the incremental rise from the bottom rung of the Hetton-le-Hole housing stock revealed.

It was his teachers whose wisdom and messages Bob Paisley would most often quote, not his father's, though you imagine that their sentiments belonged to Samuel, too. Paisley often cited the words of his headmaster at Eppleton Senior Mixed School: 'If you want to tell anybody anything, speak softly and you'll find that they're trying to listen to you. They're trying to get what you're going to say. If you shout at them, they're not interested, really. So talk softly to them.'

On the Durham coalfield, the 1920s were not days for talking. Tough times and tough places bred tough individuals. Like father, like son. There is a rare picture of Paisley at the front of the school football team, his face pinched and expressionless as he clutched a huge shield. Suffice to say the sun does not seem to be shining.

When trophies were won, Paisley, as the captain and outstanding performer, would be asked to say a few words. He had his standard lines learned off pat and could still recite them years later: 'Glad to have won the Cup. It's an honour to Eppleton School.' As he said much later, he would have been glad to keep it at that every time he won a trophy.

His schools and their football teams – Barrington Primary, then Eppleton – is where he seems to have found the characters and colour in childhood. The Eppleton school caretaker Bowler Burns was as commanding as his name suggested and provided therapeutic mustard baths in the boiler room for the boys. (The combination of mustard seeds and piping hot water were thought to warm the muscles and blood.) Paisley and the other boys who showed promise would be summoned out of class for an egg and sherry tonic when a big school match loomed.

There was a particular challenge for Paisley. He was a small boy who found himself with a size disadvantage to make up, but he was known to tackle hard and unflinchingly. Sports masters Bertie Rowe, Jimmy Johnson and Alec Wright became significant names in his world. Jack Walker was a particularly influential trainer and perhaps the wisest of all of them. Paisley never forgot Jack Walker's name.

The school team was a focus of all their lives. Eddie Burns, Bowler's brother, who was unpaid assistant caretaker, earned half a crown by refereeing the team's Saturday morning matches. Two schoolmistresses – a Miss Boyd and Miss Davison – would arrive for the inquest after the game. If they hadn't seen the match, they wanted a detailed account of it. The Eppleton Senior Mixed honours board from 1931 tells the story: five trophies for the team and Paisley's 'county cap' in that year alone. Word soon got around about the uncompromising strip of a lad with music in his feet when he took command of a football. He advanced to the Durham county youth side, earned a trial for England Schoolboys in 1933 and was just developing the sense that he could do anything, when rejection came – cold, hard and unforgiving. Sunderland, the team every self-respecting Hetton schoolboy lived for, had told him they were interested. They asked him to show them what he was made of and had him half convinced that he would be running out at Roker Park, wearing their red and white stripes in the First Division.

He was too small, the Sunderland manager Johnny Cochrane and chief scout Tommy Irwin told Paisley. Tottenham Hotspur and Wolverhampton Wanderers said the same, but it was Sunderland who broke his heart. Paisley settled for a bricklaying apprenticeship instead and had started to resign himself to an ordinary life when semi-professional football offered another avenue. He advanced to the team at Bishop Auckland, 25 miles south of Hetton, and on a salary of three shillings and sixpence a game found a team who valued him. They liked his tough tackling style and his intuition about where spaces were going to be opening up on a field.

For two hugely successful seasons, his 5 foot 7 and a half inch frame became a mainstay of the 'Bishops' midfield, where he operated as the team's left-half – the position in front of the defence, which carried the designation of stopping the opposition right-winger. This was one of the best semi-professional sides in Britain and provided the chance to run out at Roker Park, after all. The team reached the FA Amateur Cup final and Paisley was a 20-year-old in the side that won the game there against Wellington.

That was when Liverpool, managed by George Kay, became interested. Sunderland realised their mistake and re-established contact with him, too, though it was too late – Paisley had given his word to Kay. Many would later attest that there were no second chances when you seriously let Bob Paisley down. Sunderland would never be absolved of the folly of deciding he was not tall enough for their liking.

It wasn't easy, leaving Downs Lane in 1939 and taking a train to a new life 200 miles away on the other side of the country. Liverpool was another world and Paisley struggled at first. The individual who helped him find his bearings was Matt Busby, the captain of the Liverpool side who was on his way to becoming synonymous with Manchester United and whose kindness surprised the young recruit.

Busby turned out to be a compassionate manager, too. He would allow a homesick young George Best to return home. When Alex Ferguson was taking United back to the heights Busby had scaled, he allowed another Irish prodigy – Adrian Doherty – to do the same. But Paisley's homesick players would tell of a different experience. When they found themselves in digs they were desperate to be away from and would ask, in the most tentative way, whether a move might be acceptable, the answer was always, 'No.' One of Paisley's own midfielders, Ronnie Whelan, reflected years later that, 'There were very few shoulders to cry on. Their attitude was: "You've signed, we've put you in digs, now keep your nose clean and get on with it."'

They made them hard and unsentimental in Hetton-le-Hole and the troubles of Paisley's own early years and his struggles to acclimatise did nothing to change that. 'It's not a question of ability. It's all to do with adapting to new surroundings,' Paisley once said.

There was no time for him to mourn home, in any case. Military conflict was on the horizon. Paisley did not choose to join it but World War II caught up with him. He had not played a competitive senior match for Liverpool when he found himself stationed at Rhyl on the North Wales coast, then Tarporley, ten miles east of Chester, and eventually in the Royal Artillery, serving in Egypt, Italy and the Western Desert as a driver to a reconnaissance officer. He was 20 when the war came: the prime time for a professional footballer, and the few surviving images of him from those days – shirtsleeves rolled up to the bicep in the searing heat of the desert where he served – reveal the fact. The conflict took four years out of the career which, given the rejection of his teenage years, must have seem destined never to start.

The sense of precious time lost seemed a very distant consideration out in the desert, though. In 1942, Paisley was serving with the Eighth Army at El Alamein in Egypt when a plane sprayed explosive bullets over his hideout. The chaos and momentary panic in the desert left him staggering around with his hands over his eyes, leaving one of his superiors, Captain Norman Whitehouse, convinced Paisley had been permanently blinded. Whitehouse ensured the young gunner was taken away to be seen by a medical officer and within 24 hours he was back with his 73rd Medium Regiment, wearing dark spectacles. Years later, during a break on a Liverpool trip to Israel, he told midfielder Graeme Souness the story of being in a convoy of vehicles which inadvertently drove into a German camp, in a sandstorm, and came under fire. They managed to retreat and make good an escape.

Unassuming and taciturn: that was the Paisley his regiment knew, though there was no soft touch behind the young soldier's self-effacement. It was indicated to Paisley that the Major would not allow him to be in Hetton when the youngest of his brothers, Alan, had contracted diphtheria in 1944. If he was not given compassionate leave, then he would be away to Wearside of his own accord, Paisley respectfully informed the regiment. Permission was granted. Alan Paisley was 14 when they buried him.

Paisley did not bring home the demons and psychological scars which would torment so many who served, though he did lose friends out in the desert. He returned with a new perspective; he was just grateful to have life and all that it could offer him. Years later, in the front room of the home he made in Liverpool, Paisley avidly watched the Granada Television series *All Our Yesterdays*, which detailed aspects of the conflict 25 years to the precise day. He always seemed to be waiting for the episode charting the story of El Alamein. In time, he looked back with some fondness on those days. He'd joke about how he and his pal Frank Owen, who would be a lifelong friend, had 'won the war'. Later in life, he would be reunited with others he had served alongside: Sergeant Joe Bates, gunners Jack Moffat and Reg Stratton. He was proud that they had been 'Monty's boys'.

The draw of the north-east and Hetton was as strong as ever when he returned to England at the end of the conflict, even though the task in hand was to break into Liverpool's first team. A newspaper cutting from August 1946 reports of 'Robert Paisley, the Liverpool half-back playing cricket for Eppleton Colliery Welfare' against Belmont, another County Durham village. It was some performance by Paisley the bowler: seven wickets for one run conceded in 5.3 overs. Cricket would remain an integral part of his life.

It helped his acclimatisation to Liverpool that he had encountered Miss Jessie Chandler. The story they both always told of their first encounter was that they'd been bound for London on the same overnight train from Liverpool. She, a trainee schoolteacher, was travelling to visit a friend during her half-term holiday. He, the aspiring First Division footballer, was bound for the barracks of Woolwich Arsenal in south-east London where he remained stationed after the war. Paisley accidentally threw his army issue coat on her sandwiches, apologised and they began talking. The couple's children were never entirely convinced that Jessie would have acted on such an impulse. It was not in the nature of either of them to disclose the beginnings of a romance. But that was their story of how it had started for them and they always stuck to it. 'We chatted all the way to London and all the next day,' Jessie related years later.

There was a supreme modesty about the lives they led during their courtship. Their time together was limited for three years after the war because Paisley remained stationed at Woolwich, returning north at the weekends to play for Liverpool and catch what time he could with her. Jessie was an assiduous diary keeper and her entries, which offer an insight into their snatched time together, reveal no great expectation in life.

There were evidently few more agreeable recreations for the emerging Liverpool left-half than an evening's rug-making with Jessie. Paisley would work at one end of the frame they weaved around, she the other. They had not long encountered each other, yet there was no self-consciousness from either of them about setting up the frames to 'put the mat on' and getting down to work. His regimental friend Frank Owen used to sell the rugs: 12 of them on one occasion, according to Jessie's diaries.

'Bob and I stayed in – cold day – we did some of the big mat,' Jessie writes on 30 December 1945. Football and rug-making combine seamlessly. 'We did the mat. Bob played in a Cup tie at Chester. Chester 0 L'pool 2,' Jessie reports early in the New Year of 1946. 'Bob and I went to church at night. We did the mat,' reads a typical Sunday entry. Jessie was a churchgoer so Paisley went along, too.

His concerns became her concerns. He was played out of position, at outside-left, in a 2–1 defeat to Manchester United.

'He was annoyed about it,' Jessie reported. He injured his left knee and right leg in quick succession and the doctors had difficulty diagnosing a problem. 'Bob went to see about his leg. The doctor doesn't know what it is.' That would have amused the Liverpool players whose injuries were viewed so suspiciously by Paisley in future years.

Jessie seized on the write-ups of his match reports with a satisfaction that he was making his way. 'Cuttings about Bob – very good indeed – said he was the best of the 22.'

Films occupied them when work on the mats did not call: *The Seventh Veil*; *The Conspirators*; a teenage Shirley Temple in *Kiss and Tell*; James Mason in *The Night Has Eyes*; and *The Great Lie* starring Bette Davis. Jessie was the one who organised their recreation. On the few occasions when Bob did, the results were decidedly mixed. He took her to New Brighton Tower to see the wrestling, after coming into temporary possession of a friend's car. 'They looked and sounded like wild animals but funny in kits,' Jessie reported.

They were engaged on 28 January 1946, by which time Jessie certainly seemed the more capable of the two in expressing the depths of her feelings: 'Tried to show Bob how much he means to me – but I think that would be impossible.' They were married on a Wednesday afternoon, seven months later. A honeymoon followed at the Bangor Castle Hotel in North Wales. 'Bob and I were married at All Soul's Church at 1 p.m. by Rev H.V. Atkinson,' Jessie wrote. 'Feel wonderfully happy. Hope Bob does too. It rained all our wedding day but did not spoil it.'

The modesty reflected the way Paisley approached his career at Liverpool. Footballers had started to assume celebrity status by the end of the war and the media fascination with their lifestyles was reflected in the pages of titles such as the *Daily Graphic* and *Liverpool Evening Express*. Liverpool's South African outside-right

Berry Nieuwenhuys was pictured sizing up a golf putt in elegant waistcoat and flannel in one such piece. 'Wireless enthusiasts' Willie Fagan, a Scottish inside-left, and defender Barney Ramsden, were captured 'delving into the mysteries of a nine-valve set' while star striker Billy Liddell prepared to take sun-ray treatment under the eye of Liverpool trainer Albert Shelley. Paisley flinched. He wasn't comfortable in the spotlight. He was always on the margins of the photographs: the onlooker, watching others line up shots at the snooker table in several articles examining the players' favoured recreations, but never taking centre stage.

His young wife offered a slightly more colourful backdrop for Paisley's appearance in an 'Our Footballers at Home' magazine series, when a photo of her seated at the piano, overlooked by him, provided the main image. She 'charms him into the bouquet of "Galway Bay" and other songs,' readers were told, though there was no evidence that the Anfield half-back might be about to burst into song.

The same applied to Paisley's part in the team group shots. He was always on the periphery of these: bottom right in the paper's 'midday special' of 6 March 1945; bottom right again the following January 1946; top right in the same publication on 9 October that year. His demeanour was always the same: the wrinkled brow and the wide smile filling the distinctly round face. There, as in so very many of the photographs over the years, was the Emily Paisley in him. The lick of Brylcreemed hair slipping down over the forehead and the stretched crew neck of his red Liverpool shirts created the slightly ragged and uncompromising look. 'Recreation plays its part in keeping footballers at the peak of condition,' the *Evening Express* article informed its readers.

As he became comfortable in the company of his new teammates, a little comedy value emerged from the diffident and self-effacing half-back. He was known for his impersonations of the Scottish actor Alastair Sim. Faint evidence that Paisley might follow where Jessie led, on the keyboards, emerged in a small paragraph from the *Liverpool Daily Post* in January 1948. 'Liverpool fans will be surprised to know that we have an organist in the team,' it was reported from the hotel at Birkdale, Southport, where the side prepared for an FA Cup third-round tie against Nottingham Forest that year. 'Bob Paisley gave us an organ recital on the hotel organ. Several notes were off key but the tones were at least recognisable.'

Gradually, the Paisleys cemented themselves socially. He and Jessie moved from the front room of her parents' home into a Liverpool FC house on Greystone Road, close to where the M62 would be built in the early 1970s. The striker Billy Liddell and his wife Phyllis lived opposite. Liddell would sit on the outside wall, waiting for Paisley to emerge from the house, and they would catch the number 61 bus to Anfield together.

But Paisley's social awkwardness was always there. When one of the players on the United States trip of 1946 announced he had lost 50 dollars, the squad decided that there should be a collection for him and a whip-round commenced. Paisley decided this wasn't appropriate, concluding, rather oddly, that it might imply one of their number had stolen the cash. So he didn't contribute. The 50 dollars was later discovered at the back of a drawer in the team hotel.

Keeping the diary on that trip had been Jessie's idea. It also meant he committed to paper his thoughts on the footballing value of the tour. He considered the whole idea a frippery and thought the dubious quality of the opposition might breed complacency – something he would always consider a scourge for the football teams he fielded. Liverpool handed out regulation thrashings – 9–0 v a Washington side, 11–1 versus the 'Eatons' club in his own first game for two months and 9–2 v Chicago. 'This tour has proved the mentality of our directors and manager to think they have a world beating side. Time will tell,' Paisley observed scornfully.

There was no ostentation in the way he played football. It was unspectacular, uncomplicated, uncompromising, utilitarian, consistent, mindful and hard: very hard. There were no tricks or fuss. Actions spoke louder than words.

Back in his Hetton days, Paisley's friend Jackie Wilson had taught him what they then called the 'Sammy Weaver throw' – hurling throw-ins like missiles into the goalmouth in the style of Weaver, a Newcastle United and England left-half. Images of Paisley running to launch a 'Sammy Weaver' feature prominently in the newspaper discussions of him but it was his style of defending which Liverpool liked. He operated alongside Phil Taylor and Bill Jones in Liverpool's three-man half-back line, whose job was to provide a protective shield for the three-man defence – and they did so with extreme effectiveness when football resumed after the war.

Match reports repeatedly extolled Paisley's work ethic and commitment at a packed Anfield. 'The toughest man of 51,911,' he is described as in one report. He broke into the first team on 7 September 1946 when Liddell, the Scot who became legendary among Liverpool strikers, was making only his second appearance, against Chelsea. Their wait had been interminably long. Both had signed professional forms for Liverpool a full seven years earlier.

Liddell shot freely and frequently and scored twice, the first goal direct from a corner Paisley had won. Then Liddell provided for Paisley as they drove forward. 'Paisley and Liddell engineered a move which ended in Paisley shooting over the bar. These two were making a big difference,' stated one report, though proceedings were also delayed because Paisley 'received a boot thrust in the midriff'. Those who paid three ha'pennies for the *Liverpool Echo* final edition that Saturday were left in no doubt about the prime contributors to the performance watched by 49,995 people. 'Reds sail in Chelsea sunset,' stated the front page headline. 'Liddell and Paisley transformed Liverpool attack.' It was some debut: Liverpool won 7–4.

Paisley was not always so eye-catching but he was consistent, and the finest of the First Division's wingers did not seem to intimidate him. Not even Stanley Matthews, who had just made his big move from Stoke City to Blackpool when Liverpool played at Bloomfield Road in the seaside town on 1 November 1947. Matthews mesmerised Paisley's Liverpool teammate Ray Lambert that day, the *Sketch* reported. Yet, having also been skinned by the England international, Paisley 'did not let the matter rest there, but went back for a second tackle. And more often than not he succeeded,' the *Sketch* continued. 'Here is the tip for a player who will have to deal with Matthews – only [that] they will need an outsize heart to do it.'

The *Liverpool Evening Echo* agreed. 'Lambert, having suffered [Preston's Tom] Finney, now went to Matthews with a defeatist attitude common to all those whose job it is to suffer this player all of the time. Paisley was different. He went in, was beaten, and then had the temerity to go back for more. The result was that a Matthews who had left him yards behind suddenly found the second tackle the lethal one.' But Liverpool still lost 2–0.

The refusal to yield to injury, which bordered on lunacy at times, was a precursor of the way Paisley later expected his players to play through pain and felt suspicion for those who did not.

Early in one league match at St James' Park, he was hit on the side of the head and, it was reported at the time, briefly knocked unconscious by a ball struck with immense power by Newcastle United's Norman Dodgin. He remained on the field, was still so shaky by the half-time interval that trainer Albert Shelley helped him off the pitch, but was determined to return. 'During the interval, the unusual method of him walking up and down outside the main grandstand was used, in the hope he would come to,' the *Liverpool Evening Express* match report revealed. Nine minutes after the match restarted, Paisley trotted on again, to do useful work at outside-left before trying to head a goal off [sic] a [Billy] Liddell centre.' Still evidently concussed, Paisley did not last the second half. The newspapers are littered with similar such incidents involving 'Bobby' Paisley, as some of the reporters called him. He ran hard against Derby County despite 'stitches inserted in a scalp wound which bled profusely throughout the second half'.

Paisley was widely accepted to be one of the top four or five First Division half-backs of the time: part of a Liverpool side who found brief and unexpected glory after the war. The team became the surprise success of the first post-war campaign – winning the 1946–47 championship, their first silverware in 23 years, in the face of such pre-war giants as Newcastle, Sheffield Wednesday and Sunderland. He was a mainstay, playing in 33 league games in the title-winning year. The achievement was remarkable – and rather overshadowed by the success that would follow for him decades later.

Paisley could play the individualist, too. Evidence of that came in Liverpool's 1950 FA Cup semi-final against Everton, where his pre-match instructions from Kay had echoes of the kind of orders Paisley would issue to an over-ambitious Liverpool full-back, Alan

Kennedy, two decades later: 'Don't get too far forward.' Kennedy would be gratified to know that Paisley ignored instructions and did just that. He was thus in position to send in a lob which – more by accident than design – found the net in the 2–0 win which sent Liverpool to face Arsenal in the Wembley final. The newspaper reports of the game were full of allusions to how Kay had instructed Paisley not to waste possession by taking shots at goal when advancing up-field. 'Times without number, Paisley in the past has followed his own forwards . . . to make a shot. Results have not been encouraging. Mr Kay therefore chatted with Paisley and suggested that he might profitably elect in future not to court glory and marry failure.' No one was complaining when he got the team to Wembley.

He was injured in the build-up to the final and missed four games after the Everton victory, though told Kay that he had recovered full fitness in time for the big day. His confidence that he would be rewarded for his semi-final contribution with a place in the final starting XI was buoyed by the fact that his name was published in the Wembley match programme.

But it was not to be. Paisley discovered, via a newspaper report, that he had been omitted. A vote among directors – who picked the team – went 5–4 against him. He was devastated. A newspaper offered him money to tell his story, he said years later, but he declined.

It was subsequently suggested that Paisley had considered leaving Anfield in protest, though images of the Liverpool squad completing a lap of honour at Anfield after losing the Wembley final, 2–0, did not suggest the half-back was in a mood of insurrection as he walked the pitch in his immaculate dark Liverpool-issue suit, waving amiably to the terraces. Paisley was never a man for the barricades. He said the disappointment taught him how others would feel if dropped for a final, though his players would be sceptical of that comment. His managerial career would be littered with instances of them discovering in the pages of a newspaper that they had not been selected. Paisley was reminded at Wembley that the world of football was hard and unforgiving. That did not make him any more inclined to soften the blow for the generations which followed. He was, in any case, too embedded in the city of Liverpool to make a serious stand against the club. He was a 31-year-old already beginning to wonder how he could evolve his career at Anfield in order to sustain his domestic life.

Paisley and Jessie's first child, Robert, had been born at 7.40 a.m. on a Friday morning, 24 September 1948. 'Bob came to see me before he went to Blackpool,' Jessie reports in her diary. For once, she didn't record the newspaper's verdict on her husband. That was a match Liverpool lost 1–0. A second son, Graham, was born two years later and, by the hot summer of 1951, both the Paisleys and their neighbours the Liddells were becoming homeowners, leaving their club houses on Greystone Road for south Liverpool's suburbs. The Paisleys were destined for a pebble-dashed semi: 14, South Manor Way in the Woolton district of south Liverpool. Paisley, a firm if unassuming leader, was made captain of Liverpool in the summer of 1950. He was destined not to run out for England. A call-up as a reserve for an England 'B' international with Holland at Amsterdam's Olympic Stadium in 1952 was the closest he came.

Their new property was well beyond what had been his parents' means, and he wanted to get to work on it straight away. He would be into his overalls, with his bricklaying trowels out as soon as he was through the front door. He must have been the first Liverpool captain to have built a porch on the front of his own house. He knocked down the back of the garage to extend it, too, and put on a basic conservatory, after digging out the foundations.

Jessie's father Arthur Chandler was an organ-builder of repute, who worked for the firm which had installed Liverpool Anglican Cathedral's organ. He helped Paisley with the carpentry, both for the porch and for something of a conservatory – a glass-roofed lean-to – which they added. 'One of dad's constructions,' as eldest son Graham called it. There is an image of Paisley's two sons in front of the conservatory, lining up for the camera with their football.

Then the music stopped – incredibly abruptly. Paisley ought to have been looking into the middle distance by that point, comfortable in the knowledge that he had provided the trappings of the new British middle-class security. The Paisleys had the only television in the street. He and Jessie had albums full of snaps from the holidays, Jessie generally taking the pictures. They captured Paisley with the boys in an assortment of deckchairs on myriad British beaches, sometimes in full suit befitting the enduring formality of the day, sometimes suit trousers, rarely in shorts. Butlin's 1950 and 1951; location unknown 1952; both Newquay and Aberystwyth in 1953.

In another age he would have been able to contemplate easing himself into coaching – imparting the skills of a sport which, when World War II was behind them, had delighted so many people every week. But that door did not exist in the early fifties. There was no obvious next step to deliver an income. The Football Association's own coaching scheme was a fledgling one, just two years in existence at the start of the decade, and most Football League clubs did not believe there was a need for anything more than physical training. Keeping players fit and fast was the only requirement. Skills were innate and God-given, most clubs thought.

The need for an alternative course was hastened when Paisley experienced the decline which comes to all players, just as the money started evaporating at Liverpool and the team's national standing crashed. The club's wealthy and charismatic chairman Billy McConnell, a catering industry entrepreneur who possessed the vision of building the best team in the land, had died unexpectedly, and at the end of the 1953–54 season the side were relegated as the First Division's bottom club, ending 50 consecutive years of football at that level. Paisley had become more peripheral amid the decline, making only 19 First Division appearances that season, and on 4 May 1954 the *Liverpool Evening Express* reported that 'Bobby Paisley, the tough little North-Easterner who specialises in the long throw and is of the never-say-die order,' was not on the retained list of players for the first season down in the Second Division. His last game had been a 3–1 defeat to Sheffield United at their Bramall Lane ground on 13 March.

He was 35. It was the year the couple's daughter, Christine, was born. Robert was six and Graham, four, and Jessie was worried. 'We were young and unaware then, of course,' says Graham. 'But Mum and Dad both always remembered it as one of the times of most uncertainty.' It was suggested years later that Paisley had considered moving back into bricklaying, returning to the skills picked up during his brief apprenticeship in Hetton after the colliery closed, or perhaps trying his hand at running a shop. It seems improbable that he gave serious consideration to either idea. His intermittent journeys back up to the north-east vividly revealed the struggles of those with the same narrow horizons that he had known before football. The Hetton Lyon Colliery was closed by the National Coal Board in July 1950 and on a Wednesday morning in early July 1951 there was an explosion at the neighbouring Hetton Downs mine, which Samuel and Emily Paisley's Downs lane terrace overlooked. More than 500 men were working 1,300 feet below the surface at that moment and nine were killed – the youngest 25 and the oldest 54. They included Jack Walker, the football trainer to whom Paisley felt he owed much. He was a 'cutterman', operating heavy machinery where the seam was mined, and like all but two of those who perished that day, he was killed by carbon dioxide poisoning. Paisley found Walker's gravestone in Hetton cemetery, where he'd been buried like all the rest.

2

ISN'T THAT SO, BOB?

It was not so much an arrival as an earthquake when Bill Shankly first walked into Anfield as manager. The club was 'a shambles of a place', he later said, and the 40-year-old Bob Paisley must have looked a very small figure in the background.

It was 1959 and Liverpool Football Club had become moribund, marooned in football's second tier for five years, and showing little material sign of getting out. There was not even a means to water the pitch when the new manager took his first look around the place: just a pipe from the visitors' dressing-room and a tap. The £3,000 needed to put that right was one of his first investments. The Melwood training ground consisted of an old wooden pavilion with a veranda and an air-raid shelter. Instilling new life into this barren landscape needed noise, drive and monumental powers of inspiration. Shankly had them all. His appointment at Liverpool's helm was the most significant landmark in Paisley's football life because without Shankly there would have been none of what was to follow in his own career.

Paisley was still there at Anfield because, whatever it took, he had made himself indispensable. The former captain and league championship winner had certainly not been too proud to furnish Liverpool with his old bricklaying skills. He built the new manager's dugout that Shankly would sit in, as well as a section of terrace known as the 'bandbox', where the squad's unused players would stand. He plumbed the toilets at the back of the Kemlyn Road terrace and then painted them. 'Come on, you look a strong lad,' he told Tommy Smith, a trainee defender, one day in 1960. They ended up going under the Kop roof, cutting out a girder that had become an obstruction and cementing a new one in its place. He devised a system for putting up the half-time scores. The old slots which took the numbers had gone rusty. Yet Paisley also knew that being the odd-job man was not enough. He needed to find some relevance.

It was in football's fledgling science of physiotherapy that he saw it. He was aware from his playing experiences of the prehistoric way players were dealt with. Liverpool's resident sponge man, Albert Shelley, was a practitioner of the 'hot and cold towels' treatment. That entailed brandishing tweezers to withdraw a towel from a bucket of red-hot water, slapping it on a player's offending injury, then repeating the process with an ice-cold towel.

Paisley had been particularly alarmed by a game in which his old friend Billy Liddell was knocked unconscious in a collision, prompting Shelley, known for the distinctive white coat in which he carried out his duties, simply to ask the striker to run around on the sidelines. Shelley pushed Liddell back out onto the field, just before the half-time interval, to complete the game. Even by Paisley's standards of forbearance, this was extreme. He asked Liddell after the game how he was feeling.

'What do you mean?' Liddell asked him.

'The knock you took . . .?' replied Paisley.

Liddell remembered no 'knock'. He had been severely concussed at best, half conscious at worst.

Paisley had been struck as early as 1950, the year he was left out of the FA Cup final side, that this area of work might offer him a way of staying in football. By then, he had already taken up a correspondence course which would qualify him to be a physiotherapist and masseur when his playing days were over. 'We married men have to look to the future, you know,' he told the *Liverpool Evening Express* that year.

Medical practices were becoming more common in football by the mid-1950s. Some clubs had hired trained physiotherapists, and the Pinderfields Hospital in Wakefield, Yorkshire, provided a course for footballer trainers in remedial gymnastics. But Paisley found himself to be surplus to playing requirement at a newly relegated second-tier team in 1954 and needed to be imaginative if he was to catch the wave. He asked the club's board member Thomas Valentine (T. V.) Williams, a wealthy cotton broker, if he could begin spending time in the accident departments of some of the Liverpool hospitals to watch basic injuries – sprains and muscle tears – being treated. Williams, who had been enlightened enough to buy the land in Liverpool's West Derby district which would become the Melwood training ground, was a close friend of the Liverpool retail entrepreneur John Moores, who had connections in the city. Williams obtained a signed letter from Moores, asking that Paisley be granted access to the hospitals where he might pick up medical knowledge, supplementing his correspondence course.

Paisley's zeal evidently impressed the management. Williams offered him the role of reserve team trainer, allowing him to stay on after his failure to make the retained player list. The reserves were a vehicle for players recovering from injury, or young players requiring a game – winning or losing was immaterial. Paisley wanted to begin making the side competitive, and Liverpool agreed. He pasted up a note on the notice board stating that from now on he wanted a reserve team that went into every match with the objective of winning. Within a year, he had led the team to the runners-up position in the Central League, behind a Manchester United side that included many of the young players who would go on to play for Matt Busby. His second-string team were champions the following year.

From fixing toilets to running the reserve side, Paisley had made himself part of Liverpool's fixtures and fittings and, in May 1957, the club announced that he was to become 'chief coach' to manager Phil Taylor, his former Liverpool teammate, who had been dropped from the retained player list at the same time. Taylor had made manager following a year as caretaker, after the dismissal of Don Welsh.

It was now that Paisley gradually began taking over Albert Shelley's role as physiotherapist. When staff arrived for work one day in 1957, they were amused to find him sitting there in Shelley's white coat. It was the only time in his life that he would be unabashed about taking someone else's job. He felt that his own hold on a profession in football depended on it.

Liverpool's fruitless struggles to get promoted, however, made Anfield a far less secure place. One of Scotland's most celebrated coaches, Reuben Bennett, was head-hunted by T. V. Williams and also appointed 'chief coach' in December 1958, after a role working for Bill Shankly's brother, Bob, at Third Lanark, north of the Scottish border. This must have created insecurity for Paisley, whose role carried the same title.

But none of that uncertainty matched December 1959 when Taylor was sacked and Bill Shankly walked through the door as manager. Paisley submitted a letter to the Liverpool board, asking for a clarification of his position. Fatefully, Shankly concluded that the backroom team would remain intact. He could work with Paisley, Bennett and Joe Fagan, recruited from Rochdale as reserve team trainer in 1958.

Four glorious years passed, crowned by Shankly restoring Liverpool to the First Division in 1962, before Paisley provided the white-coat moment so many always remembered. He was applying electrodes to the left leg of Jimmy Melia, Liverpool's midfielder, and trying to put him at ease. 'Right, Jimmy, if you feel anything untoward just give us a shout and I'll turn it off right away . . .' the players remember him telling Melia as he walked a few yards towards a battery of dials near the window. Could he feel anything? Paisley then asked.

'No, Bob,' said Melia.

'Now?' asked Paisley.

'Nothing, Bob,' said Melia.

'Jesus Christ, Bob. Haven't you read the instructions?' asked Shankly, pacing around impatiently in the background.

'The instructions are in German,' Paisley replied.

'Weren't you in the war, for God's sake? Don't you understand German?'

'This one must need turning up,' said Paisley, fiddling with the dials.

'Bob. The plug . . . it's not on at the wall,' said Chris Lawler, the full-back who was one of the quieter ones but often compensated for lack of noise with quality of observation. A look of anxiety began to spread across Melia's face. Paisley reached down to introduce electricity into the equation and Melia's leg shot up in the air.

'Turn the bloody thing off,' shouted Shankly. The players who were not doubled up by now joined in his plea.

Liverpool trod boldly, if sometimes comically, across new sports science frontiers and the episode demonstrated how Paisley's relationship with Shankly had started to form. Shankly was the visionary who would get a scent of how Liverpool could be different – and any obstacle in his way, be damned. Paisley was the details man – left to put the idea, or machine, into effect. A feature in the *Liverpool Echo*'s *Football Pink* a few years later pictured Paisley standing in front of a bank of technology, including three models of interferential machine, a short-wave Diatherm machine, massaging vibrator and a galaxy of ointments.

The subject of attention on the day of the Melia incident was what had become known as 'the German treatment machine' – an electrical muscle stimulation (EMS) device – which Shankly had heard about through his brother. He had become convinced it could eradicate injuries and keep his players out of the treatment room – 'the Bastards' Club' as he called it – because he was always so intensely suspicious of players who were not fit. The search for the machine became Shankly's obsession. The devices were virtually unknown in British sport and were most used by Russian athletes at the time. But Shankly tracked down an early advocate – an Austrian pioneer, Dr Hans Nemec – to a clinic in Liechtenstein. Nemec referred him on to 'a man in Birmingham' and so it was that Liverpool took delivery of the portable EMS machine. It was then left to Paisley to make what he deemed to be the correct connections from the battery to the dial with wires which 'were poking out from at least half a dozen places', as midfielder Ian St John remembers.

The machine and Melia survived the plug problem. Shankly and Paisley both concluded that it had an effect and Shankly, in his overseeing role, soon became so enthused by it that he wanted the people of Liverpool to benefit. On one occasion he ran out onto the street outside Anfield, found a couple of pensioners with aches and pains and brought them in – one limping, the other with backache. 'Put them on the machine, Bob,' he instructed, and Paisley obliged. Legend also has it that one day Shankly arrived at the door with an old man and a whippet and they had concocted a plan to try it out on the dog. 'Bugger off,' Paisley replied. 'I'm not working on a bloody whippet.'

By 1964, when Shankly had delivered a First Division title to Liverpool, Paisley was the long-suffering and, as the players saw it, sometimes hapless assistant: the driver, fixer, arranger, smoother-over and general factotum who would see Shankly's ideas through and solve problems before they arrived at his door. It was Paisley who reached for his car keys on the night that Shankly – or 'Shank' as he always called him when discussing the manager with others – decided that the two of them would drive to Winsford in Cheshire to scout a player. The evening had not started well. It transpired that the player in question was actually on Witton Albion's books, leaving Paisley to calm a fulminating Shankly with the assurance that, 'I've got an AA map.' Then they reached a petrol station to find no one emerging to help them on the forecourt as Paisley scrabbled around for some money – this being the year in which self-service pumps appeared. 'You've got to serve yourself now, boss,' Paisley declared. 'Jesus Christ,' shouted Shankly. 'Another blow against the state of this country.'

Shankly was entitled to adopt this regal position. He bestrode Liverpool so hugely by the mid-1960s – having rebuilt the club and reinstated its lost pride – that you could tell within an instant of arriving at Anfield or Melwood whether he was in the building or not. Ian St John, whom Shankly made captain, had the measure of conversations between the boss and Bob: 'Shankly and Paisley walked on, deep in conversation. Well, Bob was deep in Bill's conversation,' he said, describing the pair of them, walking outside London's Hendon Hall Hotel before a League Cup tie with Watford, as the players waited to give them the slip and head out for the night. 'Isn't that so, Bob?' was Shankly's very frequent refrain. 'Yes, boss,' was Paisley's very frequent reply.

Paisley had no complaints about that. Shankly had also turned the meaning of a training session on its head – replacing the dull, utilitarian fitness routines virtually all Liverpool players had previously known with 90 minutes of work which almost always involved the ball. He had players thinking they could move mountains, and they searched his face for the slightest sign of his approval. Ian Ross, signed by Shankly in 1966 and released six years later, speaks of the Shankly 'wink' – his sign you had done your job well: 'That's what we lived for. That wink off him. You'd do anything for one of those winks.'

Trevor Birch, a 16-year-old striker in 1974, remembers Shankly shuffling over to mark him at a corner in one of the coaching staff versus apprentices' games which always wrapped up each morning session. 'I'm going to mark you, son, because you can head the ball,' Shankly told Birch. Nearly four decades on, Birch still remembers the thrill those few words gave him. 'It seems ridiculous to say it, because it was just a throwaway remark, but that's how he made you feel,' he says.

Back in the early days of the Shankly reign, when the players looked at Paisley in those sessions, they laughed. His playing days had ended only five or so years earlier but he was not the most mobile of individuals. His style of football and the ferocity of his tackling had left him with a pronounced limp, caused by an old injury to his left ankle. He would bandage it up in a figure of eight before leaving the family home on South Manor Way each morning but it contributed to the faintly comical gait on those days when it was playing up. He put on some weight, which can have consequences when you stand little more than 5 feet 7 inches tall.

At the end of the morning training session, Paisley would waddle out across the Melwood pitches to take up his customary position – goalkeeper – in the daily staff versus apprentices match: the ritual which 'Shank' had instituted. Sporting a pair of little black boxing gloves, he kept goal because it meant he did not have to run, though the games would still have to be stopped on occasions as Paisley yelped in agony because what he called his 'wandering cartilage' had gone again. That was another old injury: a piece of floating loose tissue which caused his left knee joint to jam. Someone had to push it back into place then the game could continue. When a well-struck shot once caught Paisley in the most painful place, the assembled players and staff were reduced to hysterics. 'He's squealing like a pig!' someone shouted.

His lack of objections to this stemmed from the fact that he was engrained in the football culture which dictated that you took the ridicule that was dished out. And, in any case, he had some perspective about his role at Liverpool. He'd made himself invaluable but he didn't consider himself to be management, as such. He didn't ask himself how he might lead this group of men one day, when to many of them he was often a figure of fun.

Paisley became assistant to Shankly in 1971, as part of a reshuffle which saw Joe Fagan become first-team coach and Reuben Bennett – who had been above Paisley in the chain of command through the 1960s – assigned 'special duties' which would 'probably include assessing opponents and reporting on recommended players' according to the *Liverpool Daily Post*.

None of this kept Paisley from busying himself building stud partition walls at home around this time. His sons shared the back bedroom but there would be arguments between them so Paisley built a partition straight down the middle of the room. It was an eccentric and inelegant construction which bisected the window and, rather like 'the conservatory', looked slightly Heath Robinson from garden level. But it did the job and the boys were happy. Robert's radio no longer kept Graham awake late at night.

Paisley also removed the fireplace from the front room of the semi-detached house with his leg still in plaster, when recovering from the removal of the troublesome cartilage. Shankly would also have viewed that with astonishment. His own mind was so one-track football that when he headed off to Blackpool for a few days away each close season with his wife, Nessie, he would regularly call up a member of the local First Division team for a game of 'one-a-side.' Liverpool's young club secretary Peter Robinson, who had been appointed in 1965, would also get a call within a few days of the Shanklys decamping to Blackpool in which Bill would say, 'It's wonderful here, you've got to come and see me.' Nessie would retreat from the promenade, out of the bitter wind, but Shankly would tell Robinson they should stay. ('We won't go in. This'll do us good.') He would then proceed to talk Liverpool with him. Shankly didn't know what to do with himself when there were no players around.

In contrast, Paisley didn't feel the need to call the club when he disappeared for the summer. The young family enjoyed drives out to North Wales with Jessie and the children in their black Morris 10. The car was a 1936 model, already 20 years old when Paisley bought it from Liverpool's reserve goalkeeper Dave Underwood, but it was novelty since the club discouraged players from driving at all. The children would always recall how they squealed with delight when their father drove at speed down the inclines, to ensure he got up the other side of a hill. They stayed at a boarding house in Rhyl on one occasion, Caerwys Castle on another. There was no petrol gauge, so he would park up before heading through the Mersey Tunnel on the way back and poke a stick in the tank to ensure he would not run out halfway through.

Jessie resumed her teaching career. Only a narrow window of her school holidays intersected with her husband's close-season break so they were limited to spring Bank Holiday weekends together most years. In 1964, it was a long weekend at the Cotswold House Hotel in Chipping Campden. The Paisleys stayed in the annexe and had nylon sheets, which were thought the height of modernity. When they got home Jessie bought a set. They visited Stratford and laughed at Paisley's lame joke about Shakespeare. 'It's no wonder he died young, with the prices here,' he said. There was a long weekend in Edinburgh, a trip to Blackpool and Morecambe, with all five of them crammed into a 'holiday room'.

It was the summer of 1966, as England prepared for Sir Alf Ramsey's glory, when the Paisleys branched out into a boating holiday on the Thames. As usual, dovetailing with Liverpool's pre-season international trips was complicated. Paisley had to be collected from Heathrow airport before the 45-minute or so drive on to Henley to collect the boat. Christine, 12 by then, sunbathed, Jessie cooked in the galley, the boys hopped on and off at locks. Paisley took the tiller and would also disappear off across the fields for some solitude just after dawn, to empty the toilet, reconnoitre and fetch back some milk. Family life suited him.

The overseas tours continued, though Paisley was accustomed to them by the mid-1960s: more so than Shankly, who skipped many of those trips. It was in 1965, during a tour to Canada, that news reached Paisley of his mother Emily's death. He returned home early and was in Hetton when they buried her.

He loved to return to the town, where his father reconciled himself to life as a widower. Father and son would sometimes turn up at the dog track together. Samuel would visit Liverpool, too, enjoying the simple pleasures of a trip on the New Brighton ferry from Liverpool to the Wirral peninsula, and the cigars which his son would procure for him. He would drive him halfway home – to the town square in Skipton, North Yorkshire – where Paisley's younger brother, Hughie, would be waiting to collect their father and take him the rest of the way.

If the children were in the car, Paisley would feign taking bends sharply as if on a motorbike and drive over bumps in the road so they could bounce up and down. Christine would be on Jessie's knee with the boys and grandfather in the back and she would touch the roof of the car with her head as they bounced on their way. His daughter was the apple of Bob's eye. An 11-week bus strike in 1967 meant Paisley had to take over the school run, much to his delight. The two of them would just talk, and when the strike came to an end Paisley remained her chauffeur. The joke in the South Manor Way household was that Christine had not realised the strike had finished. Soon her schoolfriend, Lesley, was being collected en route by Paisley too. She would often be late, but he didn't seem to mind.

Years earlier, it had been Jessie who would take Christine to the Santa's grotto, with the Christmas football schedule generally rendering Paisley absent. It was in one of the years he was around to take her, with a 'dancing waters' feature part of the attraction, that she always remembered. She had been nine when she became the owner of the resident family budgie, Pip, who would sit on Paisley's shoulder and on the hearth when he cleared the ashes from the fireplace.

As working life under Shankly reached its tenth year and progressed beyond, football could be put into a compartment at times. The club seemed to have its limits for Paisley. 'More often than not, after putting us on the [EMS] machine he would say, "Right, I'm off to the betting shop," remembers Ian St John. 'If he was having a good day, he might not return.' For Shankly, there was next to nothing beyond the world of Anfield, while for Paisley football was not always a matter of life and death. Horse racing was almost as important. In South Manor Way, he would slip into the hall from where his family would hear him dialling up and going through the usual routine. 'P for Peter, A for apple, I for indigo . . .' It was Paisley spelling out his name to access his telephone betting account.

His choice of friends reflected both his priorities and his discomfort in the company of those who might be considered sophisticates. They generally all loved horse racing or participated in it, though their lack of airs and graces made them unintimidating. Bob Paisley didn't want the challenge of cutting-edge conversation, about football or anything else.

His closest friend was Ray Peers, a brash, rotund boxing promoter who helped see to it that Paisley got tickets to see bouts at the Liverpool Empire in the 1960s. Peers also ran a sandwich shop on Liverpool's Dock Road and liked to say that he served a thousand cups of coffee before 8 a.m. He was a racing enthusiast, too. He lived at a hotel in Birkenhead, the Central, where he and Paisley would often drive for a drink after a Liverpool home game to talk racing, football and boxing: three of the manager's favourite topics. Paisley's disappearance there after games tested Jessie's patience at times.

In the summer, cricket became a part of his landscape. He played friendlies for Wirral XI Oxton and annotated with his teammates' names a photograph of the side he played in before what looked like a substantial crowd in 1948. As ever, Paisley was in the corner of the group shot but took his batting seriously. Though naturally right-handed, there was an ambidexterity about his cricket: he batted left-handed and bowled right-handed. (He kept a set of left-handed golf clubs, too, though the family never knew him use them.) Jessie took pictures of him during an innings on a sunlit evening, several years later. It had been an energy-sapping one, judging by the photograph of him leaving the field, dripping in sweat, when dismissed.

Racing was his passion, though. When Liverpool's trip to Ireland to play a friendly game in 1963 brought a chance encounter with the Irish trainer Frank Carr at Dublin's Gresham Hotel, the beginnings of a friendship were laid. The Liverpudlian jockey turned trainer Frankie Durr – an established St Leger and 2000 Guineas-winning jockey – became another close friend. Paisley would travel to his favourite racecourses – Haydock Park in Lancashire, York, and Newmarket in East Anglia – to see Durr race.

But it was with Carr that Paisley established a habit of spending a week or two each summer – staying at the jockey's place at Malton, North Yorkshire, in the close season and passing the days wandering around the stables, heading out on the gallops with Carr and contributing to such estate management work as dousing overgrown areas with petrol and throwing a match on it. Carr, a small man with comically large ears, came to stay at the Paisleys on one occasion, and there was no lack of suppressed mirth among the children.

This interest in racing reached further than studying the form guide, as he had always watched his father try to do. At Malton, Paisley thought he began to see patterns of behaviour and physiology common to horses and the football players he worked with for most of the year. 'You might get an older horse, like the occasional old professional footballer, looking as if he is saying, "Oh blimey, training again!" and just plodding around,' he once reflected. 'But on the big race day he'll be there showing himself off in front of the crowd and fairly flying in the race. We all know footballers like that, don't we? If you're edgy, the players will be edgy. If you're tense, they'll be tense. Players sense these things and I'm sure horses do, too. You can do too much with some horses in training and they've got nothing left for the race. Others love training and can't get too much. So it is with footballers. Some need the loud voice; some the soft. Some horses are good in any going the same as some players, whereas some are just not suited to the heavy ground. A real thoroughbred will often want a donkey or a goat to travel with it in its box. In the same way, great players need lesser lights to support and bolster them.'

In the brash world of Liverpool Football Club some laughed at this notion, but Paisley was impervious to that and it became one of the foundations of the way he viewed football. The application of equine analysis to football extended to him viewing physiological strengths and weaknesses as vital to performance in both sports. He developed a near sixth sense about opponents' physical weaknesses, which colleagues found to be spookily prescient at times. In a match at Newcastle United in September 1961, he saw Newcastle's Ivor Allchurch fall in the first half and indicated in the dressing-room at half-time that he felt the player was immobile and should be pressed. Liverpool did so and won 2–1. The Stoke City defender Calvin Palmer was another he pinpointed as a weak link – carrying a thigh injury – at Anfield on Boxing Day 1963. Liverpool won 6–1. Several players also recall Paisley identifying the way that Bolton Wanderers goalkeeper Eddie Hopkinson fell badly in a match the same season and urging the players to push harder at corners. Another Liverpool win at Anfield ensued: 2–0.

The same intuition contributed to an absorption with creating the right blend of players, perhaps using the strengths of one to mitigate for a weakness of another. 'The perfect player has never been born,' he once said. He knew that the finest players did not always bring the best results. He continued to watch Liverpool's reserves and scouted players that Liverpool thought they might sign. He looked for any way of winning.

What he'd not lost in the ten years since playing was the satisfaction that beating opponents brought in the hard game of football. Ten years with 'Shankly' – witnessing his mood after defeats – made the desire for success infectious. Winning became routine. It made Paisley a sore loser.

Others shared the sentiment. By 1967, Paisley, Joe Fagan and Reuben Bennett had been joined on the backroom staff by 33-year-old Ronnie Moran, a former Liverpool captain in the twilight of his Anfield playing days. The quartet had seen at close quarters what Shankly's football creed had achieved – and the further it took them as a club the more absorbed they became about how to extract the slightest hint of competitive advantage. Fagan worked a few evenings a week as coach for the employees of the Guinness Export brewery at Aughton, north of Liverpool, and they repaid him in kind with a healthy supply of the stout. They stored it in the little room at Anfield where the players' boots were kept and where, for week after week, Paisley, Moran, Fagan and Bennett sat on upturned beer crates and dissected the players, opponents and challenges ahead. Some of their ideas would make it to Shankly, though he was not part of the collective and didn't tend to venture into the place they called 'the Boot Room', besides occasionally arriving to seek out Bennett, his assistant until the 1971 reshuffle. He was wise enough to see that there was wisdom generated in there, though did not contribute to it.

It was in a more conventional football physiotherapist's role that Paisley became better known to the wider world. *The Kop* paper described breathlessly in 1967 how he was using 'some of the most modern equipment and medication ever discovered to keep the Liverpool lads at peak fitness'. The paper encouraged its readers to examine an image of Paisley using his aerosol on winger Ian Callaghan on the pitch – 'the type usually used to contain fly killers, air sweeteners and ladies' hair lacquer'. Paisley explained how the aerosol 'deadens the nerve ends, prevents swelling and, if there's a cut on the injury it congeals the blood'. A 'mod' is what *The Kop* called him.

He certainly wasn't always that. His enthusiasm for the sample products which the medical companies sent his way was not always judicious. 'It was torture at times!' says St John. 'And it was funny, because none of them had a degree in anything except football.'

There was an episode involving the director T. V. Williams and laxative tablets on an away trip which few ever forgot, and there were also consequences when defender Chris Lawler's cartilage locked on him during a game at Queens Park Rangers, prompting Paisley to produce an ice pack of crystals which he packed around the defender's leg and bandaged up. The team were on the train back north to Liverpool Lime Street when Lawler's knee began throbbing and burning. Lawler disappeared to the toilet to investigate the problem and removed the bandage and crystals. The crystals had fixed themselves to the skin and ripped off as he tried to take them away. A specialist who examined the leg at Anfield the next morning was dismayed by what he saw. Paisley's crystals had been a disaster and Lawler was told he must wait a month for the skin to heal before a cartilage operation. Lawler felt that his leg was never the same again and suspected that the delay to surgery was significant. He even felt Paisley had pushed Shankly to get him selected for Liverpool's 1974 FA Cup final against Newcastle United as a way of paying him back for causing irrevocable medical harm. He says Paisley told him, 'I owed you one,' after Liverpool's 3-0 win. Both Shankly and Paisley would try anything if it made winning more likely.

Over time, the two of them became complementary: one providing such vision and inspiration that the players thought they could part the seas; the other the details underpinning it. Neither of them was at his best when it came to direct confrontation, but Paisley could at least take the emotion out of those moments. Beneath the quiet exterior, he was the harder and more unflinching of the pair. It meant that he became the conveyor of Shankly's bad news, gripes and complaints.

Shankly would use Paisley as a proxy when it came to dealing with his most common grouse: players who were on the treatment table. 'Is he swinging the lead, Bob?' Shankly would generally say to Paisley in a loud voice, within the offender's earshot.

Paisley reached such an understanding of how Shankly's mind worked that he seemed to know how to head off a scene between the boss and a player. He knew there was no point entering into an argument with Shankly, because there would only ever be one winner, so he looked for more cunning means of persuasion.

'If you were unfit, Bob pronounced you as unfit, but you had to say you were fit, run around a bit and then let the boss talk you out of it,' says St John. 'He did it with me one time. I said, "I think I'll be OK, boss." When Shanks saw you it was, "Christ, son! You can't play."'

John Toshack felt that Paisley's cunning stretched to double-bluffing Shankly over team selection. 'Bob reached the stage where if Shanks said, "I don't know whether to play John or Kevin," and Bob wanted him to play Kevin, Bob would say, "I'd play John,"' says Toshack. 'Bob was very, very clever and shrewd in that respect.' St John would often hear the long-suffering assistant's account of Shank's latest far-fetched request. 'Bloody hell. You'll never guess what he wants now . . .'

More often than not, Paisley's role as the bridge between Shankly and the players simply entailed being the bringer of bad tidings. And that contributed substantially to the sense that he was the manager's lackey or hatchet man, reporting tales back to Shankly which might affect the players' chances of playing the next week. Paisley's nickname was 'the Rat' and though that had initially been in recognition of his role serving with Montgomery's Desert Rats, many of the players had a more literal and unheroic application of the term.

'Shanks's hatchet man,' is how Kevin Keegan described him. 'Shanks would load the gun and Bob would fire the bullets.' Steve Heighway, signed by Shankly in 1970, viewed the fealty of Paisley with suspicion. 'He was always at Shankly's shoulder, always trying to see through what Shanks wanted,' says Heighway. 'If there was ever any criticism it would come from Bob. If there was any toughness it would come from Bob. Not in an aggressive, big-time personality way. But when he came out, everybody was on their guard. Everyone was quite frightened of Bob in the early years before he became manager.'

It would have helped Paisley's popularity if his own powers of communication had been better. But while Shankly won people's hearts and minds, Paisley, for many, lacked a redeeming feature, and that made him hard to love. 'Shanks was the one who could build you up and make you feel special,' says Phil Thompson, who was coming through the ranks. 'Bob was the one to knock you down. He would be there, scurrying, pointing the finger at you. He was the nark.'

Toshack's interpretation of Paisley's machinations would prove to be extremely shrewd decades later but, in the early seventies, he simply didn't seem to have a relationship with the man: 'It was very, very difficult to get Bob to open out . . . to have any conversation with him – like trying to get blood out of a stone. He was a strange sort of character. There was always a little bit of a mystery about Bob. For us as players, it was all Shanks. Bob was just a physio.' John Bennett, who was signed by Shankly but never played for him, remarked that 'one stare from Bob made you go cold'.

Yet Heighway would be surprised to know that to others Paisley could be the father confessor at times, able to grasp the small personal detail which Shankly had neither the time nor patience for.

Paisley's medical samples may not have helped Lawler but the defender sought solace in him when Shankly refused to allow him to go on honeymoon after the European Cup semi-final against Internazionale in 1965, insisting instead that the full-back accompany the rest of the squad on a players' trip to Mallorca – without wives. Paisley was 'much easier to deal with than Shanks because he listened to your problems', according to Lawler – though he still had to go to the Balearics, as Shankly had instructed.

It was Paisley who talked to Ian St John, a part of the team since 1961, when Shankly dropped him to the bench for a league match as the end of his Liverpool days approached in the autumn of 1969. 'Remember how Shank has been to the players down the years,' Paisley told him. 'Everyone has to accept that the end will come.' St John got to know him through the Sunday mornings at Anfield, when he would be on the treatment table receiving Paisley's medical treatment. 'You could talk to him,' says St John. 'He always made good points. I loved that.'

In later years, when Paisley managed the team, the joke would be about his impenetrable north-east accent. 'That's footballers being piss-takers,' St John says. 'Shanks was precise and dogmatic if he was giving someone orders. Bob was different but you could hear what he was saying.'

Why did Paisley divide opinion in this way? Perhaps because the players who wore their hearts on their sleeves, like Keegan and Alec Lindsay, were the only ones this essentially awkward man could reach, and on those occasions you imagine they would have done more of the talking. Things were different with the more aloof and worldly characters, like Toshack and Heighway. With his essential shyness, Paisley did not excel at initiating social pathways.

Older players felt he was bringing technical and tactical changes to bear too. Tommy Smith always believed Paisley had made Keegan 'more tactically aware'. Paisley also worked closely with young goalkeeper Ray Clemence. In his early days at Liverpool, Clemence had difficulty kicking the dead ball and he always recalled being heckled by his own supporters in a home game against Swansea Town (soon to become Swansea City) in September 1968 for scuffing his goal-kicks in a gale. It was so bad that Swansea's players were deliberately shooting wide to concede goal-kicks as way of regaining easy possession. Paisley identified the young keeper's fear of playing in the wind and had the flags removed from the top of Anfield stadium to take his mind off the breeze. He would also work in the gym with him on boxing routines. Paisley's skill on the boxing speed balls was his only sporting attribute which impressed the players. He believed that developing a similar skill would help the goalkeeper's reactions.

It was always the quiet word from him on these occasions, rather than the group discussion, and to those who discovered this side he was the human face of the Shankly–Paisley partnership.

'He got wiser and wiser and wiser,' says Keith Burkinshaw, who played for the reserves from 1953 to 1957 and later became Tottenham Hotspur manager. 'There was absolutely nothing fancy about Bob. He just got right to the meat of the problem immediately. There were no fancy words with him and he stripped everything to the bone. The players knew this and they responded and reacted to the honesty that shone through and the plain way he said things.'

There was a Boot Room purdah which made it difficult to know whether Shankly or Paisley contributed most to specific developments in the team's playing style, though the fact that Shankly never joined those gatherings seems significant. He appears to have concentrated on getting the psychology right while the backroom staff handled the mechanics, with Paisley the most tactically literate of them all. 'We would not know what went on in there,' says Ian St John. 'And no one dared ask. No one knew what Bill or Bob suggested. It just happened.'

Paisley seems to have played a substantial role in the development of a new style of goalkeeping at Liverpool which had a lasting impact on the way the side played throughout the 1970s and 1980s. Tommy Lawrence, the keeper signed before Shankly's arrival, made up a Melwood five-a-side team also comprising Shankly, Paisley, Fagan and Bennett which regularly took on five of the first team's outfield players. There were no goalkeepers in those games so Lawrence played as a defender. The coaches realised that they were conceding fewer goals than they would had he operated in his goal. Shankly subsequently called Lawrence into a meeting in his office, at which the Boot Room members were present, and told him he was to advance out of his area in Liverpool's games as well, thus allowing the midfield to push up and play a high defensive line. The team's keepers continued to do so for the next 20 years.

Paisley's intuition about injuries helped solve some substantial difficulties in that realm, too. There was a serious problem when Keegan persistently complained of foot discomfort, soon after signing in the summer of 1971. Shankly was so irritated that he told him to his face that he was a 'malingerer' – one of his favoured terms of opprobrium for those in the treatment room.

It was Paisley who methodically searched his medical experience for a solution. 'He started to interrogate me about the strangest things,' Keegan said. 'Did I live in an attic with a lot of stairs? Was I walking up hills? Was I going horse riding? They even asked me if I had been skiing! In Liverpool?' Eventually, Keegan's new car, a green Capri, was seized upon as the suspect. 'They went out and virtually stripped the motor, lifted the carpets. It was decided that one of the pedals was too stiff. For someone who wasn't fully qualified, Bob was as good a physiotherapist as a club could have.'

Shankly later ascribed himself the leading role in the Keegan foot-injury discovery. In his autobiography, published in 1976, he said it was he who had interrogated Keegan about the Capri and then sent Joe Fagan to go out and test the clutch. 'That,' said Shankly, was 'how we paid attention to detail.' Keegan 'stopped driving that car and stopped driving altogether for a while until his foot was better.'

This reflected Shankly's descriptions and discussions of his relationship with Paisley. He rarely acknowledged the assistant. Theirs was one of those double acts which, like Busby and Jimmy Murphy, Clough and Peter Taylor, Joe Mercer and Malcolm Allison, have delivered some of the greatest success stories in football. One of the pair is generally brash; the other more contemplative and withdrawn. But Busby and Clough were far more inclined to acknowledge the quiet man's contribution. 'He was my bridge to the players,' Busby said of Murphy. 'I couldn't have done it without him,' Clough said of Taylor.

But acknowledgements from Shankly about Paisley are hard to find. The Scot's autobiography mentions just two specific contributions from Paisley, and neither has much significance. One came on the eve of Liverpool's European Cup semi-final against the Milanese giants Internazionale in 1965, when the noise from the abbey bell tower in Como, northern Italy, threatened the players' sleep, and Paisley was standing by, ready to be deputed to climb the tower and wrap cotton wool and bandages around the offending bells at Shankly's request – though they were talked out of it. 'That would have been one of the funniest things Bob had ever done!' Shankly writes.

The other came when defender Emlyn Hughes was injured in a pre-season friendly in Cologne, in the summer of 1967, after a challenge that looked likely to earn him a dismissal. Paisley was instructed to make a fuss of Hughes's injury as a stalling device to prevent him being sent off, though the strategy didn't work and Hughes was ordered off.

The myriad orders carried out for Shankly by his assistant also included pumping air into footballs the Scot was wrongly convinced the opposition bench were deliberately deflating during one pre-season tour (leaving the said sphere resembling a 'small boulder', according to Ian St John) and painting St John's testicles and groin with iodine and boot polish, allowing the manager to 'prove' to the press that a Coventry City player, Brian Lewis, had grabbed them on Boxing Day 1967. (St John had punched Lewis and been sent off.)

'Perhaps some of my psychology has rubbed off on Bob,' Shankly reflected later. 'I'm not saying that he copies me, but he might say to himself, "Well, I remember one time such-and-such happened and Bill did that. I'll do the same.'"

There were times when Paisley found Shankly's indifference to others excruciating, though there is no evidence that he ever told him so. There were no arguments between the two that any can recall. Paisley remembered a trip to play Swansea Town in 1963, and the team stayed in Porthcawl. Two elderly women were in the television room of the hotel, waiting to watch *Coronation Street* and thus preventing Shankly from watching the boxing on the other channel. There were 14 in the Liverpool group, so he called for a vote. 'Shank thought he was being democratic,' Paisley reflected. 'I walked out, I was too embarrassed to stay and watch.'

The pair once drove four hours to Lincoln to watch a goalkeeper, stopped at Doncaster to eat, arrived late for the match and had only observed a quarter of an hour's play before Shankly announced, 'I've seen enough.' 'The goalkeeper had had nothing to do but Shank had already decided he wasn't for us,' Paisley said. 'I don't know what he saw, but he saw something. [Shankly] was an impulsive man.'

Paisley seems to have challenged Shankly's thinking only occasionally. 'The business of offering advice is fraught with problems,' he said years later. 'Bill didn't give advice. He gave orders. Advice, by its very nature, must be something other people can take or leave.' In another reflection on their partnership, he said, 'The only thing possibly we had in common was we wanted to win and we were two bad losers.'

It could not be said that they were friends. Though Jessie Paisley and Nessie Shankly came to know each other better later in life, no one can remember Shankly ever turning up at Paisley's front door. There was no social visit from the Shanklys that Paisley's family can recall.

There was plenty to discuss by 1970. Perhaps it was inevitable that, having inculcated such self-belief in his players, Shankly should not have seen that they were mortal and ageing fast. A humiliating FA Cup sixth-round defeat at Watford in 1970 was the most graphic sign that the side Shankly had built up were fading. Watford won 1–0 but the indignity could have been far worse. Ray Lugg made a fool of defender Peter Wall, placing the ball through the defender's legs and crossing for Barry Endean, who had been left free to head past Tommy Lawrence.

Alun Evans, signed for £110,000 as an 18-year-old from Wolves, Tommy Lawrence, long-standing midfielder Gerry Byrne, St John and Ron Yeats were no longer good enough and this was the game which persuaded Shankly to let most of them go. 'A lot of our players were about the same age and I had given them a set time as to how long I thought they would last,' Shankly said in his autobiography. 'I had told them, "If you are a good athlete, your best seasons will be between 28 and 33. I had my best seasons during that period of my life." I thought some of them would have gone on longer than they did, because of their experience. Maybe the success they had shortened their careers. Perhaps they were no longer hungry enough. We had a mediocre time for while in the late 1960s as we prepared for the 1970s.'

Paisley had a different view of longevity. In his eyes no two players' 'best seasons' would necessarily be the same. Some of those who had delivered most for him were sold before the age of 28. None was kept until the age of 33.

If the ageing Liverpool side was a source of concern to Paisley, then he either said nothing or failed to persuade Shankly of the fact. After Liverpool had won their second championship in three years in 1966, they did not win a trophy for six years – finishing fifth, third, second, fifth and fifth in the five subsequent seasons. The runners-up finish of 1968–69 looked more competitive than it was: Liverpool finished six points off Leeds United, with the two Manchester teams', Everton's and Arsenal's titles in surrounding seasons providing a sense that there were dangers everywhere.

Gradually, Liverpool emerged from the barren years. Shankly bought young players from the lower leagues – Keegan and Clemence – and, in time, they were ready. The side won the First Division title in 1973, and the following season's FA and UEFA Cups. The players who gathered at Anfield for pre-season training in July 1974 were viewed as the ones who stood on the cusp of renewed success. The local papers offered no sense of clouds on the horizon. Heighway had scored 41 not out in 11 overs for Southport v New Brighton in cricket's National Club Knockout. The *Liverpool Echo* announced that Clemence would be switching on the Christmas lights in Skelmersdale that winter.

And then came two bombshells. Shankly told the world that he was stepping down, and Liverpool told Paisley that they wanted him to be their next manager. For the man who had spent the best part of 15 years lost in Shankly's conversation, the first revelation was shocking. The second was beyond belief.

3

NOT ME

Christine Paisley was 20 and had been at a schoolfriend's wedding in Liverpool on the day that the Anfield edifice came crashing down and her father's boss announced that he was walking away from the club which had become his spiritual home. The news about Bill Shankly was everywhere. They'd even officially announced it on the public address system in St John's Market in the city centre. But somehow she hadn't caught the news until she walked back up to the front door of South Manor Way, let herself in and her mother told her. Christine had never considered her father to be famous. The nearest she had got to such a notion was seeing him run onto the field with a sponge. The reaction of her mother, Jessie, made it patently clear that the last thing Bob Paisley intended to do was to stake a claim to be the next Liverpool manager. This was the man who still liked to do the ironing on Sunday afternoons and who often wore Jessie's 'Dame Edna Everage' spectacles for reading because he had never got around to buying a pair of his own. A man whose capacity for a life without football was evident every time he leaned back in his black vinyl swivel chair in the front room, placed his feet on the mantelpiece and watched the racing, or put on Jim Reeves or Gilbert and Sullivan's *The Mikado* on the record player.

'Is Dad going to take over now?' Christine asked her mother.

'Don't be daft,' she replied.

Paisley, back at the club that day, felt the same. His morning talk was full of the usual summer recollections – the stables, the seaside and the cricket. He would take some convincing that this wasn't just one of those standard threats to resign which 'Shank' had issued several times before this time of the year. Summer madness: that's what Peter Robinson, the club secretary who seemed to have been talking Shankly out of finishing every June since the late 1960s, always called it. The hot summer of 1974 – when the world was absorbed by the death throes of President Richard Nixon's attempts to ride out the Watergate scandal and the Turkish invasion of Cyprus – seemed no different. 'Just give it a couple of weeks and he'll be back to normal,' Robinson assured the board.

Robinson always put Shankly's loose threats about walking away down to the way the emptiness of the close season gnawed away at his self-confidence, when there were no football matches to occupy his restless mind. For all his exuberance, Shankly had a terrible fear of failure and of what that would mean to the supporters. In the six fallow years between 1966 and 1973 many fans had written to the Anfield board to say Shankly was finished. With his obsessive knowledge of every aspect of the club, there would have been no keeping that from him.

Paisley and Shankly were not the kind to share such anxieties, or how they saw the future unfolding. The only interest they shared beyond football was boxing – with a mutual admiration of Jack Dempsey, Muhammad Ali, Rocky Marciano and Sugar Ray Robinson. The only 'Bill and Bob' ever known to sit in the front room of the Paisley household were Paisley's accountants Bill Roberts and Bob Loughlin (also known to the family as 'Bill and Ben'), who were paid for their help with a crate of Guinness

Export, brought home from the Boot Room. Paisley tried his own way to talk Shankly down. 'Go off on a cruise and recharge your batteries,' he told him.

But alarm bells rang when Robinson went down to Shankly's office to remonstrate with him for a third time that summer and still could not get through. 'Look, Bill, really you shouldn't go. You're too young and useful to go. You can stay here, and I know I can persuade the directors to let you do whatever you want,' Robinson said. 'You can work one day [or] every day, be manager or, if you don't want to be manager, general manager – anything. You can literally name your job if you'll stay.'

But Shankly's mind was set. 'No. I want to go. I want to go,' are the words Robinson remembers him saying. Conversation had to start moving on to who could fill the space he would leave. As the *Liverpool Echo*'s headline put it: 'Search is on for a Superman.' This, the paper reported, was the 'biggest sensation in soccer' since England had sacked Sir Alf Ramsey in April that year.

Eventually, when it was clear he really could not be persuaded, Liverpool chairman John Smith and secretary Robinson asked the 60-year-old whom he felt should succeed him.

'Jack Charlton,' Shankly replied.

It was an odd suggestion. Charlton was only two years into his first managerial appointment, at Middlesbrough. But it was his direct style of football that Robinson and Smith – whose joint task it was to recommend a successor – felt would not fit Anfield. 'We just didn't think Jack Charlton and the way he played was right for Liverpool at that time,' says Robinson. There was a second man under consideration, as well as Charlton. It was not Crystal Palace's Malcolm Allison, even though Allison did not dispel a link between himself and the position at the time. 'No,' Robinson says of the Allison link. 'We would not have thought he was right for Liverpool at that time [either].' The second man's most likely identity is Bobby Robson, who had turned struggling Ipswich Town into fourth-placed finishers in each of the two previous First Division campaigns, having applied speculatively for the East Anglia job. Robson, who was 41 at the time, *did* fit the Liverpool mould, with his focus on good scouting, good judgement of players and 'quality time on the training ground' as he described the key to the Ipswich success which continued with a third-place finish in 1974–75. His imagination about the way the game should be played also made Ipswich one of the first sides to do away with the target-man striker at the time.

But more important to Robinson and Smith than what an outside candidate might bring was their desperation to hold on to what Shankly had built – and so the notion that there might be a successor right in front of their eyes gained ascendency very quickly. Of Shankly's backroom staff, that had to be Bob Paisley. His quiet and undemonstrative nature was certainly a world away from that of Shankly but Robinson and Smith felt that the other members of what had become known as the Boot Room meant that the then 55-year-old would not be on his own. The feeling was that the characters around him – Joe Fagan, Ronnie Moran and Reuben Bennett – were also strong.

There was not unanimity about appointing Paisley. One of the six-man Liverpool board wanted a younger man and was generally committed to the idea of appointing young people to lead the club. He felt that Paisley was too old and Robson, a full 14 years younger, was certainly of a different generation. But the dissenter on the board fell into line quickly. The contemplation of recruiting an outside candidate did not extend to Liverpool actually speaking to either Charlton or Robson.

'We did look at one or two managers who were employed at that time and, of course, thought about Bob,' says Robinson. 'It was left to John Smith and me to recommend to the board who to appoint. We thought that with the backroom staff we had we'd got a very strong set-up and we leaned towards Bob.'

Shankly made no contribution to the discussion of his successor beyond the initial answer he had given. 'Apart from when we asked the direct question who we should recommend, he didn't mention it again [though] I'm sure he congratulated Bob,' says Robinson.

From his vantage point as a senior member of the squad, John Toshack felt it was the board's fear of losing the recipe they had, rather than a deep conviction about Paisley's talents, that lay behind the decision. 'The board were thinking, "We don't want to bring in anyone new who is going to shake the bottle. Let's let the water float a little bit and see what happens,"' he says.

The problem was how to persuade Paisley to take the position on. He was part of the club's fixtures and fittings and comfortable enough in this realm to be on first-name terms with all the directors. But in two initial conversations, he made it categorically clear he did not want the role – though was not expansive about precisely why. 'He kept saying, "No, I don't feel I can do it,"' says Robinson. 'The meetings with Bob tended to be brief because he was not a great talker. He did develop as a manager, to deal with things, but initially he didn't say much. We were not sure what the exact problem was.'

Time was not on the side of Robinson and Smith. They were in new territory. No Liverpool manager had resigned before. Now, they had three weeks before the start of the 1974–75 season to find a successor. They sat Paisley down and tried to get to the bottom of what was troubling him.

It transpired that there were two concerns in his mind. The first was how people would react to him following Shankly, with an unspoken code among the backroom team at that time that one would never covet or seek to accede to another's job. The second was Paisley's aversion to the idea of handling the business of buying players and renewing their contracts. He didn't think he was capable of that. So an agreement was reached. Paisley would have the say if he wanted a player but Robinson and Smith would deal with other clubs on the buying side, while Robinson would deal with the contract renewals, or 're-signings' as those arrangements were known.

While these discussions took place in an atmosphere of anxiety at Anfield, the newspapers listed the various contenders to succeed Shankly. The *Liverpool Echo* toyed with the idea of two former Liverpool players – Coventry City team manager Gordon Milne, who was in part-time charge of England's under-18s and Ian St John, then managing Motherwell – as well as Allison, Robson, Jimmy Bloomfield (Leicester City) and Gordon Jago (QPR). Also mentioned was Tony Waiters, the former England international goalkeeper who had left a role as Liverpool's youth development manager two years earlier to pursue a career in football management and, via Burnley and Coventry, had taken over at Plymouth.

The *Liverpool Daily Post's* chief football correspondent Horace Yates led the entreaties for the appointment of Paisley, whom he knew well. 'Is Paisley the man to answer the Anfield call?' he asked. 'One of the reasons why the knowing ones claim Shankly is unique is that on the field and off it he has developed a pattern in which blows can be sustained and wounds healed without recourse to outside aid. Nobody has absorbed his ideas and patterns of play more assiduously and there are few greater readers of play and players anywhere than Paisley.'

There was not a tumult of pieces in this vein. Shankly seemed to hint at the idea of an outsider coming in. 'When the new manager comes, I go. He may not want to have me anywhere near the place.' And when the announcement of the Paisley succession came, it hardly reverberated across the land. A small article suggesting 'the board may turn to Bob Paisley' was buried amid the *Liverpool Echo*'s second-hand car advertisements – £625 for a beige 1971 Mini 850; £1,145 for a bronze 1973 Cortina 1600 – while Brian Kidd's signing for Bertie Mee's Arsenal for £100,000 seemed to capture the national imagination more.

'Paisley is King,' the *Post* declared on Friday 26 July 1974, the day his appointment was confirmed. But it did not feel like a coronation. *The Times*' report of Paisley's appointment that day ran to just 241 words.

During the annual general meeting at which shareholders received the news, on the evening of 26 July, Paisley received a standing ovation as he stood up from his seat, though it was Shankly who took the limelight that night. His speech – confident, funny, erudite – brought the house down.

Liverpool's Tommy Smith claimed that on his last day at the club Shankly typed a note and left it on the desk in the manager's office for Paisley to find the next day. The note, intended to boost Paisley's confidence, stated simply: 'Bill Shankly says Bob Paisley is the best manager in the game.' If Smith is to be believed, Paisley found it, added two commas and arranged for it to be posted to Shankly's house: 'Bill Shankly, says Bob Paisley, is the best manager in the game.' The quiet man of the partnership would take some persuading that he had not wandered into the wrong room.

4

HELLO, BOSS

It didn't help that Bob Paisley was wearing his unflattering red Gola tracksuit. It had never done much to conceal the rotund demeanour that had made him such a foil to the taut drill sergeant Bill Shankly. The kit had always been part of the faintly comical air Paisley gave off in the years when he was just plain 'Bob', the assistant manager and man in the shadows, pottering around Liverpool's Melwood training ground.

Yet now here he was standing in front of the players, on a July morning in 1974, telling them he was going to be their manager. It would have lifted the mood of stunned despondency caused by Shankly's declaring he was stepping down if Paisley had been able to impress upon them that they were all in this together. But it wasn't like that. He didn't want to be here, Paisley told them, over and over. Someone counted the times he repeated the assertion: eight, Steve Heighway thought.

Paisley related how he'd tried to persuade 'Shank' to go on that cruise but there was no persuading him this time. So 'upstairs' had been on to him, asking him to take over, he said – his term of reference for the Liverpool board. He'd refused but they wouldn't take 'no' for an answer, so he was going to have to do it and see how it went.

Kevin Keegan responded first, wearing a look of earnest concern on his face, which went against his persona as the dressing-room joker, for which they all called him 'Andy McDaft'. Paisley had to take the job. He was entitled to it, Keegan said. Then Ian Callaghan contributed. Paisley knew all there was to know, he said. The players looked across at him because Callaghan only tended to speak when there was something worth saying. Emlyn Hughes, the captain, was snivelling in the corner, still unable to accept that Shankly was going. A few of the players rolled their eyes.

Witnesses say Paisley mumbled some self-conscious thanks. He said they'd see how it went. He'd try to tide them over until someone else was appointed. Three minutes later he'd run out of things to say. That was it, then. They'd better get on with the job and make the best of it, he concluded, and ventured off, with the familiar limp they'd all come to know.

His uncertainty was something Robinson and Smith already knew all too well about. Mixed up with it was the culture embedded in the club about not knifing your boss. 'It was his way of saying he hadn't in any way stabbed Shanks in the back and didn't go looking for that kind of job,' Toshack says.

But most of the team saw a man who just didn't want to be there. For perhaps a minute after he'd gone there was silence, as the enormous collective realisation dawned on the players of what Shankly's departure actually meant. They were to be led by a manager who had never given a team talk in his life and who seemingly could not string a sentence together.

Heighway, the *de facto* shop steward of the group, tended to take the lead when there was organising to be done. It was he who broke the silence after Paisley had left. To this day he remembers what he said to the players, in a rallying speech which lasted considerably longer than Paisley's: 'Listen. Unless we pull together and make this work, this could all fall down like a pack of cards. Better to have Bob than have some bloke come in who doesn't rate half of us. At least we know there's a good chance that Bob will see something in all of us because he's has been here for ever and we have all been playing.' (Heighway was the only one who never called Shankly 'boss' – he didn't go in for that obsequious footballer hierarchy stuff – and he certainly wasn't going to give Paisley that title.)

His teammates nodded, though the fear which had gripped them most in the week since Shankly had made his big announcement is what Heighway remembers: 'At first we were worried sick that someone who didn't know us would come in, or somebody would come in that didn't rate you as a player,' he says. 'We worried that the success over the past two or three years had been down to Shanks more than the fact that we were good. It probably took Shanks's retirement to make us think that way. He was the great protector of the team. He would never criticise you in public. The group was really close. Any stuff that needed to be brought out was brought out privately in team meetings. And suddenly he'd gone, and so the next thing was that Bob came in and apologetically announced he didn't want to be there.'

Only the players know how Paisley looked at that time. There is television footage of the sensational press conference in which Liverpool chairman John Smith, reading from notes in his clipped southern accent, declared: 'It is with great regret that Mr Shankly has intimated that he wishes to retire from active participation in league football.' Tony Wilson, who within eight years would launch the Factory Records label and the Hacienda nightclub in

Manchester, was the then energetic local TV reporter who followed up with a question for Shankly. 'How can you of all people hope to survive without football?' he asked.

But Paisley does not feature. All we see of him taking up the post is a black and white image from the Liverpool papers of him walking past the empty seats flanking the room at the meeting of the Liverpool shareholders when his appointment was announced. He bites his bottom lip and there is applause from an audience of fairly ageing men, in their suits and ties. There was certainly no introductory press conference.

What was going through his mind? Almost certainly the thought of what had happened 40 miles up the road, where a mere five years earlier a 44-year-old Frank O'Farrell had stepped into the shoes of Paisley's friend and former Liverpool teammate Matt Busby at Manchester United. Paisley knew Busby well enough to have an insight into Farrell's disastrous 18 months in the post. There was enough in that precedent to know that the taking over from a legend carried the risk of embarrassment.

Years later, Paisley said he knew that United's experience carried a lesson for him. 'Bill's image had to be broken – just as in an earlier case the image of Sir Matt Busby had to be broken at Manchester United before the club became successful again.' Bold words, though they were spoken with the benefit of hindsight, when he had taken the club on after Shankly. It is doubtful that Paisley's ambitions would have extended to breaking with Shankly and the past as he stood up to tell the players he would be in charge.

It says much for Shankly's ensuing struggle to cut the umbilical cord with the club that he chose to take the team out for the Charity Shield on 10 August, leading them out at Wembley when they, as the previous season's FA Cup winners, faced Leeds United, the Division One champions. But Paisley then faced a mopping-up job after the disastrous consequences of that valedictory game of his predecessor's.

The match took place against a backdrop of national concern over hooliganism, and when Kevin Keegan and Leeds' Billy Bremner were sent off for fighting on the pitch it touched a nerve. It didn't help that the Keegan had looked like a hooligan, ripping off his shirt to reveal his torso while still 20 yards from the sidelines and, to Paisley's horror in the dugout, encountering a supporter who'd broken free to challenge him as he reached the touchline.

It looked very bad when Paisley found himself on the 7 a.m. train to London Euston with Keegan and chairman John Smith to appear before a three-man Football Association disciplinary panel. 'Shameful example' was the headline of that morning's *Daily Mail* leader column. 'Footballers who throw their fists at each other are symbolically licensing violence.'

The FA read the public mood and took no prisoners. The hearing went as badly as it could because the chairman of the tribunal seemed to have a distaste for football. 'You footballers are paid far too much money,' he said. Keegan and Bremner were both banned for 11 matches and Keegan's sense of victimhood saw him take himself off to his family in Doncaster, South Yorkshire. It was a desperate start to Paisley's tenure, considering that Keegan had been Liverpool's top scorer in each of their previous two seasons and was undoubtedly his greatest asset.

It didn't help the situation that Shankly publicly said he would have secured a better settlement for Keegan from the governing body. Paisley passed it all off with a joke; the first public evidence of a line in gentle humour which he would employ in the bad moments across the next nine years. His wit in the public sphere wasn't the sharpest and the metaphors, frequently derived from horse racing, were strained, and yet this had a habit of breaking the tension. 'The only injury we have at Anfield at the moment is my heart. It's broken,' he declared.

It was more serious than that. Keegan had scored 52 goals in the previous three years. Paisley wondered where those goals would come from in the next two months, yet he didn't reveal publicly the full extent of his anxiety. 'It sent a chill down my spine. It could have ended my career,' he said years later.

He lacked the words to coax Keegan back into the fold so operated at a more practical level, seeking help from those who could bring influence to bear. The Keegan family were his own kind of people. Keegan's father, Joe, was a son of Hetton-le-Hole. So he played that angle, telephoning him to help get the player back to Merseyside, where he could employ the quiet powers of persuasion he'd always found worked best with Keegan. The player returned.

The opening game of the 1974–75 season, at newly promoted Luton Town, awaited the new manager. Paisley adopted the Friday routine at Melwood that Shankly had always laid down. There would be the same team meeting at 10 a.m. in the little Melwood training-ground room, for which the players would gather on chairs around a table with a baize cloth laid on top of it and blue figures to mark out the tactical plan. Paisley, the improbable speechmaker, then embarked on a discussion about the players in Harry Haslam's team, who had just completed a spectacular rise from the Fourth Division to the First in a mere seven years.

It was the lack of grasp of detail which the players remembered later. Paisley's instructions for defender Tommy Smith were not to go 'wandering round like a miner without a lamp' but to keep an eye on his man, though precisely which man was unclear.

Smith didn't want to look like he was testing Paisley out, so he left Paisley to continue. Brian Hall remembered being the next man singled out for instructions. He was to 'keep an eye' on 'what's-his-name' – a player represented by the blue figure Paisley was clutching. Hall, a squad player looking to begin the season by making a serious impression, wanted to be sure who he was supposed to be dealing with. 'Who are you talking about, Bob?' Hall asked.

'Eerm, eeerm . . . what's his name . . .?' Paisley replied, still apparently unable to conjure the name.

'OK, then,' said Hall, looking around at his teammates and knowing there was no value in pushing it.

'Ah bollocks,' said Paisley. He swept the figures to the floor, told the players to just go out and beat their opponents, and left the room.

To some, this was a sign of a new manager hopelessly out of his depth. Ray Kennedy, who had only been at the club for two weeks since arriving from Arsenal as Shankly's last signing, was used to Don Howe's carefully crafted team talks and wondered what kind of future he had walked into.

But Paisley's first pre-match team talk actually had all the hallmarks of a classic Shankly stunt. Shankly, too, enjoyed upending the tactics board and refusing to dignify the opposition with a discussion of their names. His assistant Reuben Bennett had once delighted Shankly and the team by returning from a scouting mission with the names wrong, calling a midfielder 'Wheelbarrow' instead of 'Barrowclough'.

Tommy Smith offered reassurances for Kennedy. 'Listen,' he told him. 'We've done all the right things in training. Everybody knows the job. If we want to know which Luton players he was talking about, we'll just look in the match programme tomorrow.'

There had already been a hint of something different about Paisley's method, though, and no one could have failed to observe its significance.

Central defender Larry Lloyd, one of Liverpool's traditional centre-halves, had missed the end of 1973–74 season through injury and Shankly had given his jersey to midfielder Phil Thompson, a ball-playing alternative to Lloyd, who had played only a few games at centre-back for the reserves. Thompson, elegant in possession but less commanding in the air than Lloyd, had also played in central defence at Wembley in the 1974 FA Cup final.

In the first training match of the new campaign, the first XI v reserves, the question was whether new manager Paisley would restore Lloyd to the senior ranks or keep him with the second string. 'Reserves,' Lloyd was told, to his own fury. He was a big personality at Liverpool and was never slow to complain. That's why they called him 'Albert Tatlock', after the curmudgeonly *Coronation Street* character. During the practice match, Lloyd advanced into the first XI's penalty box and delivered a header which went narrowly over the bar. 'If you had a big centre-half in your team I wouldn't have had that header,' Lloyd shouted.

Thompson says he heard Paisley shout back: 'Why didn't you fucking score, then?'

Paisley sold Lloyd on 15 August, two days before his first game in charge of the club – releasing him to Coventry City at the age of 25 for £240,000 – a fee three times bigger than Liverpool had ever earned for a player. It was a bold move for the first week in a new role; a decision which did not seem to be one of an individual pushed unwillingly into a job and lacking all notion of how to deal with it.

This new central defensive philosophy was hardly unknown because times were certainly changing. West Germany captain Franz Beckenbauer had been excelling as the classy, nimble-footed central defender since the late 1960s. The Dutch World Cup team had sparkled with elegant central defenders in the summer of 1974, with Arie Haan, a converted midfielder, alongside Wim Rijsbergen. They reached the final in Munich against a host nation side captained by 'the Kaiser' Beckenbauer at centre-half. Shankly had signed off his last season with both Thompson and Emlyn Hughes, another converted midfielder, in the middle of his defence.

Paisley seems to have been more attached to the new ways than Shankly, who in 1969 had taken the decision to sign Lloyd – another stopper in the mould of Ron Yeats, whose time had passed, but a technically inferior one.

Paisley rarely involved himself in the minutiae of training but the exclusion of Lloyd from virtually his first training session went to the heart of what kind of a side his would be. 'That was Bob's biggest call and it came right at the start,' says Thompson, who went on to play 37 games that season, partnering Hughes in central defence. 'It was Paisley saying, "I want a different kind of central defender. This is what I believe in."'

John Toshack, who had been a Shankly player for four years, feels that Paisley was 'a little bit enthralled with this European style', and that the immediate effect in his first season was greater emphasis on possession and a build-up from the back. 'You might say it's a strange thing from someone from Durham who had played in the 1950s, but he decided to play Thompson and Emlyn [and] completely did away with the traditional stopper centre-back that Liverpool had always had. Liverpool became a team that kept possession at the back, built up slowly and patiently. Of all the things Bob did in management that was the biggest fundamental change. The brain centre was the understanding that the goalkeeper and two centre-backs had.' Toshack's description of the side as 'patient' is significant. There was immediately less blood and thunder about the team's play.

They won 2–1 at Luton, with goals from Smith and Heighway. A goalless draw followed at Wolves three days later – and then victory against Leicester at Anfield on a night when a new manager might have basked in the self-satisfaction of his first home win in charge. Paisley was a footnote to the main occasion, though. The match had been designated as the one in which Liverpool would bid farewell to Shankly who, with his inimitable sense of occasion and bond with the people, materialised in the middle of the Kop terrace.

None of the journalists asked Paisley whether Shankly's presence was awkward for him, nor what he'd thought of the barbed observation that he would have done better for Liverpool at the Keegan hearing. Judging by the newspaper reports, no one asked Paisley much at all on the occasion of his first Anfield match at the helm. His predecessor was the shadow on the wall in those early months.

Shankly had realised almost immediately that resigning was a monumental mistake and he could not let Liverpool go. When the players arrived by coach at Melwood at 10 a.m. each morning, maintaining the routine that he had set down, Shankly would be ready in his training kit at Melwood, his car already parked up at the front. Ostensibly, he was there to keep himself fit. In reality, he was there because he craved the life he had relinquished.

'Morning, lads,' he would greet them.

'Morning, boss,' they would reply, awkwardly, not knowing how to address him with Paisley within earshot. Shankly then proceeded to jog around the running track with them on their warm-ups and provide the encouragement that managers generally give, while Paisley watched from the sanctuary of his office: the office which Shankly had once occupied.

There was a collective state of mourning for Shankly in Liverpool at the time. The local papers were dominated by plans for a permanent reminder of his work. A local Liberal councillor, David Alton, wanted to rename the recently pedestrianised Bold Street 'Shankly Parade'. The first of Shankly's ghost-written *Liverpool Echo* columns described the evening he'd spent in the company of supporters at the Vines pub in Liverpool city centre and the Mons establishment in Bootle.

'Keep at it, son,' Shankly told Ray Kennedy when he encountered him at Melwood one morning. Kennedy became convinced that Shankly was privately expressing doubts about laying out £200,000 to buy him from Arsenal. Word got back to him that he had asked Bob Wilson, television pundit and one of Kennedy's former Arsenal teammates, 'Should I have spent the money?' Kennedy was one of life's worriers.

There was an exchange in those early weeks between Shankly and the young teenage striker Trevor Birch, who was last in the Melwood dressing-room and lacing his boots when Shankly strode in.

'Alright, son?' Shankly said, leaving Birch searching for something to say in such stellar company.

'Bob's doing well, isn't he, boss?' the teenager replied, seizing on Paisley's first weeks since taking Shankly's old seat, which by then had yielded five wins and a draw. 'They've won a few games now.'

'Jesus Christ, son,' Shankly retorted. 'I could have left a monkey in charge.'

Paisley said nothing to Shankly about this awkwardness. Verbal confrontations were never his game. With Shankly, there would only be one winner and with innate respect for hierarchy, he would still have considered him his senior. It is why they had never argued down the years. Paisley did make his feelings known to Robinson when he met him back at Anfield after training, though.

'It's very difficult with him there. He doesn't say too much, but it's just the players,' Robinson recalls Paisley saying. 'It's awkward. The players don't know what to say or call him.'

More revealing than this embarrassment was the fact that he did not want Shankly back in. Had Paisley remained reluctant to manage Liverpool, Shankly's return to the scene would have been the perfect route out; the ideal opportunity to hand back the reins and disappear back into the shadows. 'Shank' would have had the two-month break Paisley had proposed, only minus the cruise.

Paisley's disinclination to do that revealed that the quiet man was also an unyielding one. Once he had taken up the position, he *did* want to be manager and, what is more, he was not inclined to ask for his predecessor's advice. Paisley tried to encourage Shankly to look for work elsewhere. He suggested some scouting missions to Scotland. He raised the idea of him taking Nessie along with him and Liverpool paying their expenses.

None of this worked. Paisley then agreed with Robinson and Smith that something needed to be done. After several conversations with them, he left 'upstairs' with an agreed plan of action which they would put into effect. Shankly would be telephoned at home about the situation, rather than invited into Anfield. This unenviable duty fell to Smith who, in line with what he, Robinson and Paisley had discussed, pointed out to Shankly that visiting Melwood was fine, but could he please do so when the players were not there.

There was no way of avoiding causing mortal offence. Shankly abandoned his Melwood routine, never to resume it, and began turning up at Everton's training ground instead. Years later it was suggested that Shankly had called Smith and asked for his old job back. But he did not. 'That definitely didn't happen,' says

Robinson. 'He might have wished for it, but knowing Bill and his pride I don't think he could have done that.'

'I had to take into account the fact that it was Shank,' Paisley said in hindsight. 'I knew it would be difficult for him to do anything but the top job in any club. If he advised you, you had to take his advice. Bill was a boss man – and I don't mean that in any derogatory sense. If he had been elected onto the board at Liverpool he would have wanted top position; wanted to be in charge. His word was law – and that's not advice.'

Paisley was hard enough to go his own way, but wise enough to follow Shankly's. The creed of football he had had laid down was socialist and collectivist in ethos – its founding principle being that every player be subsidiary to the team effort; running, supporting, anticipating, covering and generally delivering to others on the field. You passed the ball to a red shirt and ran to take up a position to receive it. You were subsumed by the team ethic. Paisley had lived and breathed that for 15 years. It was a philosophy heaven sent for Liverpool, a socialist city where pomposity and swagger had always been viewed with suspicion and where there is always an acute antennae for pretentiousness and arrogance.

The first team were universally known by the coaching staff as as the 'Big 'Eads' – just so they knew that Shankly was always watching for signs of swagger. There would be no 'Billy Bigtimes' at Anfield. There was no time for anything that might be considered an affectation. The training kit was dowdy. The idea of building an indoor pitch, like Everton had, was scoffed at. 'This was a proper, run-down workingmen's club,' says Phil Thompson.

Complex tactical talk was viewed as pretention – even the practice of set-piece corners or free-kicks. When Shankly had, against his better judgement, been persuaded to attend a training course in 1971 at the Football Association's Lilleshall base with Paisley and reserve-team coach Joe Fagan, he lasted a day before telling Paisley, 'That's enough, Bob. We're going home.' And sure enough, Paisley accompanied him back home to Liverpool while Fagan stayed to satisfy his curiosity about the new ideas on coaching.

The Liverpool rules were simply that, 'You get the ball; you give it, you move,' says Steve Heighway. 'It was the ultimate team game. You were only as good as your last game. You never got ahead of yourselves and you learned that the way you play is a waste of time without the physical effort.' And what a physical effort it was. Liverpool was a school of hard knocks played by hard men. 'If we tried to play the way we wanted to play without the physical effort, it wouldn't work. So the ideas of heading, running, tackling, competing [all] came before anything else. You earn the right to pass. You earn the right to play. If you are playing against somebody who is working just as hard as you are and negating what you do, it might be the 85th minute before you wear the opposition down. If the opposition are negating what we do, we don't change what we do.'

Brian Hall, a university graduate like Heighway – the pair were known as Big and Little Bamber, after the *University Challenge* host Bamber Gascoigne – observed something in the ethos of the place that was beyond intellectual analysis. 'I can't explain it. I can't explain how they instilled into us a system of play, a pattern of play and the role of the individual within it. It became almost instinctive. You knew your little role within the system. I was never told too deeply what I had to do when I went out there. You quickly learned it.'

As the first season developed, it did not take Thompson long to absorb what Paisley wanted to see in a centre-half. When the

20-year-old was stretchered from the field after twisting his knee against Stoke City at Anfield, eight games into the First Division season, newspaper photographs captured a look of deep concern on the manager's face. 'Six-weeker,' Paisley said, as he surveyed the player in the treatment room. Fagan gently twisted the knee and unlocked it, to Thompson's delight. It was two days later that a specialist diagnosed cartilage trouble. 'You'll be out for six weeks if all goes well,' he told Thompson.

For a time, the transition was seamless, though Paisley's life was changed utterly. His new role encroached on the family existence he once knew. Jessie saw him less, though she roped him into events when she could. It later became an annual tradition that he would bring one of Liverpool's trophies into the primary school where she taught and eventually became deputy head – St Mary's, Grassendale. Children – and very often their parents – would queue up to have their photograph taken with the silverware and manager.

Paisley opened the garden fête every year at St Hilda's school – though Christine had moved on by then – and provided an autographed ball. It was a Church of England school run by Anglican nuns, the Order of the Sisters of the Church, with one of whom, a Sister Mary Grace, Jessie formed a friendship. It amused Bob that she would accept his offer of a little sherry.

He cherished his Sunday afternoons away from Anfield – the only time of the week he properly saw the family, though Jessie related to the father of one of her pupils at St Mary's that her husband was beginning to regret giving out his home number to journalists because of the number of calls he would receive on a Sunday. The parent, John Toker, asked why they didn't get a second line installed. She looked at him with disbelief. 'Mr Toker,

I could never ask Bob to do that,' she replied. 'He already thinks that one line is an extravagance.'

Eventually Paisley asked that one designated individual from the press corps telephone on a Sunday and share the information, to preserve his sanity when he sat down after his lunch at South Manor Way. Football rarely entered the home. His sons would watch football and if something about a game or commentary vexed Paisley he would make an observation, though not often. Denis Law was 'past his sell-by date', he announced on one occasion. 'He's kidding the public.' He'd occasionally comment on a big transfer deal for a player he didn't rate. 'You'd swim across the Channel with him on your back to get that kind of money,' was one of his popular refrains in the household – meaning he'd have be so glad to get rid of a particular player that he would have dropped him off at the purchasing club himself. (He certainly felt Manchester United got good value by selling Ray Wilkins to Milan for £1.5m in 1984.)

There was a car accident four weeks into his first season. Paisley collided with a petrol tanker and badly damaged his vehicle, emerging unscathed. But there is no evidence that escalating stress might have contributed to this. The only inconvenience was a clash of duties, with the wedding of his eldest son, Robert, scheduled for October 1974. That had to be shifted to a Friday so the Liverpool manager could attend. At that stage, the performances were good, Liverpool sat top of the league after six games and bookmakers offered 11-1 on against them winning the title.

But then came the reality check: a visit to Manchester City, managed by Malcolm Allison, in front of a crowd of 45,000. Liverpool's 2–0 defeat – their first under Paisley – revealed that a new defensive philosophy isn't made in a day and that defenders need to defend as well as pass. Both City's goals were very poor from Paisley's perspective. Colin Bell chested a ball past the static full-back Alec Lindsay to cross for the first, with Thompson and Hughes both absent as a tame Clemence parry was sent straight back past him into the net by Rodney Marsh. Dennis Tueart was equally free to exploit a cross and score the second.

Results started to fluctuate, with a setback at home to Burnley one of two defeats in the following three games. Leeds United, struggling after Brian Clough's whirlwind 44-day managerial tenure had ended, were beaten at Anfield. But a third defeat, away to Ipswich, convinced some of the newspapers that Paisley at Anfield wasn't going to work. The *Daily Mail's* Jeff Powell concluded that football was witnessing a shadow of Shankly's great team. 'Liverpool, naturally enough, resent suggestions that they are not the same team without Shankly,' he wrote. 'But the fact remains that something vital, urgent, alive and irresistible has gone out of football. The new manager, Bob Paisley, was always an influential figure in Shankly's administration at Anfield. But Paisley without Shankly is something else. A compendium of foibles is emerging in players suddenly released from Shankly's grip.' Lloyd's unhappy departure was being equated with the Keegan controversy as examples of indiscipline and the more pragmatic build-up was seen as evidence of a less visceral Liverpool.

The garish headlines that were emerging from the Sunday newspapers after Paisley gave his post-match Saturday press conferences also concerned him. 'I learned my lesson with one or two quotes when the Sunday print comes in after Saturday's game and it's in black and white,' he ruminated later, referencing Jessie in the way he often did. 'The wife used to say, "You know, you didn't say that." I'd say, "Well, I did, but I didn't mean it that way." It's so different when it goes down in black and white.'

But none of this had the same effect on him as the work of Frank Clough, chief football writer of the *Sun*, who was the most strident critic and didn't have time for Paisley. Clough articulated most often the thought that the lack of blood and thunder in this Liverpool team made them drab and that they were a shadow of Shankly's side.

Paisley could handle the local reporters, but he saw the influence those writing from further afield was having and felt a deepening sense of gloom. He was so unsettled in the autumn of his first season that he walked into Robinson's office and told him that he wanted to step down. The precise date of this development is unclear. The 1–0 defeat at Ipswich on 2 November was certainly a cause for concern because Bobby Robson's side were one of Liverpool's prime title contenders and the result took the East Anglian club within a point of them at the top. The defeat at home to Arsenal seven days later was actually more damning and there then proceeded a sequence of four draws, running into December, which left the team fourth.

For the Liverpool board, Paisley's declaration was a calamity in what had been a deeply difficult autumn with the Shankly–Melwood situation to deal with. They sat Paisley down once more and tried to understand what they could do. The conversation revealed a frustration which ran deeper than one journalist submitting Paisley to the indignity of unflattering comparisons with the Shankly era. Paisley also said he felt exposed by the volume of press appearances. He was embarrassed by requests he was receiving to speak publicly. He felt he did not have the grasp of language to do that, he told Robinson. Results cannot have helped his self-confidence at this time, though it was the ancillary work, not the football, which seemed to be the problem.

Robinson and Smith again cast around for a solution. They asked themselves whether there was a chunk of the public role which they could relieve Paisley of, having done so to convince him he could manage the team in the first place. Was there someone within their ranks who could help with the public face of the job? Joe Fagan was certainly more comfortable with the press. He always seemed to be on first-name terms with most of them and had an uncanny knack of speaking comfortably without ever giving any information away.

Fagan was needed in the Paisley coaching set-up, though. They decided on someone else to help with the work, who would become a more important part of the set-up than any of them could then have known.

Tom Saunders was a former headteacher, Liverpool Schools and England Schoolboys coach, who had become Liverpool's youth development manager a year earlier when the incumbent, Tony Waiters, had left. Liverpool had been surprised that Saunders was willing to give up a strategic educational role to join them, and he clearly had potential.

It was put to Paisley that 'Tom would help'. He would be put alongside him to assist with the public speaking, though at the outset no one was terribly clear how that would work. With his more refined background in education, Saunders certainly possessed the erudition that Paisley lacked. Yet he was modest enough to bring subtlety to the support system. Saunders was a very good judge of human nature and social situations and he became the one who tried to fit in. The Liverpool board were struck by how he purposefully avoided pushing himself upon Paisley. He sat in press conferences, offering the occasional joke or piece of levity to break the ice, and began preparing notes for Paisley to help him deliver public speeches. Gradually, he refined the note-making when it became clear that if there were copious notes Paisley would stumble over them. Saunders provided brief points instead, to which Paisley could apply his own words.

Paisley found Saunders's presence a deeper source of help than any had expected. Both he and Liverpool's players found him grounded and reluctant to flaunt his academic background. A local solicitor, Tony Ensor, was appointed a Liverpool director several years later, and approached Saunders to discuss further education in a loud voice one day. 'Tom, what university did you go to?' Ensor asked. 'Tony, I went to the university of life,' Saunders replied, to the amusement of the players who overheard.

This characteristic in Saunders appealed to Paisley – an individual whom life had not equipped for conversations beyond the fine points of football and racing and whose social awkwardness sometimes often limited what he had to say about those subjects, too. He was not a sophisticated man but Saunders's easy manner put him at ease. A few weeks after this new arrangement was put in place, Robinson was surprised to find Paisley asking the former headteacher if he would be willing to move his desk into the manager's office at Anfield. Saunders, needless to say, agreed.

Saunders's role developed to include scouting opposition. Paisley found the brevity of the notes he provided practical and effective. With their uncomplicated methods, Liverpool had never wanted an essay on where the threats lay. In time, scouting opposition evolved into scouting new players. Saunders's assessments proved to be excellent on both counts.

Another calamity had been averted, though how seriously Paisley meant his threat to leave is unclear. His family had never been aware of it, and if he ever discussed it with Jessie then it was not something she had made known to them. Robinson's attempt to talk him around was not as torturous as the task of persuading him to sign up for the manager's job in the first place. There is no evidence that Paisley was seriously determined to walk away.

But there was another clue to his frustration in one of his daily encounters with the locally based journalists, whom Shankly had always accommodated when they arrived at Anfield in search of stories. When the usual group loitered in the Anfield foyer several days after the home defeat to Ipswich, they found Paisley unwilling to engage in convivial chat.

'What's the team this weekend?' Mike Ellis, the Merseyside-based journalist of the *Sun* asked, grinning. 'Same as last week with a few out,' Paisley replied flatly, and walked away. They knew something was wrong.

A conversation ensued with the reporters in which Paisley again expressed frustrations with the media side of his role. He told them he was finding he had little to say, day after day, and that meant they had little from the gatherings to write. In truth, what the journalists really hoped for, to fill out their reports, was an encounter with one of the players in the corridor.

The group put an idea to Paisley. A general discussion would take place with him, in which they would help shape the thrust and tone of what he said and at the end of it he would make it clear which elements he was happy to have them publish in his name. He would not have to do all of the talking. He agreed. An accommodation was struck that was always to be maintained with this trusted group: John Keith of the *Daily Express*, Ellis of the *Sun*, the *Daily Mail*'s Colin Wood, the *Daily Mirror*'s Chris James, and Nick Hilton of the *Liverpool Daily Post*. The evening *Liverpool Echo* made their own arrangements to call him.

As these relationships grew closer, the reporters intuited what Paisley would want to say. Keith often led off the discussions and perhaps knew Paisley best, though it was Ellis who would later travel with him, ghostwriting columns at the 1980 European Championships in Italy. Sometimes Paisley might want to know:

'How would you put that?' The arrangement worked, though it could be an unusual experience for newcomers.

When young reporter Ian Ross – no relation to the player of the same name Shankly signed in 1966 – replaced Hilton at the *Daily Post*, he discovered how difficult it was to participate in a press conference where the manager says so little.

'Newcastle on Saturday,' someone said, to open things up.

'Aye,' replied Paisley.

'Same team?'

'Aye,' said Paisley.

'Newcastle are playing well. What do you make of them?' interjected Ross.

The rest of the room looked surprised – as did Paisley – and the interview then followed a different course. The reporters trooped out a little later and one of them approached Ross. 'Better not to ask him questions,' he said. It was not quite the lesson Ross had expected to take away from a meeting with the manager of a top First Division side.

There might have been less talking and stage presence but Paisley was quietly maintaining Liverpool's standards. Despite the bumpy autumn, Liverpool were top at the turn of the year, though in February and March came six successive draws, include a goalless Merseyside derby at Anfield. The sixth, at Filbert Street on 19 March, was against relegation threatened Leicester City, who had won only two in 11 games since the turn of the year. Liverpool sat fifth, four points off the top with eight games to play. Though they had scored only 52 times in Shankly's last season and would manage 60 by the end of Paisley's first, the feeling still persisted that a light had gone out at the club. The argument struck a chord with fans. 'We all met in the Abbey [pub] and for the first time in my life of watching the Reds people were saying things that were less than polite about the manager,' one reflected in a supporter magazine. 'Not really nasty things but, well . . . you know, was he up to the job and all that.'

The supporters were so uncertain of the future that the *Liverpool Echo* reported that Lawrenson's Coaches had cancelled all its match-day services a few days in advance as they had received no bookings for the trip to West Ham United in February. Five 'football specials' were put on by British Rail but only one left Liverpool's Lime Street station.

The *Echo* was full of debate about the reasons why. Some contributors blamed the midweek scheduling for a London away match. It was a time of deep economic uncertainty, with the trauma of the recent three-day week and miners' strike a prelude to the era of Margaret Thatcher, who that month became the first woman to lead a British political party. And there was the ever-present spectre of Shankly. Some claimed the poor turnout was a protest against the club's treatment of the man who had not been welcomed back into the fold. The newspapers remained fascinated by what Shankly's departure had removed from Liverpool. A reminder of him appeared in the headlines after a 2–0 defeat at Arsenal, engineered by the London side's Alan Ball. Shankly had written a piece for the Highbury match programme. 'Ball shows just how much Shankly is missed,' declared the *Daily Mail*.

Toshack felt a failure to qualify for Europe by finishing runners-up could have left Paisley's continuation as manager in question. Though Robinson insists there was no set target for that first season, there had been 11 consecutive seasons of continental football under Shankly.

Where oratory failed him, Paisley would employ a little homily. Several players recall one of his that winter. 'Always remember, the football press is like a swimming pool: all the noise is in the shallow end,' he told them.

He continued to dispense his eerily accurate wisdom on players' weaknesses. One day he wanted to know why reserve-team player Jeff Ainsworth was not out on the training pitches.

'Pain in the bottom of his back,' he was told.

'Do you drink vodka?' Paisley asked Ainsworth, to the player's astonishment. He nodded.

'That's why, then. That's in your kidneys, lad.' The diagnosis proved accurate.

There were obsessions about diet which came from the Shankly years and were always maintained under Paisley. You could always have toast with soup, but would be castigated if you ate bread. They thought the players digested fresh bread less well and it could affect an individual's weight.

Paisley's eyes were open to others. The Anfield maintenance foreman, Bert Johnson, mentioned a sign he'd made, for no better reason than there was some red and white paint and wood he couldn't find a use for. In white letters on a red background, it read, 'THIS IS ANFIELD'. Johnson thought he might place it above the players' tunnel. Paisley agreed.

The playing style did not differ hugely from what Shankly had bequeathed. The philosophy was still to pass the ball to someone in a red shirt and then take up another position in which you could receive it – and that was not as elementary as it sounded. The distributor needed the vision and intuition to accelerate or delay the pass to allow the recipient to receive it comfortably and, in turn, send it on well. 'Who needs time on the ball?' Paisley would occasionally ask a young trainee if he encountered one. And before they could answer, he would tell them. 'It's the one who's going to receive it.'

There was a clue to how else he would evolve the side in the purchase of a 23-year-old, Phil Neal, from Fourth Division Northampton Town in October 1974. Neal anticipated a period acclimatising to his new club, in the reserves, and certainly didn't expected to be given a first-team debut against Everton, at Goodison Park, within a month of signing.

Shankly, still very much a Greek chorus despite his departure from Melwood, was with newspaper journalists at the game and, in remarks published afterwards, said he worried about the idea of fielding Neal. 'It's not a place to test a player,' he said.

But Paisley was interested in finding an attacking wing-back for Liverpool. The benefits of such a player had been established as long ago as Nílton Santos's performance in the 1958 World Cup and Ray Wilson's for England eight years later, but Liverpool had never employed such a player, and there were few in the First Division. Midfielder Ian Callaghan seemed aware that Neal may be a different kind of left-back, as he sat on one side of him in the dressing-room. 'I'll cover you,' he said. The more unreconstructed central defender Tommy Smith was the other side. 'Just kick them,' he said. Neal's dipping shot at Goodison's Gwladys Street end towards the close of the match demonstrated the attacking dimension he brought to the full-back's role. Neal would play 650 times for Liverpool.

There was evidence of Paisley's propensity for little psychological ploys, in the way he tried to put Neal at ease, by omitting to tell him he was playing until an hour before the game began. Neal thought he would be facing Everton's reserves when Saunders was dispatched to his digs on the morning of the match. The pair collected Neal's boots from Anfield, then walked half a mile across Stanley Park, which separates Anfield and Goodison, with them concealed in a brown paper bag. Paisley was waiting behind a door when they arrived. 'Do you want to play?' he asked, grinning at Neal.

That childlike pleasure of offering a young player a chance never left him. Many players say that the most warmth they received from him came before they kicked a ball – and, perhaps, before he would judge them. 'Do you want to play for Liverpool?' he asked Joey Jones, another new full-back, when making the eye-catching decision to sign him from Wrexham for £110,000 in the summer of 1975.

The inclusion of Jones in the team illustrated Paisley's fascination with finding the right combination of players – those 'lesser lights' to 'support and bolster' the greats, as he described the scene in the Malton stable yard. 'You need the extroverts in the dressing-room and the loners,' the manager reflected years later. 'It didn't worry me that Joey might have lacked a bit of footballing ability. He more than made up for that with the type of person he was. You couldn't give him any important jobs to do . . . but he was a real comedian and sometimes it is good to have that in the side.'

As often as not, these players would be signed on the basis of what Paisley thought they would deliver in the future, however much frustration that might bring them in the reserves, learning the way that Liverpool played. Terry McDermott – his second signing (£175,000 from Newcastle United in November 1974) – would become one of Paisley's top players by the late 1970s, scoring 15-to-20 goals a season, displaying superb technique behind the forwards. But in Paisley's first two seasons he had a minimal role.

Paisley was equally clear in his mind about which players he had no place for – and Lloyd was not the only one. John Toshack had scored 41 goals in the previous three seasons and been among the club's top three scorers on each occasion, but Paisley had always been suspicious about the time he spent in the treatment room. Toshack's £260,000 transfer to Leicester City – which would have been a new record sale for Liverpool – was so far advanced in March 1975 that the player had even been introduced to his new teammates.

Toshack felt that Paisley had never liked him. His first day as a Liverpool player, after signing from Cardiff City in 1970, had been spent in the treatment room with him and the striker felt that from the start Paisley had considered him something of a lightweight. 'I never really felt that I had won him over,' Toshack says.

The player's medical at Leicester proved that Paisley's distrust of Toshack was unjustified. X-rays showed the striker had a chronic problem – calcification of the muscles in his legs – and the deal fell through. He returned to Anfield and embarked on a lighter training regime, resigned to playing fewer games, though there was never an acknowledgement from the Rat that Toshack's time in the medical room had been genuine. His first impressions were always hard to dislodge and the lack of empathy did not surprise Toshack. He had always found Paisley to be a closed book. 'He was a strange character and a hard one. There was no warmth.'

Toshack didn't help the situation when, after the Leicester move had failed, he told Paisley that he intended to play a match for Wales in Budapest, ahead of Liverpool's penultimate game of the season, against Middlesbrough, where the team needed to win to secure the second spot that would guarantee them European football. 'If you play for Wales you'll be dropped for Middlesbrough,' Paisley informed him. Toshack assumed that Paisley may need him too much to follow through on a threat like that, so ignored the warning and travelled to Hungary anyway. It left Paisley with a decision to make, because Toshack had been his second top scorer in the First Division that year. He dropped him for Ayresome Park and Liverpool lost 1–0.

Everything then fell on winning the last game of the season, against Queens Park Rangers at Anfield. Prouder managers would have left such a player out in the cold, though a moral victory was not the kind he was looking for. He selected the striker for the game and watched him score twice as Liverpool won 3–1, squeaking into the European qualification places by the narrowest conceivable margin: a 0.038 superior goal average over Bobby Robson's Ipswich Town.

'I do wonder if Shanks, with his pride, would have found a place for me,' Toshack reflects. 'But that was Bob. He could take the emotion out. He would definitely hold a grudge. But he wouldn't hold a grudge if he knew it was going to work against him.'

It had been a tumultuous nine months, in which Liverpool had equalled the runners-up position of Shankly's last season, though accumulated six points fewer. There was certainly statistical ammunition for those who doubted the new manager. At Anfield, where in Shankly's last season they had won all but three matches, Liverpool had been materially less impressive. Away from home they were only marginally better, drawing more games than any side in the division.

As Heighway left for his summer break he felt an acknowledgement was due to the players. 'Credit the squad for not taking the piss,' he says, looking back on that season. 'It would have been easy to take the piss out of Bob – not because he was weak but because it was somebody doing the job who didn't seem to want it and didn't seem to have the skills for it.'

That might have been the impression left by a manager whose press conferences were sometimes assisted, who rarely appeared on television and who had claimed in the first place that he would rather be somewhere else. But appearance and reality were different entities. Being observed in plain sight did not interest Paisley. The quiet persona and undemonstrative exterior obscured an individual who very much did want to manage Liverpool and take the decisions that came with it. Changes were under way and it suited him fine if others wanted to think otherwise.

5

ROOM WITH NO WINDOWS

The away team dressing-room door at Queens Park Rangers was shut and the inquisition going on behind it was loud, angry and full of recriminations. Many of those taking part in it wondered where things were heading for Liverpool.

The opening day of Bob Paisley's second season had just started with a 2–0 defeat and it wasn't just the result which had left two of the established members of the squad disgruntled. Tommy Smith, aged 30, and Alec Lindsay, aged 27, had been left out of the side by Paisley in favour of Joey Jones, the 19-year-old just signed from Wrexham, and the barely blooded Phil Neal. Smith had been at that club since 1960 and was one of the few Paisley would easily converse with. They would talk if they passed each other at Melwood, but there hadn't been a word of warning from the manager that he was to be dropped for a new campaign. Even Smith was not averse to calling Paisley the Rat.

Not for the first time in the last 12 months, the decision raised eyebrows and suggested that Smith and Lindsay, two members of the Bill Shankly old guard, might soon need to look for new clubs. Paisley's assistant, Joe Fagan, had been talking before the match about Neal and Jones getting forward to join in the attacking side of Liverpool's game. Everyone knew that Smith and Lindsay were not the quickest men on two feet.

But the problem had been Emlyn Hughes, Liverpool's supposedly dependable captain, who'd spent much of the game charging around all over the pitch and leaving wide open spaces in defence. The consequences were disastrous. With Hughes out of position, Gerry Francis had played a one-two around a stranded Phil Thompson, the 21-year-old centre-half, and scored. The game was settled with 20 minutes to play when Hughes charged forward again, was dispossessed and Rangers' Mick Leach doubled the lead after a clear run on goal.

Paisley had taken a seat in the main stand at the start of the game, but with the prospect of victory vanishing he'd headed down to the dugout and told Smith, the substitute, to prepare to go on.

Smith was just taking his tracksuit off when Fagan told him to put it back on again, which puzzled him. Wasn't the manager supposed to be the one in charge? Smith always remembered the force of Fagan's instructions, though. 'I'm not letting you go on and be associated with this shit. Go and sit down.' So he did as he was told.

The recriminations came thick and fast after the game. Paisley had not shared his true feelings with the press. The Sunday newspaper reporters were in the room when he gave his press conference and, having learned his lessons about them, he employed a lame joke to take the temperature out of the situation. 'Everyone charged off to do someone else's job, including selling the programmes,' he told them. His face when he arrived in the dressing-room told the real story.

'What the fuck? What the fuck were you doing?' several players remember him shouting in Hughes's direction.

The captain had missed the pre-season through injury. He needed to 'have a good run around' is several players' recollection of how he justified his positional indiscipline to Paisley. That certainly raised a snigger. Hughes always had a lot to say for himself. It never escaped some players' attention that if you were at Anfield on a Sunday morning to have an injury looked at, Hughes's car would be parked up on the forecourt, signalling that he would be in Paisley's office, dispensing some wisdom.

'So that's how you thank me, is it?' said Paisley. 'I got you the two faster full-backs you said I should buy. That's the last time I listen to you . . .'

Silence dropped on the dressing-room like a stone and suddenly every eye in the room was boring into Hughes, who stared at the floor like a man who wanted it to swallow him up.

'What did you just say?' Smith demanded of Paisley. '*He* told you to buy new full-backs?'

Never at his best in these situations, Paisley stammered out an attempted retraction. 'Didn't mean that' and 'wasn't like that' were the only fragments that were audible. He was fighting a losing battle, because his conversation with Hughes was out there now.

'You bastard,' Smith said, marching towards Hughes. 'I should knock the living daylights out of you.'

Lindsay stepped in front of him. 'Not before me,' he said.

Joe Fagan intervened before punches were thrown, but the team coach was shrouded in silence as it pulled through the streets of London that night. *The Times* reached its own conclusions about the Liverpool performance. 'The Anfield army are not their old resolute selves. Where once they would have ground out a narrow victory they were defeated by wit and invention,' it declared. But the story behind the scenes was more dramatic than correspondent Geoffrey Green knew.

The episode revealed one of the substantial chinks in Paisley's armour. He was not effective when it came to verbal sparring. 'He didn't get into conversations because he didn't trust himself,' says Phil Thompson. But it also demonstrated that by the outset of his second season as manager his players had a voice in a way that had been inconceivable under the hugely motivational management of Bill Shankly.

Paisley always felt that Hughes, his first captain, might have been a better player if he hadn't had quite so much to say for himself. Hughes always wanted to be 'a charge hand', the manager once said. But he was still free to suggest new players and ideas to Paisley. In the Anfield canteen Hughes and the 27-year-old goalkeeper Ray Clemence were, by the start of Paisley's second season, sometimes to be found sitting at the coaches' table. In the dressing-room voices could be heard far more often. Team talks had started to involve the players.

Even some of those who thought life would never be the same after Shankly saw that a quieter manager could be a more democratic and empowering one, who would hear them out. 'Shanks used to dominate these [team meetings] but Bob encouraged the players to participate fully,' Keegan would say years later. 'Even the lads who had kept quiet began to add to the discussion. Bob was willing to let the lads stamp a little of themselves on the club's ideas. Bob was big enough to accept the fact that maybe a player could give a reason why a certain thing should be done in a certain way.'

The air of independence extended to the players being allowed a mid-season night away in 1976, where the talk carried on. They chose Llangollen in the North Wales Vale of Clwyd, an hour's drive from Liverpool, with a meal at the Bryn Howel Hotel, a round of golf and some drinks at night. 'We had never done anything like that when Shanks was the boss,' said Keegan. It would become a regular practice.

The environment meant that players answered to each other as much as to Paisley. When Leeds United's Eddie Gray had caused both Neal and Jones problems at Elland Road, it was Keegan who later took the defenders to task in the dressing-room. Paisley listened and five minutes had elapsed before he added his own slightly eccentric rider. He told the team that he would have had no problem with Gray that day. 'Give me Eddie Gray in a confined space and he wouldn't beat me,' he said. That certainly took the heat out of the scene. The thought of Paisley facing Leeds amused some of his players.

'I don't know about that, boss . . .' said one.

'I'm telling you! If you put him in a confined space...'

Some headshaking ensued.

'I'm telling you . . .' Paisley said, and walked out. His self-effacement had its limits. He would not let them impugn his reputation as a Liverpool half-back.

Though Neal and Jones had struggled at Leeds, Hughes's original observations were valid. Smith was not mobile and, though no one would say it, Lindsay was one of the slowest players at the club. The two new defenders' contributions – especially wing-back Neal's – would show the value of a manager prepared to listen to his players, rather than assume he knew best.

Hughes was by no means the most popular man in the squad. Some of the players thought he was always out for himself, and he also made the mistake of putting himself at odds with Tommy Smith, the bedrock of the squad's Liverpudlian contingent, which meant that some of the local players were against him too. Smith used to call him 'a creep', and those in the Smith camp felt Hughes's high-profile display at QPR reeked of self-publicity. 'It was all designed for the fans – "Look at Emlyn!"' Thompson still feels.

None of that bothered Paisley. To his mind, there was nothing wrong with creative tensions in a squad. In any case, he had not introduced the new full-backs on Hughes's advice alone. The contents of conversations like that were fed, like everything else, into the poky, windowless room down the corridor from his office which had been a place to commune years before he became manager. The forenames of the select few who sat together in the Boot Room – Bob, Joe, Ronnie and Tom – were as ordinary and unaffected as its surroundings: upturned beer crates for seats, a calendar of topless models, a threadbare carpet on the floor, a kettle. Tom Saunders added a little gravitas but Joe Fagan and Ronnie Moran could have easily been mistaken for the caretakers, given that they always walked around Anfield with bunches of keys hooked to their trousers.

That was how Paisley wanted it. Their values, laid down by Shankly, were based on working for one another and not getting ahead of yourself – and their room reflected precisely that. Footballs and training kit were stuffed onto grey metal shelving. A Perspex notice board appeared in the room a few years later and was considered sophisticated. 'Just like Real Madrid,' read the ironic message Moran scrawled across it, just in case anyone thought the Boot Room was getting above itself.

That's not to say there were not hierarchies, because Paisley, like Shankly before him, believed in them, too. It was always the job of the assistant manager's wife, for example, to wash the reserve team's kit. Everyone knew that Bob's seat, where he would nurse a glass of Scotch, was the one on the far left, as you entered.

When Melwood training was done – usually by 1 p.m. – and they had driven back to Anfield, this group had hours at their disposal. Though Paisley might have some calls to make, including to his bookmakers, the backroom staff had little else on their minds but talking football. In the empty afternoons after training they would sit for as long as four hours and leave at around 5 p.m., reflecting, arguing, planning all that time.

Part of the process on those occasions would be to log details of the training sessions in the black notebooks known as the 'Anfield bibles', which Paisley and Moran had begun keeping in the Shankly days, containing details of drills, injuries, opponents – the kind of stored collective memory which would today be called a database. The notes were a continual reference point amid changing times: a stored collective memory as to what had worked. No other club had anything like it.

Saunders became an increasingly significant part of it, establishing himself as a key confidant and adviser to Paisley: the *consigliere*. But Moran and Fagan were the manager's main football authorities. They were the ones who had played the game. Both were Liverpudlian to their core, though Fagan, who was born within a mile of Anfield and underwent a trial with Liverpool, joined Manchester City, believing he would have more first-team opportunities at left-back there. He had returned to his home-town club 18 months before Shankly's arrival and, for many players, provided the avuncular quality and powers of communication that Paisley lacked. On the many occasions when players left Paisley's team meetings struggling to comprehend his instructions, Fagan would provide the translation.

Moran had the career as a Liverpool left-back that Fagan believed was beyond him, playing 379 times between 1952 and 1965. He was captain when his monumental enthusiasm led Shankly to invite him onto the training staff during the 1966–67 season. Alongside them in the ranks was the unremittingly tough Reuben Bennett, a Scottish former goalkeeper who was nothing less than Shankly's henchman until 1971, given the task of driving every last ounce of effort from the players.

In time Fagan, Moran, Saunders and Reuben Bennett would be joined in the Boot Room by Roy Evans, who was brought up in the Bootle suburb on the bank of the Mersey and who had lost his place as a full-back when in 1974, at the age of 25, he was asked by Paisley to join the staff as reserve-team manager. Paisley saw the way he instilled sense into the younger players. Evans loved Sundays in the Boot Room when, having examined injured players and sorted out the kit for the next day, there would be time to reflect on Saturday's game. 'We'd sit there for 15 minutes,' says Evans. 'And then someone would say, "What about it? What did you think about yesterday?" Someone [else] would throw a player's name out: "I thought he could have been better." That's how it started.'

Evans never initiated the conversation because he was the junior party: those hierarchies at work again. 'He [Paisley] would talk to you about it, ask your opinion,' Evans says. 'I'm a 25-year-old guy and he is asking my opinion. He is saying, "You might not get it right but you might get one little thing we don't." They gave you your voice, your confidence, and that's the only way you could learn, really. They say, "I know what you mean but no, that wouldn't work that way." It showed he wanted the people below him to have a voice and to speak. At the end they've all had their say and put their bit in but you as the manager have to make the final choice.'

The players knew they must not cross the threshold or breach the sanctity of the Boot Room unless invited to – which they almost never were, with the sole exception of when they were collecting their boots before leaving for international duty. Tommy Smith had the temerity to put the carpet out for sweeping one day. He was told in no uncertain terms to put it back.

If the players, and especially the younger ones, were making a noise outside, a head would reach around the door and issue the order: 'Fuck off or shut up.'

The five of them ran the team together. Paisley's word was not gospel and nor did he think it should be. He always sat in the stand during the first half of games and only took to the bench if things were not working. Sometimes, he would come down the interior staircase at Anfield and out to the dugout and suggest a substitution to Fagan, though it was not obligatory – as Smith discovered at QPR. If there was a shift in the pattern of the game before he could get Paisley's recommended substitute on, Fagan would leave things as they were.

Fagan was Paisley's contemporary and perhaps closer to him than Moran. They knew him as 'Smokin' Joe' because he was so often dragging on a cigarette. He would spot the smallest drop-off in performance effort and, like Paisley, could put the fear of God in a player without saying too much, but it was he who offered thoughtfulness. He didn't often swear. 'You buggers!' was one of his catchphrases when something had got away from him at Melwood. He could also be something of a pessimist when watching from the bench. 'Oh, they've shit it!' was another of his sayings, signalling that he thought the game was lost. When Fagan let you have it, you knew he meant it and you knew there was trouble.

Ronnie Moran was the bad cop, the rabble rouser – generally effing, blinding, cajoling and demanding and always available to dish out a bollocking. 'The fuck-off man', they called him. His linguistic inelegance was matched by a very physical approach to the daily staff versus trainees games. His nickname – 'Moransco' – was the nearest they got to having a laugh at his expense. Moran is the only man the young striker David Fairclough knew who could shout 'give and go' continually for half an hour. He'd employ any device to get more out of players and get under the skin of the edgier ones. He became the feared man who would take the ball away from you and run you to death if you were not putting in the maximum effort – though many say the tough exterior obscured something subtler. On the occasions when Moran would give reserve-team player Owen Brown a lift to Anfield, the young forward would hear his tactical ideas in the car, but then would see him revert to type once they had arrived.

Paisley was not interested in annexing the territory of these men – each of whom, in their own way, formed the bridge to the players that Paisley once had for Shankly. He left them to run things. He would make the drive back from Melwood to Anfield in the brown Austin Rover which he drove in his early years as manager while the players, Moran and Fagan would be on the coach. Another ritual retained from the Shankly era was that the coach windows must remain up. The environment was rank but it was deemed unhealthy to left fresh air flow in. The players showered at the stadium.

There would be an hour or so for Paisley to deal with business in his office – another unpretentious, windowless affair, with a couple of grey and black telephones on a shelf on the wall, next to an unsightly ventilation pipe. 'Like a foreman's office on a Wimpey estate,' Paisley's rival Brian Clough called it. And then they would join the others back in the Boot Room.

There was plenty to discuss at the start of the 1975–76 season. After QPR, the early weeks lurched from bad to near catastrophe. The first of two home games ended 2–2 (against West Ham), then Liverpool trailed 2–0 to two goals in 16 minutes before half-time against Tottenham. Emlyn Hughes was still not fully fit and both he and Thompson were too adventurous for their own, and

Liverpool's, good. The opening goal deflected in off Hughes's shin, the second left the two central defenders out of position. Liverpool mustered no chances before half-time.

Yet Paisley resisted any temptation to introduce substitutes, and the Anfield crowd contributed to a comeback, with three goals in 18 second-half minutes securing a 3–2 win. 'I think we should have slaughtered them,' said the Spurs manager Terry Neill. Paisley opted for one of his little homilies. 'I wouldn't like another 39 minutes like that,' he said. 'There'd be a few thromboses about.' Privately, he knew he had more decisions to make.

One of the club's biggest signings was struggling. Liverpool had hoped that Ray Kennedy would be a new partner for Keegan, with Toshack struggling for fitness. But it hadn't worked. Kennedy wasn't happy. The hard, self-regulating Liverpool environment was a different world to the one he had known at Arsenal. He'd started feeling odd muscular spasms, too. His right hip would push involuntarily when he walked, leading him to feel awkward and off balance. His right foot had a habit of scuffing the floor and he felt strains in his right arm and leg which he couldn't explain. When speculation surfaced in the newspapers that he might be transferred to Leicester City, Kennedy asked to see Paisley. He told him he thought he was being singled out for indifferent form when he wasn't the only one not playing well.

Kennedy had become accustomed to the niceties of life at Highbury. He liked the smoked salmon and chocolate cake they laid on for away trips. But Paisley's response was cold and hard. Something along the lines of, 'You need to lose weight and work harder.' He didn't pull any punches when the newspapers asked him about Kennedy, either. 'If Ray wants to play for Liverpool then he can, but I only want those people who want to do well for this club,' he was quoted as saying. It was a calculated manoeuvre.

Paisley wanted a reaction and provoking one was a use he found for the newspapers. Kennedy seethed, learning for himself why they called him the Rat. He didn't mind admitting that he hated Paisley at that time.

But Paisley liked Kennedy's spatial awareness on the field and his range of passing. He thought him honest. The player had been born 20 miles due north of Hetton-le-Hole and, for Paisley, that kind of birthright was always a good sign. He wasn't ready to sell him unless he had to.

By chance, the manager had come across Kennedy's former secondary school games teacher, Rob Brydon, on one of his trips back to the north-east. Most PE teachers have plenty to say during a random encounter with a First Division footballer manager, and most managers look for a way to limit their exposure. But Paisley listened. Brydon mentioned that the schoolboy Kennedy had been a midfielder. Paisley thought about it. He might just try that.

He called Kennedy back to his office and told him that because he had lost some of his sharpness in attack he intended to take him back to where he had started on the field. Kennedy's recollections of their exchange revealed that Paisley did not invite much conversation on the matter. "'You're going to play in midfield in future. You'll do better when facing the ball,'" he said. He encouraged him to be more aggressive and put more fight into his game. 'You don't argue with a man like him,' Kennedy reflected years later.

He was suspicious by nature, though. His nickname among the players was 'Susser' because he always seemed to be trying to 'suss out' an ulterior motive. His first instinct was that this might be Paisley's way of putting him out to grass.

There was a five-game try-out in the reserve team's midfield. Then the new role was put to the test in the First Division against

Middlesbrough in November 1975 – a 1–0 win at Anfield. It was clear that this metamorphosis would take some time. Kennedy instinctively neglected the defensive side of his role and allowed players to get past him. In the Boot Room, they looked for a way to compensate. Joey Jones, who was less inclined to advance upfield, was asked to switch from right-back to left-back and Phil Neal was moved to the right. That bolstered the left side of defence and helped cover the spaces created by Kennedy's runs.

There were others players to weigh up. No player was evidently discussed more in the Boot Room in the early months of the 1975–76 season than Jimmy Case, who combined his football with an electrician's apprenticeship as a career back-up option. Case saw himself as a striker, though the options up front seemed scarce. His slight frame created questions about his ability to hold up a position in midfield. They worried about his physique.

He'd scored in the 3–2 comeback against Tottenham but was then put back in the reserves for a month. He was picked again, scored two in three games, and dropped again. There was little explanation from Paisley. On one occasion the manager just threw Case the number 9 jersey and said, 'All right, lad, see if you can handle that one.'

Paisley knew more about the prejudice against shorter players than most, but still took some convincing about Case. Fagan seems to have argued the player's merits harder than anyone. There'd been a punch-up involving the 21-year-old and Alec Lindsay, who had stuck out a foot after Case passed him one time too many in training, prompting him to respond with a right-hander. Case was summoned the next day before Fagan, who tore into him, reminding him what the consequences would have been had he been playing in a European game.

But the episode appears to have convinced Fagan that his physical contribution might complement the more languid Kennedy. 'That Case boy, he's got some aggression, hasn't he?' Fagan observed at the time. 'I think we'll have some of that.' They didn't mind fighters, in the Boot Room.

The only player who seemed to get much of Paisley's attention during that 1975–76 season was a young local striker, David Fairclough. Several times, Paisley offered him advice on the way he shaped to score in training, and he also wanted the young Liverpudlian to try out the speed balls as part of his fitness work.

'He used to take me aside from time to time and offer ideas, little tips,' says Fairclough. 'That was odd because he didn't do that with other people. It was a joke for a while. People used to say, "The Rat's got a soft spot for you!"'

What Paisley wanted most was to balance defence and attack. He still sought more patience from the players and asked them to hold the ball more, rather than run themselves into the ground. It meant a slower tempo than some had become accustomed to under Shankly. The team was going to be playing 60-odd games a season in all competitions and this was a much better way to play, he said. They were starting to drop Keegan into a withdrawn midfield role away from home. For a second successive season, this was by no means popular. Coventry City were equally unambitious when the teams met at Highfield Road in mid-October, though the most absorbing drama was the sight of Larry Lloyd, the defender Paisley had dumped, proving not to be 'overfriendly in his manners or tackles to former colleagues'. Liverpool lacked intensity and rarely threatened. 'All a game of Paisley patience,' the *Daily Mail*'s headline stated after the 0–0 draw. The accompanying report criticised the way the side 'pack their defence, congest midfield and invite opponents to lose patience. It is unadventurous and unattractive.' The withdrawal of Keegan from the conventional forward's position that Shankly had found for him was 'unpalatable', the newspaper declared. 'Liverpool guaranteed continuity when they replaced Bill Shankly as manager with their assistant Bob Paisley,' the *Mail's* Jeff Powell wrote. 'But in time teams come to reflect their manager's character. Shankly was full of passion and an overwhelming belief in the greatness of his team. Paisley is quieter, a more detailed planner, steadier. Now, so are Liverpool. They no longer frighten the life out of the opposition.'

Twelve months earlier the endless comparisons with Shankly had led Paisley to inform Robinson that he couldn't deal with the press. But his robust defence of himself at Coventry suggested that he had underestimated what he was capable of. 'It may not be good for football and perhaps it's not entertaining,' Paisley declared. 'But to win the championship you have to find the happy medium between adventure and the need to get results. We are committed to playing in a certain way at Anfield because of what our fans expect. If we have to play like this away from home and inch our way to the title, that's how it will have to be.'

Paisley did not always know the reporters away from Anfield, but his discussions were none the worse for it. He was clearly trying something substantially different away from home than at Anfield, where the old spirit was intact. Liverpool scored 11 goals in their first five home league games of the 1975–76 season and four goals away.

Though Paisley 'never used two words where one would do', as Keegan put it, the players began to take some pleasure in the fact that his vocabulary had a life of its own and that his sentences never quite seemed to finish, often tailing off with ''n that . . .' His most emphatic catchphrase was, 'What the fuck?', though it took a lot to get him agitated enough to say it.

'Tactics' sessions were also something to savour. There was talk in a Melwood briefing one day of 'Tony Currie's far flung one'. This, it transpired, was Paisley-speak for a long ball from the Sheffield United midfielder.

On another occasion Paisley accused Tommy Smith of 'hitting the slow ro-lo'.

The term had been allowed to pass when Smith interjected. 'Hang on. What the fuck is a "slow ro-lo"?'

It was possibly rolling a pass across the pitch, possibly under-hitting a pass – no one ever quite got to the bottom of that one. Paisley grinned as he delivered some of these esoteric expressions. They did have some meaning but they reflected the deeply embedded ironic disdain for fancy tactical talk, which Paisley saw as the height of affectation.

David Fairclough heard the manager tell him on one occasion that he was to be 'the lone star ranger'. He took that to be Paisley-speak for playing as the lone striker.

If Paisley heard a piece of so-called technical football terminology used in the media, he would ask his players what on earth it meant. 'Leading the line' was one of his favourites. The term 'blind side run' was another; many was the time he would walk off chuckling to himself after hearing that one and asking what it meant.

His scepticism was also reserved for those players whose reputations were bigger, to his mind, than their contributions on the field of play. 'Doing a Huddy' derived from the Boot Room view of Alan Hudson, the Stoke City midfielder much fêted as a midfield technician. Paisley was always adamant that Hudson should hold no fear as he operated deep in midfield, from a position where he would not be challenged by opponents and therefore cause no harm, thus 'doing a Huddy'.

Another of that ilk which always tickled him was England manager Sir Alf Ramsey's description in 1968 of West Ham midfielder Martin Peters as 'ten years ahead of his time'. Paisley was still grinning at the notion ten years later.

A journalist talked about Leeds United's Duncan McKenzie having 'flair' before the match against Jimmy Armfield's side at Anfield in February 1976. Flair, Paisley replied, was something you found at the bottom of a pair of trousers. Others that would set him off included: 'We must be more positive' ('Time to call an electrician' was his stock joke); 'giving the ball enough grass' and 'doing the business in the final third'.

Paisley's own vocabulary could be a mystery, too, because of his struggle to recall a name and the thick north-east vernacular which made him hard to comprehend. For reasons which have never been entirely clear, he disclosed before a game against Aston Villa that he had been speaking to one of their scouts, whose surname eluded him. 'I've been speaking to Duggie . . . Duggie . . . Duggie doin's,' he said. The players dissolved into laughter and from that day on, Paisley was collectively known to them – sometimes out of earshot – as 'Duggie Doin's' – or sometimes plain 'Duggie'.

His players also adopted the 'Bob walk'. The troublesome ankle of Paisley's created a tendency for him to sway from side to side as he moved, with a pronounced swing of the arm. This was recreated to great comic effect by players who complemented the routine with his favourite expletive: 'What the fuck! What the fuck! What the fuck are you doing?'

The great mimic was Terry McDermott, the Liverpudlian who had been signed in the autumn of 1974. McDermott had only been at the club a few months when, with the players gathered in the Melwood dressing-room ahead of one of the manager's weekly Friday morning tactics talks (always a brief affair) he assumed the 'Duggie Doin's' pose, waddling around the tactics board, forgetting players' names and dropping the miniature player figures on the floor, while keeping a close eye on the door in case Paisley walked in. But there was a back door to the room and he entered that way instead, catching McDermott *in flagrante*. 'Would you like to give the talk then, Terry?' Paisley asked, deadpan.

The laughter took the edge off and brought some warmth to what was an unsparing and hard environment. Paisley didn't mind the jokes, even though his own were not exactly cutting edge. One of his favourites was about the chairman of Bishop Auckland, the great amateur team he'd done so well with, deciding to send the result of one of the club's away games back by homing pigeon so that the scores could go on show. Except the chairman wasn't sure how homing pigeons worked, so he looked the bird in the eye one day and dispensed with written instructions. 'Tell 'em we won 3–1, pet,' he said.

Phil Neal, one of the more serious-minded in the dressing-room, recalled more than the malapropisms which seemed to stick in other players' minds. The level of detail garnered from Saunders's opposition reports impressed the young defender. He would be detailed to pick up a particular player from set-pieces on the right, on the basis that the player had slipped his marker a couple of times the previous week. A decoy runner in the opposition ranks would sometimes be identified in advance. There would be reminders of Liverpool's failings against the previous week's opponents.

They were all better listeners than talkers in the Boot Room and that became clear after matches, when they started inviting opposition managers into the room. Visitors would come to include Elton John, who had brought his Watford team to Anfield before his curiosity took him down into the sanctuary. 'Do you have pink gin?' asked the singer. Paisley always liked to relate their reply: 'Sorry, we've only got Export.'

But a pop star was insignificant. To Paisley, Moran, Fagan and Saunders, the ten minutes spent with opposition managers at 5.15 p.m. every other Saturday mattered hugely. 'We tried to find out what other people did,' says Evans. 'Travel, food. And then later, when they'd gone, we might say, "We should think about that."'

Years later, Paisley would present the idea of inviting opposition managers into the Boot Room as a sign of sportsmanship. 'At the end of the day . . . the only thing you can do is say, "Look, come in, have a drink; win lose or draw, you can come in, irrespective of what words we've had, or anything." The game's a sport, really, and that's the attitude.'

That was economy with the truth on Paisley's part. For him, this was another intelligence-gathering exercise. Southampton manager Lawrie McMenemy saw that in the end. The little reception committee in the Boot Room left him feeling that Paisley was one of the nicest individuals in football, but he came to realise that their offer of cheap beer and talk was a hustle.

On one occasion McMenemy arrived wearing a fashionable new light-coloured raincoat, and when Paisley told him to 'sit there, son' and pointed to a dusty beer crate, he felt he was being tested for a reaction. A glass of Scotch from a cup or a beer were the offerings. McMenemy, 'wanting to be one of the lads', took a seat and started talking players, teams and systems with them. Five minutes in, he discovered that he was imparting information about his own players – 'best foot, ability in the air, his personality'.

Only when he was on the way home did it dawn on McMenemy that he'd given away secrets. 'You'd been getting the third degree without realising it. If you'd said anything positive about the player in question then you could expect them to turn up at your next home game to scout him.'

In his pursuit of football knowledge Paisley wanted to know exactly what other managers thought of his own players, too. 'There's a lot of talk goes off in there [the Boot Room] and that's interesting because you're always interested in what people think about your own players. They tell you more about your own players than you really know yourself, or vice versa,' he later reflected. No manager recalls leaving the Boot Room armed with Liverpool's view of his team.

The one exception to that rule was the night when one of the Manchester City coaches, Jimmy Frizzell, arrived in the Boot Room and proceeded to suggest City's manager Billy McNeill, didn't know what he was doing. 'Hey, hey don't be telling us, mate,' Moran said. 'Be telling your manager. It's easy to criticise.' An assistant bad-mouthing his own manager ran against the Boot Room respect for hierarchies and of never trying to steal your boss's job.

Nobody else seemed to be on to the value of this fact-finding opportunity. The only person who Paisley remembered asking a meaningful question during all those years in the Boot Room was Arsenal's Don Howe. 'What are your methods? How do you do training?' Howe asked. Bob, Joe, Ronnie and Tom always respected him for that. They would not have missed the opportunity to ask Howe about Ray Kennedy.

This information-gathering began to yield results, and the little pieces of wisdom coming their way were not lost on the players. Liverpool played at Tottenham in mid-December and again began the game with caution. Some compared it to a European away game, Liverpool drawing Spurs out, 'wary of having run into a booby trap' as the *Daily Post*'s Horace Yates put it. Jimmy Case had scored a hat-trick in midweek, against Ślask Wroclaw in the UEFA Cup, but had been located deep in midfield, which seemed puzzling.

When Keegan scored an opening goal, Liverpool began to show more ambition and the afternoon turned into an exposition of what attack-minded players breaking through from midfield might offer. Kennedy had remained in the reserves along with Joey Jones, who was taking time to reach the Liverpool level. But Case burst forward to score a fourth goal in two games, and substitute David Fairclough looked dangerous. The value of the attacking full-backs Hughes had wanted revealed itself, too. Neal advanced to exploit space and scored his first Liverpool goal. A 4–0 win took Liverpool from 5th to 2nd on goal difference.

Fagan had been right about Case. It was becoming a breakthrough season, in which he would score 12 goals from midfield. Tommy Smith was the surprise package, adapting himself to the new ball-playing style in a way few thought possible. 'He was handier with his feet than people realised,' says Ian St John. But Hughes's goal in the win over Stoke at Anfield – taking the ball from the halfway line, beating three defenders, exchanging passes with Keegan and beating a fourth man to score – underlined why Paisley considered him a player of class, if a little too much conversation.

The decision to reposition Kennedy eventually began to reap results. In March 1976 Paisley walked into the dressing-room and asked Kennedy if he wanted to play for England. The manager, Don Revie, had been on the phone. He won his first international cap against Wales that month and scored his first international goal. He masterminded the 5–3 home win over Stoke City in mid-April which took Liverpool to the top of the table. 'What a great player Kennedy has become,' reported Yates.

Fairclough – the only one Paisley had seemed to coach – proved to be the difference, though. After a surprise 2–0 home defeat to Middlesbrough had restored the doubts about whether Paisley could take this team to a league title, the young striker embarked on a run of four goals in three consecutive league games. He had already seen off Norwich and Burnley when he beat five men to finish with a low shot into the net against Everton with three minutes remaining. It was a hugely resonant and long-remembered strike which kept Liverpool two points off leaders QPR with a game in hand and five games to play. Liverpool had won seven and drawn one of a vital eight matches.

The goal also created a finale which had seemed beyond any expectation on that opening afternoon at Loftus Road – the possibility of a First Division and UEFA Cup Double. Liverpool had progressed steadily through the European competition, securing a place in the two-legged final against Belgian side Club Brugge by overcoming Barcelona with a shrewd tactical display which brought them a 1–0 victory in the Nou Camp stadium.

The televised Club Brugge home tie came first and in the television studio George Best looked at a Liverpool team now populated by players who, Keegan aside, he had hardly heard of. He just could not see them finding a way past the talented Belgians. 'You look at some of those players and wouldn't really say they were world-class players,' he said.

One of Paisley's young additions – Neal – did struggle at Anfield, at the hands of the Belgian international Raoul Lambert. Liverpool were two goals down inside 12 minutes.

Paisley had little to offer by way of words at half-time. 'Nothing that I remember and nothing like Shanks,' says Toshack of his interventions. But he employed a tactical switch for the second half which changed the course of the night. Toshack was removed, Case sent on and Liverpool attacked down the flanks instead. Case immediately scuffed an easy opportunity on the mud-caked Anfield pitch but went on to deliver a command performance. He and Kennedy ran the midfield, both scoring as Liverpool found the net three times in five minutes around the hour mark to take a lead into the away leg.

In Belgium, Lambert sent Club Brugge ahead with an early penalty, but Keegan's crashed 15-yard equaliser was enough and the side held out to clinch Paisley's first trophy. For many, the converted midfielder Kennedy was the stand-out player.

There was a lack of ostentation about the way Liverpool paraded the UEFA Cup around the new Olympiastadion in Bruges on the night of 19 May 1976. The base of the trophy fell off. 'Paisley's hits are so composed,' stated one corny headline, reflecting on the unglamorous way Liverpool had found their way to victory.

Toshack was devastated to have been removed from the action so early at Anfield, yet he would later reflect that Paisley's decision was visionary and not something he could argue with. 'A change of approach was needed and the final scoreline was a tribute to the tactical knowledge of Paisley as much as anything else,' Toshack says.

The arithmetic for the last First Division match of the season, at Wolverhampton Wanderers, underlined how tight the league season had been and the significance of Fairclough's contribution, in what was a spring-time like none other for him. Paisley's players could afford to draw 0–0 or 1–1 in the Midlands and still win the league, but 2–2 or defeat would hand the title to QPR. For Shankly, this would have been a moment for steadying minds with the big speech. For Paisley, it was another moment of unintended comedy gold.

Vast numbers of Liverpool supporters had turned up without tickets that night, including Phil Thompson's brothers, Owen and Ian. Thompson was worrying about them getting in and, since the door of the dressing-room at Molineux opened out onto the main road which runs past the stadium, he kept disappearing out through it to see if he could find them. A message then reached him that his elder brother was at the main stadium door so he ventured off again, returning five minutes later with a plea for Paisley. 'Boss, you have to help,' he said. 'My brothers have been to every game this season and now they can't get in.'

Paisley went out into the corridor, buttonholed the elderly steward for a key to the door out onto the street and, after returning with it, told Thompson to 'get them up here'. Thompson jumped onto a bench, spotted his contingent through the high window which gave a view onto the street and signalled to them to come to the door, which Paisley duly opened. It was not just the two Thompson brothers who stepped through it. Friends and extended family numbering eight walked in and, to their astonishment, found themselves standing in the dressing-room where Paisley was attempting to prepare the players for his most significant night in 36 years at Liverpool.

It was while Thompson was placing his entourage into the company of a police officer and asking him to see them to the Liverpool end that Emlyn Hughes – never one knowingly to pass up an opportunity – stepped up onto the bench Thompson had used and informed Paisley, 'Boss, my mates are out there as well.'

Paisley opened the door once again, and this time a procession of around 40 people filed in, carrying flags, banners and horns and singing their Liverpool anthems in the dressing-room. What was supposed to be an environment of organised calm was now becoming bedlam. Paisley started to panic. 'What the fuck. What the fuck?' he shouted at no one in particular, single-handedly attempting to force the door shut. 'How many are in your family? This has gone too far.'

The consequences were more profound than he probably knew. 'We were in pieces,' says Thompson. 'It was typical Bob and it relaxed us more than any team talk.' Keegan felt the same. 'I doubt that a team of players have ever worked more closely with their manager than Liverpool did with Bob,' he said. 'We willed him to win the league. We wanted to win it for him.'

And they did. An early goal for Wolves, who needed a win to avoid relegation that night, set Liverpool back on their heels, but Keegan scored the equaliser, Toshack swivelled onto a shot to score a winner and Kennedy rounded off the night with a third as Paisley's side clinched the title by a point from QPR. Paisley did not look like a man in his element when he made a rare appearance before the TV cameras that night.

Emlyn Hughes ended the season with far more to say, just as he had started it. 'He's got to be manager of the year. He's just got to be,' he told the same television interviewer from amid the euphoria of the Liverpool dressing-room. By then, Paisley had vanished into the background and was nowhere to be seen. They'd done all their talking in the Boot Room. He could leave the discussion to others now.

6

WE NEED TO TALK
ABOUT KEVIN

Bob Paisley said that he had discovered quietness did have a place in running a football team. 'I believe I have mastered the side of management which worried me,' he told the *Liverpool Echo* in the aftermath of the league and UEFA Cup Double. 'I had no experience of handling the players in other ways. Bill had always done that: that was the manager's job. I had to learn to deal with the manager's problems and I have found that it is easy to get involved in an argument and that it is better to be tactful. Never say anything that you might live to regret.'

But despite the warm afterglow of his own breakthrough season, there was unchartered territory ahead. The next problem was beyond his very limited managerial experience.

The UEFA Cup campaign had opened Kevin Keegan's eyes to what a life beyond Liverpool might look like and left him determined to get a slice of it. After helping to carry the wobbly European trophy off the field in Belgium he told Paisley that he wanted to leave Anfield. Players generally only wanted to arrive there, but here was a player seeking a move for a reason other than having given up on a place in the team. He was Liverpool's best player, too.

There were few others Paisley considered remotely good enough to replace Keegan, though the forward did not seem to be in the mood to wait around in the summer of 1976. He had been particularly taken by Barcelona's Nou Camp stadium, where Liverpool had played their UEFA Cup semi-final in late March. Keegan looked around at the dressing-rooms in wonderment – 'almost as big as Liverpool's training ground' – as well as the club's own little chapel, the magnificent surface of the pitch and the crowd of 85,000.

It was a time of financial rewards for football's great players. In the summer of 1976 the newspapers were full of Johan Cruyff's new £10,000-a-week contract at Ajax. The best paid British players, meanwhile, had an 82 per cent domestic super tax rate to deal with. Keegan collected a bonus from Liverpool of £2,000 for his contribution to Paisley's second season, though that was reduced to £400 after tax – and then there were surtax demands from the previous year. The pound was sinking, too, despite the swingeing spending public cuts and higher interest rates announced in July 1976. Keegan being Keegan, he didn't bottle up his thoughts as he left the Nou Camp. He wandered up to the press reporters who'd covered the match and told them how he felt, and his thoughts filled their reports. 'Don't get me wrong,' he'd said. 'I'm all for Liverpool. But in a couple of years' time I think my inclination would be to play in Spanish football.' His urge to leave was actually far stronger than that.

A petty argument between Paisley and Keegan suggested that the manager would struggle to deal with a challenge of this size. Keegan had discovered that a member of the administrative staff, Ken Addison, whose role in Liverpool's commercial department included charitable work, was not travelling to Belgium for the UEFA Cup final second leg against Club Brugge because Liverpool had not – as Keegan understood it – invited his wife. Keegan, with his very acute sense of right and wrong, went to see Paisley and told him this should be sorted out for Addison – though the manager was not interested. 'She doesn't like flying,' Paisley replied flatly, with total disregard for Keegan. Even as the team manager he was never inclined to criticise 'upstairs'.

'It's a disgrace. Extra press and all sorts are coming along on the plane and this bloke, who'd do anything for this club, isn't invited,' replied Keegan, irritated by Paisley's tone.

'None of your business,' said Paisley. Keegan stormed off and when Liverpool lifted the trophy in northern Belgium he could barely bring himself to look at Paisley. 'Well done. You deserve it,' was the most enthusiasm he could conjure. These were the moments when Keegan missed Shankly's warmth most desperately.

The dispute was quickly smoothed over – Paisley was not generally inclined to sulk with a star player who could get results for him, so he and Keegan were rarely at odds for long. But keeping the player at the club was not so easily brushed away.

For most managers of the pre-war generation, steeped in Anfield as Paisley was, the idea of Barcelona appealing more than Liverpool to a player so idolised as 25-year-old Keegan would have been a source of indignation. But though Keegan was contracted to the club for another three years, Paisley knew a flat rejection would not work. He wanted to find an answer and looked for someone who could provide it. 'We'll talk to upstairs,' he told Keegan.

Paisley knew that there was a relationship between Keegan and Peter Robinson, stemming from the part the club secretary had played in getting Keegan to Anfield in the first place.

That had all started with a phone call Robinson received in the office in the spring of 1968 from Scunthorpe United, where Keegan's career was starting. On the end of the line was Jackie Brownsword, a Scunthorpe coach who held the distinction of playing a few games short of 600 for the club. He had called, as clubs often did, to ask Robinson for tickets for a Liverpool game. Bill Shankly was in the background and gestured to Robinson that he wanted to speak to Brownsword, too. He didn't know him but was always very taken with how he had managed to play until the age of 42. After arranging the tickets, Robinson put Shankly on the line and it was then that Brownsword recommended his club's best prospect – Keegan. Liverpool had some reports on him but Scunthorpe had only very few games left to play that season. 'I'll send Joe and Bob and if they fancy him we'll sign him,' Robinson remembers Shankly saying.

Paisley didn't need to watch the player twice. He returned from the trip – a Friday night match at Grimsby – and urged Shankly to conclude a deal. Keegan never forgot that. 'My best recommendation came from Bob Paisley,' he reflected. He also always remembered the part Robinson had played. Years later, when managing Newcastle United, Keegan arranged for Brownsword to be at St James' Park for the occasion of a Liverpool match. 'There's someone I want you to meet,' he told Robinson.

Persuading Keegan to stay took more ingenuity than signing him had. Robinson conceived a plan by which the forward would stay for one last season and in return Liverpool would do everything possible to get him to a foreign club that suited him, whatever the price.

Keegan took a little talking around but with Paisley's persuasion became agreeable to it. Paisley was satisfied with the idea. It would at least buy some time. The club concluded there was no point trying to keep it a secret.

The announcement that the player was to go came on the morning of the 1976 Charity Shield against Southampton, and he made no secret that he had a sense of his own value. 'Yes, I know my worth,' he was quoted as saying. 'The rewards of playing for some club like Real Madrid are so staggering that by going out of the country I could be a millionaire in five years. I'm not pleading poverty now – it would surprise me if many other English players had a more lucrative contract than mine. But with income tax at 82p in the pound for me, what's the point in sticking around indefinitely?'

It was a forthright declaration which would have made some managers flinch, though Paisley was more interested in trying to extract another season of high performance from Keegan. 'He'll have to be in top form to make European clubs go for him,' he observed. Raising the prospect of there being no takers was his way of challenging Keegan to give him one more quality campaign.

'Upstairs' were proving invaluable for Paisley. First, Robinson had helped resolve his anxieties about appearing in the public realm, and now Keegan was sorted for the short term, even though several informal inquiries that winter about an individual Paisley felt perhaps could replace him – Glasgow Celtic's Kenny Dalglish – met with firm rejection. 'You won't get him,' Liverpool were told, several times.

The significance of keeping Keegan and keeping him happy did not take long to reveal itself. He was one of the outstanding players in the autumn of 1976 and the best of the Liverpool side in the 3–1 win over Everton in which, almost inevitably, he scored. The influence of Ray Kennedy was becoming increasingly significant in his new role, too. He also delivered against Everton and was widely commended for his performance in a hard-fought 1–1 draw with Leeds United. His 'courage' in midfield was what one of the Sunday papers highlighted.

Winning the title had created a greater air of confidence around Anfield. Paisley's public discussions revealed further advances from the reticence of his first season. He was the reigning manager of the year now. Saunders was needed less.

'We had no biorhythm,' he told reporters when Liverpool lost 1–0 to Newcastle United on 25 September. There was glint in his eye when he said it. It was his way of sending up the pseudo-intellectual explanation for Liverpool's second defeat of the season, which had not dislodged them from the top of the league. 'We didn't play well,' he then added, by way of translation.

Paisley had more prosaic notions of football wisdom, based in the very small details, though they took some comprehending at times. Before the league game against Norwich City in January 1977, he offered some odd advice to penalty-taker Phil Neal about Norwich's Indian-born goalkeeper Kevin Keelan. Keelan had 'short arms' when he dived to his right for penalties, the manager observed. It was his way of saying that when Keelan leapt to his right, he used his stronger left arm to attempt to stop the ball, rather than his right, which would have extended out further. It seemed like an obscure observation to make but Liverpool happened to win a penalty against John Bond's Norwich side that afternoon, which Neal placed beyond the 'short arm' of Keelan.

Paisley also took to employing the occasional double bluff. Joey Jones, who was generally discouraged from advancing too far up the field, was puzzled to find the boss asking him one night to 'go up for the corners'. The manager of the Aston Villa side Liverpool were playing three days later was in the stadium that evening. It transpired that Paisley's instructions were a decoy intended to convince him to feature Jones in his match preparations. 'I was nowhere near the six-yard box the following Saturday,' Jones says.

With Keegan in his last season and Toshack physically capable of playing only half Liverpool's games, Paisley had moved boldly into the transfer market, when a club record £200,000 was paid to bring the striker David Johnson from Bobby Robson's Ipswich Town, four days before the start of the 1976–77 league season. Johnson was an England international and one of the new breed of striker who broke the old centre-forward mould by providing something other than height and brawn in the penalty area. Robson had experimented with deploying two mobile strikers – Johnson and Trevor Whymark – to good effect.

But though picked to start the first eight league fixtures, Johnson was deemed in need of assimilation time. He was frequently the substitute.

There was no explanation of this from Paisley, whose austere management style took some adjusting to for the forward. 'Having come from a man like Bobby Robson who was a great manager, who dealt with players and spoke to them and inspired them it was very different,' Johnson says. 'Bob was the complete opposite. He wasn't a motivator. He couldn't talk.'

Liverpool did not immediately need a new record signing. The only setback came just before Christmas in a heavy midweek defeat at Aston Villa – who were 4–0 up in half an hour and 5–1 up at half-time – which served another reminder that Paisley came well down the order of merit when it came to oration in the midst of a crisis.

'That result just blew Bob's mind,' Heighway says. 'He couldn't even speak in the dressing-room afterwards. He was shell-shocked. He couldn't even be angry. He didn't do angry. There was just an astonished dressing-room with Bob shaking his head.' This struggle for self-expression struck Phil Thompson, too: 'No, he didn't say too much.' It was Joe Fagan who read the riot act. 'I'm not detracting from those Villa boys,' Paisley told the press. 'They did well. But my defence – I didn't think they could play so badly.'

He kept virtually the same side for the next game, at West Ham, and Liverpool went down 2–0, conceding top spot. He convened a 'squad discussion' after the defeat in east London, though it was brief and he does not seem to have raised his voice like Fagan. He promptly picked the same side yet again to face Stoke City at home, the day after Boxing Day, and Liverpool won 4–0, climbing back to the top spot they had surrendered by the defeat in London. Keegan dominated once more, lofting a difficult opportunity over goalkeeper Peter Shilton's head for one of the goals.

The world around them was becoming a more challenging place in the winter of 1976 – a time when Harold Wilson's surprise resignation as Prime Minister reflected surging unemployment which topped 20 per cent in Liverpool, with inevitable effects on gate receipts. Kevin Keegan was not the only one frustrated by the strictures placed upon him in football's burgeoning commercial environment. Liverpool's earning power in Europe was limited by the fact that they were able to sell only highlights to BBC or ITV for the domestic audience, rather than live televised coverage, and the two broadcasters were not exactly turning it into an auction. Liverpool could sell their own overseas TV rights – with the countries which lacked quality teams proving the keenest – though UEFA, European football's fledgling organisation, took 4 per cent.

Liverpool needed new ways to generate the money for the transfer market and the announcement, in Paisley's third season, that there would be a mid-season trip to Gothenburg underlined that. A mid-season exhibition match provided a one-off opportunity to generate extra money that was too good to miss. The Swedes were not the only club wanting to host the First

Division champions. There was interest from Saudi Arabia, Dubai, Israel and Ireland. Each of the games generated the equivalent of a single First Division game gate receipts.

Paisley was receptive to the idea of travelling away in mid-season. 'He knew that anything we made was spent on players or on the ground,' says Robinson. 'There was no one taking sums out of clubs like there were in some places.'

Informing the players they would be heading off abroad was not always straightforward, though. Steve Heighway wanted to know what they would be getting when it was announced that the side was to play in Gothenburg. Tommy Smith backed him.

As Paisley hesitated, Heighway tabled a bid. The players wanted £300 each for going, he said.

'I'll see what they say upstairs,' Paisley replied.

The next day Heighway inquired what the reaction had been.

'They'll give you that,' he said.

A few months later, Paisley announced they would be playing in Israel, and Heighway moved to broach the question of an even higher fee.

'There's no discussion. That's what it is,' said Paisley, at the limit of his willingness to negotiate. Deference on the Rat's part – sometimes it seemed like subservience – to 'upstairs' felt rooted in class consciousness at times, and his players would have liked him to fight the management for them. Some felt he was a small figure when it came to taking on their paymasters. Shankly would have done more. It is hard to imagine him tolerating mid-season overseas excursions.

But the travel brought good income in and Paisley came to enjoy it. The trips to Israel were the start of a long attachment to that country, in which his experience seemed very different from the ordeal which the United States had been after the war. A mid-season postcard from Jerusalem's Wailing Wall to Jessie revealed as much. 'Darling,' Paisley wrote. 'A quick note after our visit to Jerusalem and Bethlehem, where we spent a really interesting five hours. The weather is good with a slight breeze which makes it more comfortable. Will drop you a line later on. Love, Bob.'

The players were amused to know that Paisley earned some commercial income of his own. Gola wanted him to wear their tracksuits. One of those he sported was personalised, with his name stitched beneath the logo. He managed to get Gola deals for the coaching staff too, though since the club's Umbro shirt deal was one of the best around, this became a little delicate on match days. On those occasions Paisley just had to settle for his Gola boots and dispense with the tracksuit. He also wore a Gola tie.

There were other signs that Bob had gone up in the world. He and Jessie moved house in 1977, leaving behind the house in South Manor Way where they'd raised the children for a new home, at 29 Bower Road in the picturesque heart of Woolton village. They'd paid off the mortgage on the old house, though Paisley was becoming more recognisable and people would be looking in to see where the Liverpool manager lived, so it was seclusion they wanted, rather than luxury. The new place was detached but not much larger: a dormer bungalow with two large rooms in the roof space reachable by ladder rather than stairs. There was also a greenhouse for Jessie.

Their lives were not ostentatious. Paisley's Christmas present from Christine was often Brylcreem and a comb. His hair was always brilliantined, though Jessie sometimes cursed at the mark this left on the head-rests of his chair. The antimacassars didn't do the job they were intended for.

The partnership Paisley and Robinson were forming saw Liverpool announce at Christmas 1976 that both of them were to be offered new seven-year contracts, running until 1983. For Paisley, the new deal was worth £105,000 over its entire seven-year span. He would earn in seven years what Cruyff earned in ten months.

That same press conference provided another sense of the new commercial landscape. Plans were announced for an export drive to market the club and its merchandise overseas. Anfield would have a new executive lounge for shareholders. The club's first sponsored match would take place later that season, when Bell's would pay for an association with the match against Manchester United on 3 May. Perimeter adverting would be introduced at Anfield. Robinson also made Liverpool the first league club to secure shirt advertising – first with Hitachi, then Crown Paints.

A ban on shirt advertising in televised matches, FA Cup ties and European games, however, did frustrate Liverpool. It was estimated that the Hitachi income would have been £250,000 without the strictures. Paisley viewed this as another way of earning money for players. He seized a paintbrush and wore a replica crown for the publicity shots with Crown Paints, grinning over his shoulder for the camera.

The burgeoning working relationship with Peter Robinson was significant in the complex commercial landscape that football began to occupy. It was an improbable one: Robinson, the educated, erudite and ambitious football executive who had gravitated from positions at Stockport, Crewe, Scunthorpe and Brighton to become club secretary aged only 29, in June 1965; Paisley, the trained County Durham bricklayer 17 years his senior who had worked his way up at Liverpool the hard way.

For Paisley there had been an awkwardness about this at first, whereas Shankly, who had generally been first into Anfield each morning, would typically be straight into Robinson's office and would call him four or five times a day, sometimes in the evening just to discuss a programme he must watch on television. It was different with Paisley. He and Robinson would speak just once a day. The conversations usually entailed Robinson heading downstairs to seek him out and see if there were issues on his mind. They didn't generally last long. It was not Paisley's natural realm. Many a time when there was a problem 'downstairs', Tom Saunders would discreetly head up to see Robinson about it on Paisley's behalf, sparing Bob the awkwardness of having to broach some gripe or complaint felt by the players. Saunders was a bridge to the board, too.

Robinson always felt that his own relationship with Shankly might have contributed to Paisley's gaucheness. 'He had seen the relationship I had with Bill and was probably apprehensive about how I would react to him,' he says.

The arrangement Paisley and Robinson had struck with Keegan continued to serve the club well, though. Keegan basked in his soon-to-be continental status, appearing with Anderlecht's Robbie Rensenbrink on the cover of *Shoot!* in March, though he continued to be the player around whom points accumulation was built.

A rare blemish came with a bad miss in a goalless spring-time draw at Stoke. But he was instrumental to Liverpool winning a potentially title-defining game at Manchester City, scoring soon after firing into the side-netting. Liverpool sat second on goal difference, with a game in hand on QPR and through to the semi-finals of the FA Cup and European Cup, leaving Paisley to observe that, 'We must be in with a chance of something.' He was still not one for earth-shattering disclosures to the press.

The club's attempt to make every penny count always made spring a busy time for Paisley. High corporation tax rates made the club determined to minimise the profits they made and find any available means of doing so. At that time, all of a player's transfer fee could be written down into a year's accounts, rather than spread across the period of the player's first contract, as it eventually would. In a good year of revenue earning, buying in the spring helped reduce the profit and tax liability. The Football League's deadline for buying players was mid-March, to ensure that clubs did not distort the end-of-season run-in.

The battle to keep the taxman at bay was helped by the arrival of a 21-year-old defender, Alan Hansen, from Partick Thistle in the spring of 1977. Liverpool had indicated their interest in him on 3 May 1977 and concluded the deal on 5 May, 24 hours before their tax-year ended. The club's accountants were happy. 'I was tax deductible,' Hansen later said. Paisley was happy to fit in with the accounting system. 'Lost in tax' was how he described these deals, some of which were gambles with money which the club would otherwise have lost to the Inland Revenue.

The players were looking for their own ways of making money, too. The tax demands meant that every penny that could be earned was earned, though the energy with which Keegan monetised his superstar status was extraordinary. It reached a level which would have made working life difficult with a less *laissez-faire* manager than Paisley.

Keegan had always possessed an acute sense of his own worth. His record 'It Ain't Easy', with the Liverpool band The Fourmost as backing singers, pre-dated Paisley's time as manager and was a source of rich amusement at Anfield. It sold 12,000 and, Keegan liked to say, reached number seven in the Merseyside charts. By the mid-1970s, Keegan was getting so much mail that he set up an office in the back room of a junk shop run by a friend, Lennie Libson. It was there that he based his limited company Nageek

Enterprises – Keegan spelt backwards – which he set up when he realised that he was paying far too much tax. It helped that newspapers paid cash for interviews.

In the space of a week before the start of his last season, Keegan racked up 1,000 miles for a promotional trip to the Isle of Man, studio analysis for London Weekend Television's live coverage of the Czechoslovakia v West Germany European Championships final, an appearance in an all-star XI with Billy Bremner, his 1974 Charity Shield *bête noire*, against Brazil to mark the sixth anniversary of the founding of the Paris Saint-Germain club, plus the opening of a fête in Rhyl, in North Wales. Then came an appearance in a heat of the BBC's *Superstars* entertainment programme, which pitched the continent's sports stars against each other in a multitude of pursuits, and saw Keegan crash from his bicycle in a race to reach the first corner of the track ahead of the Anderlecht captain Gilbert Van Binst – yet still become the first footballer to win the heat. He collected his prize money, collapsed from nervous exhaustion at Newport Pagnell Services on the way home, and spent three days on an intravenous drip at Northampton General Hospital. 'He's young but I hope he'll learn that he can't move mountains,' Paisley said.

This was extraordinary equanimity given that pre-season was almost upon Liverpool. Paisley would not have stood for that with a player so invaluable. For some of the squad at Liverpool, it seemed that the stars could do what they wanted without jeopardising their place in the team, while the rest of them fought for the remotest sense that he would see what they had to offer. Those outside of the elite felt an injustice. Paisley's calculation was hard but pragmatic. He was less willing to antagonise those most likely to help the club win.

For those on the periphery, the Rat's indifference was maddening. Liverpool's performance-related salaries meant that players earned £300 per point, which made a precious place in his 12-man squad so important to them. But he remained impervious to those who did not feature in his plans. He was so absorbed by how he would win the next game that, on occasions, he even forgot to tell the unlucky 13th man that he would be watching from the stands. (Teams had only one substitute then.)

This was becoming a particular frustration to David Fairclough who turned 21 midway through the 1976–77 season. Fairclough's burst of speed had earned him the nickname 'Whip' and he was a regular sensation from the bench, with a goal against Saint-Étienne at Anfield proving crucial to Liverpool securing a place in the European Cup final against Borussia Mönchengladbach in Rome. But Paisley was not convinced by his consistency. Tommy Smith later said that Paisley had told him there was a psychological problem with Fairclough, who was excellent when arriving from the bench with a point to prove but less so when playing from the start, in what Paisley described 'a comfort zone'.

The greatest agony for the peripheral team members came whenever Liverpool were on a poor run of form. The team would not be announced on a Friday, as usual, but 13 appointed players would have to wait until they arrived on a Saturday to find out which of the 12 of them would be changing into their match kit. This gave Paisley, Fagan, Moran, Bennett and Saunders an extra evening to deliberate. The suspense was increased by a little routine in which the boots of the 13 players were lined up underneath the treatment table before the match. Fagan would then send the players out 'to look at the pitch' and when they returned the 11 starters' boots would be under the shirts with the remaining two left underneath the table. It was torture for those without Keegan's certainty of playing.

One Saturday, early in 1976, Fairclough and Heighway arrived back from their 'look at the pitch' to find both of their pairs of boots still under the table. Heighway, an agitator when he felt the need, approached Fairclough. 'If this is what they think of us let's just go and have a cup of tea in the players' lounge,' he said. They both walked out of the dressing-room. Five minutes later, Fagan arrived there – presumably dispatched by Paisley. 'Dave – it's you. You're sub,' he said. There was no explanation for Heighway, whose afternoon was over.

The players could fulminate as much as they wanted but it made no difference: results did the talking for Paisley. They would put up with his coldness because they craved a part in the winning side his Liverpool were becoming. The players he was increasingly turning to – Kennedy, Case, Neal, Thompson – were flourishing, so demonstrating that when it came to recruiting and selecting players, Paisley came into his own. From the turn of the year to the end of the 1976–77 season, Liverpool lost only twice in the league, while also progressing towards the finals of the FA Cup and European Cup.

It was the turn of David Johnson to feel the chill of unexplained rejection before the FA Cup semi-final against Everton, his first club, a game in which he was expected to play. 'Was I excited?' recalls Johnson. 'You bet I was. In my head I was playing.'

Three hours before kick-off, he and his room-mate Keegan were heading down for the midday pre-match meal at the Lord Daresbury Hotel in Warrington, the team's traditional pre-match base, when Paisley sauntered along the corridor towards them.

'Good morning, boss,' said Keegan.

'Good morning, Kevin,' replied Paisley.

'Good morning, boss,' said Johnson.

'You're sub,' Paisley said, scuttling straight on to his room, opening the door and disappearing behind it.

'I wondered if I'd heard him right,' says Johnson. I asked Kevin, "What did he say, Kev?"' There was no, "Can I come and have a chat with you?" I didn't think that was the right way to do it. I was looking for a taxi to go home but Joe Fagan and Ronnie Moran came out and talked me around. I think it was in his make-up, though. He was a man of very, very few words and half of them you couldn't understand anyway. I have to say there were times as a player when you really didn't like him.'

Liverpool drew 2–2, won the replay 3–0 to reach the final and by April were also well on their way to a second successive title. A 1–1 draw at QPR in early May was significant, with the well-established Case scoring, and a goalless home draw against West Ham a week later secured the prize. Liverpool had won the league through sheer consistency of performance and effort, though had not been the most dazzling. Five sides had scored more First Division goals than them; none had conceded fewer.

Then came the FA Cup final and another decision for Paisley. Would Johnson or Fairclough, the star of the previous campaign, start at Wembley? Fairclough's reasons for believing it would be him reflect Paisley's dissembling when picking a team – a failing which often compounded the blow for the unlucky player. He'd not selected Fairclough for a league game at Coventry, promising him, 'You'll be in my Cup final team,' according to Fairclough. In the course of going back on that promise, Paisley then revealed the comical consequences of bringing his limited conversational skills to bear to soften a blow.

The day before the final, Fairclough opened the door of his room at the team's Sopwell House hotel in Hertfordshire to find Paisley loitering, rather suspiciously, outside. The manager beckoned him up the corridor towards his room and he was about to wave him inside when he evidently gave up plans for the consoling speech and said what he had to say to the 20-year-old there on the landing. 'You won't be playing tomorrow,' Paisley told Fairclough. 'But I will need you in Rome.' And so the discussion ended.

It was a better attempt to break bad news than most of Paisley's players were treated to. His own experience of being dropped from the 1950 final may have played a part in this unusual inclination to speak to Fairclough. But the suggestion that the 20-year-old would have a place in the European Cup final against Borussia Mönchengladbach was quickly forgotten when Paisley announced his team in Rome. Fairclough was one of five substitutes. He sank back in his seat in desolation and was not sent on there, either. Though it seemed the wrong time to make a scene, he would reflect years later on how that had 'cast a shadow over what should have been the greatest moment of my career'.

For a man who was usually so clinical, Paisley's unnecessary empty promises were odd – perhaps his way of avoiding at all cost the kind of verbal challenge for which he was ill-equipped.

Entirely unaware of the manager's dissembling behind the scenes, supporters were confident ahead of the FA Cup final. 'Smith and Jones – United Funeral Directors' stated one of their banners, in celebration of Tommy Smith and Joey Jones. But Liverpool, whom Paisley had organised in an attacking 4–3–3 formation, could not capitalise on their first-half superiority and then went behind after Stuart Pearson ran across Joey Jones and fired the ball past Ray Clemence. Case equalised but almost immediately a Lou Macari shot cannoned off Jimmy Greenhoff to win the Cup for United.

There were recriminations. In the confines of the dressing-room, Paisley blamed Jones, wanting to know why he had not brought Pearson down before the opening goal. Jones, revealing the flinty personality that helped persuade Paisley to buy him in the first place, did not accept the criticism. 'Well, you've been telling me all season not to bring players down,' he replied. Paisley apparently didn't return fire. 'I think he was just surprised I'd answered back,' says Jones.

But it was one of the few major games in which Paisley said he felt he had made a tactical miscalculation. The Football Association had announced before the game that if the final was drawn, a replay would not take place until 27 June – the problems of rescheduling having been caused by Liverpool's European final in Rome.

Paisley, furious about the notion of waiting 33 days for a reply, decided that Liverpool must win the game there and then at Wembley. He opted for a very attacking set-up, with a three-man forward line – Keegan, Johnson and Heighway. 'My worst ever tactical decision' is how he later described his decision to field Johnson, rather than Callaghan as an extra midfielder.

The players, rather than their manager, found a way of lifting themselves from a gloom that seemed to deepen as their journey home began. They were bussed to Watford station, where their 7.45 p.m. chartered train north to Liverpool became stuck behind a broken-down football special and remained stationary in the middle of Hertfordshire for two hours. In the hiatus, Ray Clemence threw a wrapped sugar cube across the carriage, and then another. Someone threw one back, and then another. Drink was taken. It evolved into a party on the motionless train in the middle of nowhere, interspersed with choruses of the team's 1977 FA Cup record 'We Can Do It'. That seemed enough to erase the disappointment of Wembley.

Paisley's immediate concern was Keegan. He was the individual most capable of a moment of class to deliver Liverpool a European Cup but he was racked with uncertainty about his future. In football's complex new commercial world, the move to Europe that he, Keegan and Robinson had talked about was just not materialising. One of the difficulties of signing or selling players in the late 1970s was the lack of agents to help facilitate a move. Keegan was one of the first British players to have a commercial agent and Liverpool had thought that might help him find a team. But the club, placed in the unusual position of needing another side to come forward for their best player, found that the work being done on Keegan's behalf only entailed finding him commercial appearance opportunities. No one was on the telephone trying to secure him the move he wanted.

Keegan, on the other hand, suspected that Liverpool were stalling, waiting for the right valuation. He noticed that Bayern Munich had made a reported £500,000 from the sale of Franz Beckenbauer to the New York Cosmos, so had ready money to buy him. Keegan made direct contact with John Smith on 5 May, two weeks before the FA Cup final and in the midst of the title run-in, in a state of concern that the club chairman may be trying to play him. 'I told him that if he didn't keep his word [to sell me] I would quit. The season was running out and my patience was running short, though I knew Liverpool were hoping to receive an offer closer to their valuation.'

Paisley was keen to see developments. Intermediaries seemed to be everywhere but none were reliable. Rumours of interest from Bayern and Real Madrid failed to materialise into anything concrete. Paisley was also concerned that nearly 12 months had elapsed and there was still no obvious successor to Keegan. He had been monitoring Kenny Dalglish but the word from Glasgow was that Celtic were still not selling.

'I have to admit I was becoming quite worried,' Keegan later reflected. 'What if no one came forward? Imagine the embarrassment of going cap in hand to Liverpool and asking to stay.'

Finally, at the 11th hour, on FA Cup final weekend, an approach was made – from Hamburg – the only club remotely able to make the deal happen, and, as things turned out, the proposition was better than the Anfield board had anticipated. The German side paid £500,000 in cash.

Keegan thought it had not been a good season for him. He felt he was a marked man in many ways. Defenders were out to stop him and Anfield had grown suspicious of him. 'People eventually accepted that I was leaving and while that was a good thing it also had its disadvantages,' he reflected. 'I began to feel that some of the supporters were turning against me. When a substitution was about to be made, I sensed that some people wanted me to be brought off, although I cannot be sure whether that was simply a psychological reaction on my part.'

It was to Liverpool's benefit that Paisley was willing to accept that his prime striker would rather be somewhere else in the 1976–77 season. Because of the agreement struck between Keegan, Robinson and himself the previous summer, Liverpool were equipped with a top scorer who found the net 20 times that season. This resolution would have been less straightforward under Shankly, much though Keegan had idolised him. 'I wondered if I could have approached Shanks in the same way once I had said I wanted to go,' he reflected. 'He might have just laughed it off and not wanted anything to do with it. Bob knew I meant it when I approached it.'

His goals tally was one that none of his teammates came close to matching and it would have been hard to see Paisley winning the title without it. Yet Keegan's contribution had become so integral to Liverpool's push for the title that it barely carried the headlines. Against Arsenal, during April's title run-in – a 2–0 Anfield win which enhanced Phil Neal's claim on an England place – it was Keegan who pounced on goalkeeper Jimmy Rimmer's failure to collect a ball, and scored. In a controversially physical match at Ipswich in early April, it was Keegan who delivered the decisive second goal, rising to head home David Johnson's cross. The sum of money secured for Keegan at the end of the season allowed Liverpool to be competitive in their search for a replacement for him. But he had not yet quite fully repaid Liverpool for the imagination they had shown in keeping him. There was one last night in Rome yet to come.

7

MUNCHING GLADBACH

Keegan was the last man aboard the plane for Rome and the send-off must have made it seem worth that year's wait in Liverpool. In scenes reminiscent of The Beatles at Speke airport, a balcony at the little terminal – a preferred vantage point as the players and staff made their way across the concrete to their plane – was packed. Liverpool had chartered a British Airways flight to get everyone on board for their first European Cup final, against Borussia Mönchengladbach. Club secretary Peter Robinson had taken steps to ensure a smooth passage through Rome. After Paisley's side had reached the final, he'd received a telephone call from an established London-based Italian football fixer and agent, Gigi Peronace, who had also played a part in most of the big deals that saw British players – John Charles, Jimmy Greaves and Denis Law – transferred to Italian clubs. His reasons for calling Robinson related to the Italian journalists. Peronace told Robinson that Liverpool could have 'a difficult time' with the Italian press out in Rome. But he could work for the club to make things easier. He would need 'some small gifts' to give to the journalists, but it would be in the club's interests.

Robinson asked Peronace what he had in mind. '£2,000,' he replied. Good money, if not a fortune, and worth it, Robinson thought, if it meant an easier ride for Paisley and his players during the build-up to the match. The Italian press had been aggressive the last time Liverpool had played in the country, 12 years earlier, and Paisley, of course, was not at his most relaxed in a media environment. An agreement was struck and, with Paisley's knowledge, Peronace set to work.

After the two-hour flight to Rome, the players disembarked to a battery of flashbulbs and hordes of journalists waiting for them at the city's Leonardo Da Vinci airport. One of the Italians opened with a benign question for Paisley, just as Robinson had hoped.

Was this his first time in Rome? he was asked.

No, he replied. The last time he'd been here was in a tank.

It amused him that he'd last driven in to liberate the city in 1945, though not all of the Italians felt the same way. Many of them were old enough to remember Benito Mussolini leading them into war on the side of Nazi Germany and the atrocities carried out on their nation by Adolf Hitler when Italy surrendered to the Allies after their forces had landed in Sicily. Mentioning the war was a diplomatic minefield. Robinson winced, as did Smith, Case and Ian Callaghan. Tommy Smith, more worldly than Paisley in this environment, spotted that a group of Italian journalists was looking to build up an angle out of the comment when they spoke to the Liverpool players. Smith had been nominated as the best person to speak to them, so before he left the airport he found himself explaining that Paisley was simply proud to have been a part of the Allied liberating forces and felt a compassion for the Italian people because of that. The 'I invaded Italy' line did not make the Italian press, thanks either to Smith's diplomacy, Robinson's investment or a combination of both.

Paisley meant no harm, though if it had been pointed out to him that he shouldn't mention the war then he didn't appear to take much notice. He mentioned the liberation several times more before the trip was done. 'Rome was a place that I'd been to during the war and I'd had a particular fancy for the whole city,' he repeated years later.

The *faux pas* that he had been oblivious to reflected the treacherous waters that European football always held for him. The continental challenge appealed to Paisley the football strategist, and from the start his more pragmatic approach was suited to the competition. A four-man Liverpool defence replaced the side's usual three at the back for the first European Cup campaign of 1963–64. But it was a suspicion of European football, rather than a fascination with it, which most informed Paisley's thinking – as it had Bill Shankly's. In an era when very little European football could be seen on television and the only available information on opponents had to be brought back to Liverpool by scouts, usually Tom Saunders, Paisley's approach was principally to emerge as unharmed as possible from overseas trips and get the thing finished at home. Shankly and Paisley 'hated it in the beginning,' says Ian St John. 'They felt the opposition were all cheats.' Paisley made it Liverpool against the world.

The roots of the suspicion lay 350 miles north of Rome, in Milan, where on the evening of 12 May 1965 he and Shankly had experienced a 3–0 defeat they would never forget, to Internazionale in a European Cup semi-final in San Siro. The result, in front of a 90,000 home crowd, overturned a 3–1 first-leg win at Anfield and sent the Milanese into the final they had so badly wanted – scheduled, as it was, to take place in their own stadium.

Smoke bombs – 'purple things', as Shankly described them – landed in front of Paisley and left him reeking of smoke. There had been another diplomatic incident, when the Milanese press had somehow taken offence at Liverpool parading the newly won FA Cup at Anfield before the first leg and described the Liverpool fans as 'animals'. But the match left the distinct suspicion that referee José María Ortiz de Mendíbil had made decisions intended to ease the Milaneses' safe passage to a final against Benfica.

The conspiracy theory stemmed from the sense that decisions – free-kicks, throw-ins – went almost entirely against Liverpool. Two of the Milan goals were highly contentious and Tommy Smith was inexplicably sent off at the end. Liverpool's doubts were fuelled when evidence later emerged of systematic bribery of referees by Italian officials from the 1960s. It was an experience which Paisley often recalled, hardened him to the vagaries of Europe and convinced him that in foreign fields you must check under your bed as well as under your pasta.

He was certainly a more accomplished traveller than Shankly, though. There had been the Liverpool American tours of his twenties and thirties, which acquainted him with time differences and new cultures. Shankly, on the other hand, refused to put his watch back on one transatlantic trip, remaining steadfastly on English time. He generally skipped pre-season trips abroad and left Paisley in charge.

The type and standard of opposition was often more technical than the First Division blood and thunder. Rather than relying on pace and strength to drive through teams, European sides demonstrated a high standard of ball control to find spaces and score. Defeating them required a more subtle blend of attack and defence. Even when they had won in Europe, Liverpool had sensed that the size and nature of the challenge was changing. They'd played Borussia Mönchengladbach four years before the Rome final, in the two-legged 1973 UEFA Cup final, and thought they were cruising, only to realise how mistaken they'd been.

In the Anfield first leg, Liverpool won 3–0. The Germans struggled to deal with John Toshack, a player Paisley would make much use of in Europe because opponents were unaccustomed to the target man. But then they found themselves overwhelmed in Germany, 2–0 down at half-time and, as the *Daily Telegraph*'s Robert Oxby described it in his match report, 'tottering under successive waves of attacks'. Bernd Rupp and Jupp Heynckes combined to particularly devastating effect but others – Günter Netzer, Herbert Wimmer and Dietmar Danner – joined in the fast shifting of the ball. Shankly whipped his players up in the dressing-room at half-time, insisting the Germans had gone and 'shot their bolt'. After the game, he told journalists that he could see Borussia were tiring, even in that first half, and that, 'I knew it would be all right.' He was the only one in the Bökelbergstadion who did. It was psychology beyond the remotest imagination of Bob Paisley.

'You've got to hand it to Shanks,' striker Roger Hunt later reflected, drawing on his experience of a decade playing for Shankly before he left Anfield in 1969. 'You know he's wrong but somehow you can't help believing him.'

The tactical switch that saved Liverpool that night against Mönchengladbach seems to have been of Paisley's making. Kevin Keegan was moved into midfield and space was denied to the Germans, who could not find the all-important third goal in the second half. Liverpool squeaked home.

Shankly's rhetoric alone could not always save a side who were still in the foothills of their continental journey of discovery, nine years after their first competitive fixture in Reykjavik. He described Ajax as 'too defensive' after they took Liverpool apart 5–1 in Amsterdam in 1966. That match was played in thick fog and, as St John recalls it, resulted in Shankly taking to the pitch while proceedings were still on-going and urging his players, who could not see each other, to 'stop charging up the field. We've still got the game at Anfield.'

The game should never have been played and the fact it took place offered more ammunition for the view that the foreigners were not to be trusted. In the Anfield programme for the second leg of the Ajax match, Shankly told a Dutch journalist that 'most continental teams do a lot of bluffing'. There were echoes in that statement of Shankly's comments after the 1966 European Cup Winners' Cup final, in which Liverpool played Borussia Dortmund at Hampden Park. The Germans had been 'frightened men' Shankly said. His side lost that one 2–1.

In the autumn of 1973 came a 4–2 aggregate defeat to Red Star Belgrade – a 2–1 scoreline in both legs – in the European Cup second round, which confronted the club with the distance they lagged behind the best when it came to the elite continental competition. Liverpool couldn't get close to the Yugoslavs' slick superiority as they navigated the ball around the last third of the pitch. 'That was real football,' purred Gerald Sinstadt, commentator for the highlights of the match on BBC's *Sportsnight*.

Red Star were prepared to play a waiting game and stunned Anfield with two immaculate goals from distance in the second leg. It didn't help that Toshack missed several good chances from close range. It would be Shankly's last shot at the biggest European prize. Eight months later he stepped down.

His successor wanted the build-up in Europe to be slower and more conservative, particularly away from home. Denying the opposition scoring opportunities would also quieten the home fans and put home sides under pressure, Paisley told his players. That, in turn, would force them to take chances and open up spaces. Shankly had shown pragmatism, with his four-man defence and instructions on the field at Ajax, but Paisley took that to another level.

So, almost immediately, Liverpool laid siege far less, even though the effect could be particularly metronomic and dull on foreign fields. Defender Tommy Smith said Paisley had told him before an early European game that 'the quickest way forward is to push the ball back and frustrate your opponents into making mistakes'. Phil Neal recollects a conversation, probably in 1976, in which Paisley told him that 'keeping the opposition quiet' was paramount: 'Do that. Make plenty of passes. Deny them scoring chances in the first half and their fans will start to get fidgety.'

The ball-playing centre-halves, Phil Thompson and Emlyn Hughes, and keeper-sweeper Ray Clemence were an important part of the new strategy. Paisley saw that the continental sides had fewer of the strapping target-man centre-forwards who were such an important part of the artillery in England. It meant that central defenders did not need to be built like barn doors; deploying more mobile, less physical men did not constitute a risk.

For Toshack and Keegan, higher up the team, the slower build-up took some adjusting to. 'I remember Kevin saying to me in one game that we needed to be more patient. There was no point continually making runs,' Toshack says.

Paisley's views on foreign countries varied according to where Liverpool happened to be going. He liked Scandinavia, where the club regularly journeyed for money-spinning friendlies, generally scouring the cities where Liverpool played for keepsakes to bring home for the family. There was always a doll of some description for Christine, though the troll he brought home from Norway is the one the family always laughed about. Arriving back at South Manor Way in the early hours, he left it on the living-room table and gave Jessie the fright of her life when she walked in on it the following morning. It was not an object of beauty, though he liked it and in time it gravitated to his Anfield office.

Eastern European trips were a different story. On the morning of a European draw, Paisley would wait in his office to discover what fate had in store. Once he knew, he would be out across the pitches to tell the players. If there was no spring in his step, they knew they were heading out to the east. Paisley always called these trips beyond the Iron Curtain 'missions'. If there were raucous supporters outside the team hotel, he generally assumed it was an organised attempt to prevent his men sleeping.

Though it was Tom Saunders's role to undertake the reconnaissance mission, Paisley also ensured that two Liverpool hoteliers and friends of the club, Alan Glynn and Harry Wright, travelled to check out the food on offer and ascertain whether Liverpool needed to bring some of their own. Players knew better than to consume any of the local produce or drink the tea at half-time in a communist country. A mauve soup was served up in Romania. 'Don't touch it,' Paisley told his players. 'It's probably drugged.'

The strategy was to be in and out of enemy territory in minimal time. Robinson realised that chartering flights would make the process quicker. When he first raised the idea there was some anxiety, because it was a charter flight that had crashed in Munich with Manchester United's young squad on board in 1958. That was still part of the collective memory. But Robinson satisfied Paisley that it would be preferable, allowing the side to fly in and out of the places where they played European games in one day. They would nearly always leave Liverpool's Speke airport on Aer Lingus BAC111 flight, with the same appointed pilot, Barney Croughan, in the cockpit. If the flight would not return them to Speke airport by 2.30 a.m. they would stay overnight, but otherwise they would always be out after the game. The plane was always blessed and carried the lucky shamrock. It amused them all that Paisley always checked the door. He'd been on a flight to France with Liverpool in the early days when the door flew open.

Occasionally, the plane might be diverted to Manchester and Jessie would set out to collect him in the Rover, with Christine for company, then Paisley would drive them home. After one trip, Paisley and Liverpool director Sid Reakes sat in the front, while Jessie, Christine and Emlyn Hughes crammed into the back.

Paisley always sought to elicit what information he could on the opposition from his network of friends and contacts. Before a particularly inhospitable trip to play Trabzonspor of Turkey in October 1976 he spoke to the Chesterfield manager Arthur Cox, who had been coaching in Istanbul, and Malcolm Allison, who was managing the Turkish club Galatasaray at the time. Liverpool lost 1–0, a margin overturned with a 3–0 win at Anfield, taking them another step towards the Rome encounter with Mönchengladbach.

There were times in the hotels of Europe when Paisley's apparent struggles with the new-fangled complexities of international travel seemed comically gauche. Butter and sauce packets in restaurants always seemed to be beyond him, and if he did open any it would be at the wrong end or in such a way that the contents would squirt out everywhere.

He had a little routine, when they were away, of throwing peanuts up in the air and trying to catch them in his mouth. They always seemed to miss and bounce off his chin instead. At times, he seemed to be deliberately adopting the figure of fun character. If it was a Friday night at the Daresbury, BBC2's *Pot Black* would often be on the television and Paisley would predict the pocket a player would aim for. 'Bottom left,' he would say, matter-of-factly, before a player aimed bottom right.

But there was serious intent, where the football was concerned. The first demonstration that Liverpool were making progress in

Europe under Paisley came on 30 March 1976 in the UEFA Cup semi-final at Barcelona's Nou Camp, in his second season at the helm. The Spanish side's West German manager Hennes Weisweiler was under pressure, yet the UEFA Cup semi-final still posed a huge challenge.

Liverpool had conceded only three goals away from Anfield in the four preceding rounds of that run, with what the *Daily Mirror*'s Derek Wallis described as a 'safety first' approach in his third-round report from Śląsk Wrocław in Poland. Paisley described the 2–1 win there as, 'The most difficult match we've played in Europe.' The strategy that Liverpool had employed in that second half against Borussia Mönchengladbach in 1973 – packing Keegan into midfield to make the team more secure – had become the default mode on away trips to the continent.

But Barcelona posed a more material threat than anything encountered beforehand and Paisley's usual encouragement of Neal to push up from full-back did not apply. Neal still recalls Paisley approaching him in the dressing-room beforehand that night to tell him, 'No attacking from the back for you tonight, my lad.'

The Spaniards' Carles Rexach, the man Neal was up against, contributed to Paisley's conservatism. It was one of the Barcelona players – and probably Rexach – who elicited another of those baffling Paisley assessments which had his players in stitches and contributed to the tension being eased in the dressing-room beforehand. 'He's not fast but nippy,' Paisley told his players. What he meant by that none of them were ever sure.

But though the reputation of the Spanish preceded them, and they had Johan Cruyff in their number, Paisley had a surprise in store. He felt that there were weaknesses in their defence, so rather than pull Keegan into midfield he deployed him in the striker's role and tried to strike early, as if this were a First Division match.

It worked. Barcelona were rocked back and conceded in the 13th minute, when Toshack knocked down a long Ray Clemence clearance into Keegan's path, took the return pass and scored. Then the Spanish had to come out and respond and left gaps. Liverpool did not push it. 1–0 was quite enough. After taking that lead, they gave a composed display of possession football. The Nou Camp fans contributed to the escalating pressure on their own side, expressing their displeasure by hurling white cushions onto the pitch.

It was cue for a wild Joey Jones moment. He proceeded to throw the cushions back. On this occasion, Paisley was the better acquainted of the two with local tradition. 'What the fuck? They're throwing them at their own players. Put that cushion down,' he told Jones, or words to that effect.

The dispatches from reporters in the stadium after the match that night revealed how much this performance had meant to Paisley. Chris James of the *Mirror*, one of the Merseyside group who knew him so well, found him 'emotional' in the aftermath. Needless to say, that was not reflected in the words he offered to reporters. Paisley was matter-of-fact about a Barcelona being 'a bit suspect at the back'.

Paisley had also dispensed with the wingers that the continentals tended to use and operated more narrowly, using workmanlike contributions from Case, Ian Callaghan, Heighway, Kennedy and Keegan – to pack the midfield and prevent the Spanish from creating chances. The commentators saw Paisley's role as substantial. 'Mr Paisley, the architect of this great victory, laid down ideal tactics and the players carried them through to the letter,' said one. Cruyff knew the quality in what he had seen. 'You've always got to hope in football,' he said of the prospects of overturning the deficit at Anfield. 'But let's face it. Liverpool must get through now. I don't want to talk about Liverpool individuals but they have great individuals to make up the great team they are.' Cruyff's prediction was prophetic. A 1–1 draw at Anfield sent Liverpool through to the final against Club Brugge.

Pragmatism – the key to the change in fortunes from the Shankly era – was still being preached when Graeme Souness arrived at the club a year later. 'My job on really big games was to have a good look at it,' Souness says. 'Bob, Joe and Ronnie would tell me, "See how the game pans out. Don't go chasing it."' In one unguarded moment Paisley seemed to reveal a desire to be playing less cautiously. 'I can't wait to get home and play some proper football,' he told the *Guardian*'s Patrick Barclay after one particularly attritional trip.

Paisley's tactical vocabulary for these occasions was, needless to say, not exactly sophisticated. 'We'll do the European One!' he said before one match, prompting the usual quizzical looks from the players. This, it transpired, was nothing more than an overlapping run by the full-back – usually Neal, the wing-back – from a dead-ball situation. Or perhaps it was just sardonic Paisley displaying his usual disdain for tactical labels. Paisley was generally very reluctant to practise set-pieces at all, so the fact that he was suggesting one indicated that he felt Europe was different and needed a little more ingenuity. 'It hardly needed a name but maybe they felt we'd catch European teams out,' says Steve Heighway.

'I did not think Liverpool played as I had expected, being more defensive,' reflected Club Brugge manager Ernst Happel. The *Mirror*'s Wallis also noted the more pragmatic Liverpool approach, killing opponents with their possession. 'Many might argue that the performance here was a copy of the displays that some have found distasteful this season,' he wrote. '"Not enough flair," they said. "Insufficient adventure," they argued.' Yet who could really argue when the trophies are there to be admired? The side had been 'composed rather than colourful, sound instead of spectacular'. The defeat of Club Brugge over two legs in May 1976 was another exhibition of the developing European collective. The ultimate continental challenge – the European Cup – came in the following season and it was the quarter-final against Saint-Étienne, the previous season's finalists, that would test Liverpool to the core. The French were pragmatists themselves and had conceded only once in ten previous European ties.

What the *Liverpool Echo* described as the 'tactical battle' of the first leg in the Massif Central began well. The febrile home crowd had been silenced by a display in which Thompson and Hughes were the stand-out players, yet the French had more of the ball. There were only ten minutes to play when a miscued cross from Gérard Janvion presented Dominique Bathenay with a goal, and a 1–0 lead to take to Anfield.

In the home leg, the away goal rule left Liverpool needing to score two in 40 minutes after Bathenay equalised out Keegan's early strike. Paisley immediately left his seat in the directors' box for the dugout. Ray Kennedy scored, leaving Liverpool one goal short of their requirement, and he gave substitute Fairclough 14 minutes to conjure something.

Again, Paisley offered no specific instructions to cloud Fairclough's mind. 'He just made me feel good and said he simply hoped that I would get a chance,' Fairclough says. 'He said, "Get a piece of something. See if you can turn this one."' Considering what Smith says Paisley told him about Fairclough being more motivated to prove something when arriving from the bench, the manager was pushing the button he felt would work.

And it did. A deftly measured long ball was laid into his path from the left foot of Ray Kennedy. Fairclough ran onto it and scored. 'Allez Oops,' declared the back page headline in the *Echo*, above the iconic image of the leaping 20-year-old, arms outstretched. It did not require the greatest intuition to know that Fairclough was needed, but it was one of the many Paisley substitutions that worked. 'I thought he was the lad to upset their defensive patterns,' Paisley told reporters. 'Dave has the pace, ability and skill I was looking for to take to the French defenders, who were tiring.' Paisley preferred to use strikers as substitutes. He felt that a midfielder arriving from the bench could upset the finely calibrated function of the team by adding too much energy and tiring the rest out.

The semi-final against FC Zürich was an anti-climax after that – a 6–1 aggregate win sending Liverpool to Rome for what would be Kevin Keegan's Liverpool valediction against the Germans.

The preparations and the superstitions for Italy were like none other. Tommy Smith's wife, Sue, had been eating spaghetti with the children on the evening of one of the early round games, so maintained the same routine. A sprig of lucky heather was pressed into Paisley's hand as he made his way across the concrete at Speke airport in brilliant sunshine, for the flight to Rome. He took it, briefly looking serious until he made the final stride towards the plane and the broad smile materialised.

The players mostly wore Gola polo tops and flared jeans and Paisley, limping a little, his old ankle injury probably playing up, a loud brown checked tie to match his jacket. It was a modest departure point for a side setting off to claim European club football's greatest prize. The squad walked past a red Ford Popular and a Morris Marina estate, both parked up a few dozen yards from the runway. The players were mobbed by autograph hunters in the airport building. Friends of the club and family boarded the plane with the players. Jessie Paisley's fear of flying meant that she watched the game at home with Christine.

Across land and sea, supporters followed them in their thousands, selling possessions to make the pilgrimage, so the story goes. Eight-hour delays at Ostend railway station were no impediment. They basked in the sun at the Colosseum and around the Trevi Fountain, and what greeted the players when they arrived at the Stadio Olimpico took their breath away: a vast bank of red and white chequered flags carried by the 24,000 Liverpool supporters who had amassed there. The most vivid banner of all, homemade by supporters Phil Downey and Jimmy Cummings, proclaimed Joey Jones's role in Liverpool's journey past Saint-Étienne and FC Zürich.

JOEY ATE THE FROGS LEGS
MADE THE SWISS ROLL
NOW HES MUNCHING GLADBACH

The banner was testament to the humour which always made Paisley feel that Liverpool was his natural environment, and its people his people. Downey and Cummings had made up the first two lines as individual banners for the European quarter- and semi-finals against the French and Swiss but had struggled for something apposite for the final. It was Downey's mother who came up with the idea of running all three together.

This challenge in Rome was something new for the manager completing his third season: a one-off game on neutral territory, when the balance between attack and defence must be precise. Too much caution and the tie would be over; too cavalier and the consequences would be unthinkable. Paisley took what he could from the grapevine of rumour and talk. Denis Law had told Tommy Smith that Borussia Mönchengladbach were vulnerable in the air. No one knew why he should be such an authority, but Paisley looked to feed on German fears. Toshack was injured and had no chance of playing, but he must feature in the pre-match talk, Paisley decided. He put out the notion that the Welsh striker would be available for Liverpool's line-up.

It was Paisley using the media to affect the opposition's thinking. In the Boot Room, they developed a term for disseminating information for the other side to chew on: giving them 'toffee'. The squad also included another target man whom Paisley had never intended to use – Alan Waddle. It was known to the BBC's match commentator Barry Davies by mid-afternoon that Toshack would not feature, though the message did not seem to have reached the Germans, whose players were on a win bonus of £3,750 per man. (For Liverpool, the figure was £1,600 each.)

Paisley told the press that Mönchengladbach were a threat on account of having 'five really good players; outstanding players' – though he did not elaborate on this very specific number. They and Bayern Munich had been the artists of German football, the two clubs that dominated it for most of the 1970s through a creed of technical excellence: passing and playing, rather than mere efficiency. But Liverpool's opponents arrived in Rome having established genuine superiority over Bayern, eclipsing the three Bundesliga titles the Munich side had won between 1972 and 1974 by taking the next three titles while scoring goals in abundance.

'It will have to be a typical European job that will get us through,' Paisley said. It was no secret by the summer of 1977 that Liverpool's strategy was to choke off space in the centre and play a waiting game. When it came to team selection, Ian Callaghan was recalled in place of David Johnson – a more conservative approach than the FA Cup final, for which he had reproached himself. There was a little more discussion of the opposition than usual. Allan Simonsen, the mercurial 5 foot 5 inch Danish striker with a vision to create goals and score abundantly, and Uli Stielike, the central midfielder whose distribution was behind much of Mönchengladbach's attacking thrust, were the two the Boot Room had talked most about. It struck the players that there were no forgotten names, no 'Duggie Doin's' that night. 'Simonsen's the danger,' Paisley told Hughes. 'Watch the lad Stielke,' he said, looking in McDermott's direction.

There was a rare set-piece idea, too. It involved Tommy Smith, who was detailed to go up for Steve Heighway's corners and position himself at the near post to get some of his head on the ball, sending it on for Keegan behind him to meet and deliver a header. All of this must have been discussed at Melwood because Paisley did not have much to say in the Stadio Olimpico's vast subterranean dressing-room. Joe Fagan and Ronnie Moran did most of the talking, though Paisley did insist on mentioning that tank he'd sat on during the liberation of Rome. 'We were laughing at him and that relaxed us,' says Phil Neal. 'I'm sure that was the purpose.'

Liverpool opened the game out in their usual style for a European away match, easing the ball around, getting the measure of the Germans until such time that gaps might start to appear. 'Patient skill. Inter-passing until the time was right for a forward move of penetrating efficiency,' as the *Liverpool Echo* match report later described it. Paisley felt from the outset that Mönchengladbach looked too rigid in their thinking. They seemed prepared for the aerial onslaught which, with Toshack injured, rarely came. But that attacking threat they posed became evident early, when the West German international Rainer Bonhof, provider of the winning goal in the World Cup final three years earlier and presumably one of Paisley's dangerous five, struck a shot which skimmed the surface of the turf, flew beyond the outstretched hand of Clemence and struck the post.

It was through their rapid counterattacking pass-and-move football that Liverpool finally spotted a gap and went ahead. Heighway advanced into a space opened up on the right and slipped the ball between two defenders to find Terry McDermott, who had cleared 50 yards of turf to receive the ball and score right-footed.

It was the contribution of Ian Callaghan to the goal that Paisley liked best. The 35-year-old's presence drew away a defender, creating the pocket of space which Heighway exploited. Wing-back Neal, flying down the right on the overlap, can also clearly be seen distracting the German defence. The quality of the Heighway pass surprised Keegan. The goal-net was not taut as at home so the ball nestled into it beautifully when McDermott scored. Keegan always remembered that.

But McDermott's awareness was the finest aspect of the move. He had demonstrated that ability to see opportunities early, before a defender, and taken up a natural position in the box. 'That's nice. That's McDermott. That's a goal,' was the BBC commentator Barry Davies's way of describing it. The camera did not focus on Paisley, though there were no prizes for guessing his sentiment. Here was the Melwood pass-and-move mantra made flesh. He would have been delighted.

The Germans' vulnerability helped. It was a poorly defended goal. Herbert Wimmer, whose role was to offer defensive muscle to midfield, had departed with an injury after 24 minutes. Hans-Jürgen Wittkamp was weak in the air all night. Hans Klinkhammer, Wittkamp's partner at the back, was careless in possession. The *Guardian*'s match report observed that Bayern Munich, winners of the European Cup for the three previous years, always had Franz Beckenbauer to organise and clear up after mistakes. But Mönchengladbach's captain, Berti Vogts, had his hands full. The

Germans had decided that Liverpool's stand-out threat, Kevin Keegan, must be man-marked, and Vogts was allotted the task. His struggle to deal with the Englishman became a game within the game – an even more absorbing duel than the publishers of the match programme could have anticipated when they devoted the centre pages to these two players. Keegan didn't mind Vogts' close attentions. He said after the game that being man-marked had actually given him confidence.

For all their first-half superiority, it took a momentary lapse in concentration from Liverpool to allow the Germans back in and demonstrate why Allan Simonsen was enough of a threat for Paisley to have remembered his name and related it to his players. Case, in attempting to play the ball to Neal from in front of his own defence, sent it straight to the diminutive Dane, who seized it and scored with ruthless left-footed efficiency from a position just inside the left-hand side of the penalty box. Case was desolate. Smith still remembered the look on his teammate's face years later. When the Germans' goal spurred them and helped their fans find a voice, the consequences seemed grave indeed. Simonsen could not quite find the elevation to head in a searching cross from the right by substitute Christian Kulik. 'And thank heaven he wasn't a taller man,' said commentator Davies.

When Simonsen turned provider, crossing right to left across the Liverpool box for Uli Stielike, who won a 25-yard footrace with Tommy Smith to reach it, Liverpool fans held their breath. Clemence raced out to save with his legs.

Then came the unscripted variation on the Paisley set-piece which would be stamped across the club's history for all time. Liverpool won a 64th-minute Heighway corner and Smith advanced up the field for his much discussed flick. But Heighway, for reasons which have never been entirely clear, stepped across the perimeter running track to deliver the ball at such velocity that no flick was possible. It reached Smith smack on the forehead and flew in.

It was 18 minutes later that Keegan, whose personal battle with Vogts had seemed more challenging for him after the interval, finally escaped the German right-back's shadow, running beyond him into the box and drawing a foul and a penalty. Several Liverpool players were confounded by anxiety as Phil Neal prepared to take it. Neal looked at Wolfgang Kneib and wondered whether the goalkeeper would assume the spot kick would go to the same side Neal's had in the Zürich semi-final. Should he try bluff or counter-bluff? Ian Callaghan was on his knees, closing his eyes and praying.

Neal had converted ten penalties that season, two of them in the European Cup. He struck the ball right-footed, just inside the left-hand post from the keeper's viewpoint. He did the job.

From his commentary position, Davies spotted Paisley near the end of the game, up out of his seat, 'shuffling his feet, poised to do something that even Bill Shankly could not quite achieve', as he put it. When the whistle sounded, and euphoria came, Paisley wandered out onto the pitch in his brown suit and light brown coat, beaming. He sought out and hugged Callaghan, the player with whom he went back furthest. The image of the two of them – toothy Callaghan and round-faced Paisley – would be one of the most remembered of that night. There was a similar embrace from Paisley for Keegan. There is also an image of the Boot Room team together, with Paisley, Moran and Evans shaking their fists, and Saunders holding up his own a little more demurely. For some reason, a pristine Gola bag, clutched by Fagan, features very prominently in the photograph. The backroom team's sponsors must have been happy with that.

The subsequent television footage captures Paisley wandering around the fringes of the euphoria, the limp evident, not quite knowing how to join in as his players prepared for what they would always remember as the night of their lives.

The celebration was held in the banqueting hall of the St Peter's Hotel, off the Via Aurelia Antica. The numbers were already substantial when Joey Jones really got the party started by opening the fire escape with Alan Waddle. It was an open house after that. Keegan received a black eye for all his efforts. Neal caught him with his hand, just under the eye, as he tried to prevent four teammates throwing him into the hotel pool. He was wearing a pair of leather shoes he'd just bought and was trying to get them off before he took the plunge.

No one could sleep. At 2 a.m. Peter Robinson gave up all efforts and left his room to sit outside, reflecting on the size of the accomplishment: how this football team, from a city so economically deprived, had seen off competition from all the major cities in Europe and won this Cup.

Paisley was reflective, too. Never at his best in a crowd, he was seen by half a dozen people that night in a seat in the corner of the St Peter's banqueting suite, not venturing to take a drop of alcohol. 'I didn't want anything to affect the moment. I wanted to take it all in,' he said later. Friends and players drifted in and out of the small corner where he sat. For Robinson, who had seen Paisley through those difficult early months, there was half an hour of conversation with him. The awkwardness of the early weeks, when Robinson sought the manager out once a day and Paisley was not always sure what to say, had evolved into a comfortable friendship.

Fagan and Moran were with him, too. No one was witness to that particular conversation, though how they might replace Keegan was surely a part of it. They'd collectively nursed him through this difficult final season, which had included some negative reaction from fans, and had been handsomely rewarded for it in the Stadio Olimpico where Keegan delivered the defining performance of his career and was, for most, the man of the match. 'Keegan stood out,' declared Paisley. 'He's played his finest game for Liverpool in his last game for the club.' The search for his replacement could be put off no longer now.

It was the accomplishment which most merited reflection; not the next challenge. Only two other British clubs – Glasgow Celtic and Manchester United – had won the European Cup. A mere three years after he had taken up the job of manager, Paisley had redrawn the way that the team played. His Liverpool side had combined the control and technique of the continental passing game with the aggression and work rate of British football – a combination that Europe would feel the full force of for years to come. The side's greater tactical awareness since 1974 had certainly been down to the blossoming influence of Paisley. Seven of the side in Rome – Clemence, Hughes, Thompson, Smith, Keegan, Callaghan and Heighway – had played in the Liverpool first team under Shankly.

When the squad returned to Liverpool, a hero's welcome awaited at the city's St George's Plateau, though it was a sign of the abiding affection for Shankly that his name was the one being called by many – not Paisley's. As so often during Paisley's years at the helm, Shankly was with the Liverpool team and staff. Immaculate as always in his suit and red tie and heady in the euphoria of the moment, the Scot's instinct was to respond and he moved forward to take the microphone. From his position at the back of the plateau, the reserve-team manager Roy Evans saw this. He'd taken a drink or two already and it was that which give him the Dutch courage to step in and stop Shankly. 'Boss,' Evans said. 'It's Bob's turn first.' Shankly knew Evans was right and, for a brief moment, the realisation left him overcome with emotion. 'He went to blub a bit,' Evans remembers now. But Shankly heeded Evans request and stepped back.

There was no desire on Paisley's part to deny the stage to the man who'd laid the deep foundations for all this. After he had spoken, he handed the microphone to Shankly and he had his say. It was the next day that Shankly sought Evans out. 'By the way, son,' he said. 'Thanks very much for doing that. That was right.'

8

TRANSFER COMMITTEE

The reverie of Rome did not obscure the underlying problem: how on earth would Liverpool replace Keegan, whose performance in the Stadio Olimpico demonstrated what a monumental space he would leave behind? The newspapers had plenty of suggestions for Paisley. Much of the talk was about Trevor Francis, Birmingham City's 23-year-old who had just broken into the England team. Geoff Twentyman, Liverpool's chief scout, had monitored the striker over a long period though his notes were hardly a decisive testament to the need to go out and buy him. 'Very promising player. Worth noting,' Twentyman wrote. 'Lurks up front. Could become good.' Both those entries were from 1971, and Liverpool were still no closer to signing him six years later. Francis had a poor fitness record and that was something that made Paisley, like Shankly before him, suspicious.

A solution was found for no greater reason than Peter Robinson attended a county cricket match in late July 1977, a few weeks before the new season began. He ran into a Sunday newspaper journalist who was fishing for stories. The Sunday sports desks were always more anxious for material than the daily papers at that time given the substantial space they had to fill on football. How Paisley would replace Keegan was, inevitably, the main topic of consideration.

'Have you asked about Dalglish?' the journalist asked Robinson.

'There's no chance. They won't sell,' he replied.

Dalglish's name had first been knocked around at Anfield a year earlier, when Keegan announced his intention to leave. Celtic's Jock Stein was one of the few managers Paisley got on very well with – there was a mutual interest in racing – so Paisley rang him. A few other informal inquiries were made, too. 'You're wasting your time,' the Liverpool contingent heard. It was against this background that Robinson was sceptical about what he was told next.

'You'll get him now. Things have changed. You should go back,' the journalist told Robinson, hinting that Dalglish's hankering to move south of the border had intensified to such an extent that the 26-year-old would wait no longer.

The picture was complicated by Stein's desperation to hold on to the player. It was made clear to Robinson that the Celtic manager was adamant he wanted Dalglish to stay, so Paisley's friendship with Stein was of no help in coercing the Glaswegians to sell. Liverpool needed to get to the Celtic board before Stein got wind of their move. Robinson knew the chairman so he made the call and discovered that the journalist's tip-off had been correct. There was now also a greater need for money at the Scotland end than Liverpool had anticipated.

The new season was imminent, so Robinson moved swiftly. Celtic were persuaded to consider a bid and by the time Stein became aware, the wheels were in motion. Stein then made several attempts to reach Paisley – first calling Anfield, and then the house at Bower Road, but Paisley had headed to Mallorca for a break with Saunders. Robinson needed to get him back to Merseyside. It was Ray Peers who called Paisley and told him that he should take the first available flight. There was an air of resignation in Stein's voice when the two managers finally spoke. He had told Paisley two years earlier that he expected the striker would want to leave one day. Though he'd hoped to hold on to him one season longer, it was an uphill task. If Dalglish refused to go on Celtic's pre-season tour of Australia then his time in Glasgow would be over.

The most disquieting part for Liverpool – for whom this was a more important deal than any undertaken – was that they had been led to believe there was competition for Dalglish. They needed to conduct the negotiations with utmost secrecy. But the journalists knew Liverpool's workings all too well. When Paisley and Robinson headed off anywhere together it was often because they were involved in buying a player. Three years into Paisley's tenure, reporters who suspected a deal was in the offing had taken to calling the club secretary's office to help establish if Robinson and Paisley were absent at the same time.

So it was decided that Robinson would stay at Anfield, leaving chairman John Smith to travel to Scotland with Paisley, thus limiting suspicion, though that was not the limit of the subterfuge. First, Paisley disappeared off to a hotel in North Wales, telling only Peers where he was going. Then he and Smith headed to Scotland, checking into a hotel in Moffat, an hour south of Glasgow, under the names 'John and Bill'. Paisley later claimed his cover had been immediately blown because someone had asked for his autograph in the lobby.

Paisley and Stein met after a Celtic match with Dunfermline, both entering the club by a back door, and, with the Keegan cash already deposited, a British record £440,000 fee was agreed upon.

It didn't take long to appreciate the wisdom of the decision the club had taken. The Melwood training ground could immediately see why Paisley wanted to buy Dalglish. Keegan had been the man of speed and indefatigability who ran through walls for the team, making himself the target for whom the midfielders could aim and then scoring freely: precisely 100 goals in 323 games. Dalglish was a more cerebral type of player, who brought technical excellence, spatial awareness and peripheral vision as well as exceptional strength. He drew those around him into attacking play. 'The first five yards is in the head,' Paisley once observed. The Scot happened to be a very good finisher, too. He scored seven minutes into his First Division debut at Middlesbrough and found the net again in Liverpool's next three games. He could poach goals or score them from distance.

The purchase of Dalglish reflected the way Liverpool had come to operate in the transfer market with a manager whose absence of ego meant he did not make the selection and pursuit of players a personal fiefdom. By the beginning of the 1977–78 season they had established a system – agreed upon by the club's board – by which Paisley, Robinson, Smith and Tom Saunders would look after player recruitment collectively, meeting up once a fortnight in Robinson's office to go through possible targets. Saunders's significance to the quartet cannot be underestimated. Though he'd been asked to help Paisley communicate publicly, it quickly became clear that his work as a youth-development coach for the Football Association had established in the former headteacher a keen eye for players, too. It particularly impressed Paisley that he was so very decisive about those he scouted.

Chairman Smith, who also sat on the Football League board, was not always available, so often it was just Paisley, Robinson and Saunders discussing targets. Paisley had the veto and the casting vote on any player. Each of them, with their various contacts, came to contribute significantly to a process of finding and buying players which rarely – if ever – brought duds through the door. Liverpool were ahead of their time, in this respect. Throughout the era when Paisley managed, the entire responsibility for transfers at other clubs tended to be vested in the manager.

Peter Robinson was a businessman, not a football man, though the work he had undertaken fostering relationships with his contemporaries at other clubs played a big part in buying players. Smaller clubs would ring and asked for tickets and Robinson always made a point of supplying some. As the purchase of Keegan had shown, those clubs would then be more willing to let Liverpool know first about their young talents.

Robinson's relationship with Scunthorpe had paid dividends before Paisley became manager, and even before the Keegan purchase. He had previously worked for the club and it was that connection which brought the call from one of Scunthorpe's directors to say that Liverpool should look at Ray Clemence. Robinson built up other relationships through offering them exhibition games against Liverpool. A string of Irish players arrived through that route: in 1977–78, Synan Braddish, Brian Duff and Derek Carroll were all picked up after a Liverpool friendly with Dundalk. A year later Ronnie Whelan arrived from Home Farm, an Irish club with which there had been a strong relationship; and so, too, Avi Cohen from Maccabi Tel Aviv, in the same year, following another of Liverpool's tours to Israel.

With such an absence of agents, there was no obvious way of establishing contact with a player, so Liverpool also found the press an invaluable part of the process. They would discreetly inform a Sunday newspaper journalist of their interest in a player, prompting a story. Often was the occasion when that player rang Liverpool to see if the story was true, and the line of communication the club had sought was thus opened. Robinson had a small group of journalists in Manchester and London whom he could trust. Shankly would never have harboured the notion that a player could be signed by first letting the press in on Liverpool's interest.

Of course, Paisley, with his knowledge and network of contacts, was the prime mover among the transfer committee quartet. It was Jock Stein who told him he should look at Alan Hansen, suggesting that the defender might not be cut out for the more physical Scottish game but would possibly settle in England. It was Paisley who felt that the club must sign Graeme Souness, a player he enthused about endlessly before bringing him in during the 1977–78 season. But Paisley's eye for a physical flaw often also made him the one who pointed out why a player should not be signed. 'He doesn't run right,' he would say. Or, 'There's a problem with his left leg.'

While chief scout Geoff Twentyman had been the main assessor of players in the Shankly years, the quiet influence of Tom Saunders came increasingly to the fore under Paisley. Saunders was the one who would be sent out to cast a final look at any player Liverpool had monitored. It was he, through his contacts in youth development, who discovered from Chester's secretary that one of their young prospects, Ian Rush, was worth looking at and would be available for sale. The decision-making was certainly not always entirely analytical. The purchase of the 'tax-deductible' players each spring, to offset the substantial corporation tax meant that some gambles were taken without any great certainty that they would bear fruit. Rush – whose £300,000 transfer fee was very substantial for a 19-year-old – would not have been signed at such a price if the tax system were less punitive. Braddish, Duff and Carroll, just like Hansen, arrived this way. Joey Jones heard Paisley call the Irish trio a 'job lot'. None of them ever played for the first team and they had vanished back into obscurity within two years. As always, Paisley had little time for those beyond the spectrum of who he might pick in his first XI. He remained below the radar, narrowing things down to the biggest job of all – picking the team, developing the patterns and assessing the weaknesses of those they would play.

That is certainly what Saunders saw in him. 'When a goal's scored, he'll have the complete move analysed in a flash and he'll often emphasise the contribution of players running off the ball who were not directly involved,' he said. 'You might not have been fully aware of them yourself. Every scrap of information is stored in his memory. He astounds me by recalling incidents of matches we saw a long time ago. He's not given to idle chatter and, after we've watched a match together, often he'll hardly say a word for long periods on journeys home. That's probably when he's concentrating and reflecting.'

How Paisley also helped the system was by selling players surplus to his own requirements whom other clubs felt could do a good job for them. As he entered his fourth season at the helm in August 1977, he was calling less than ever on those players inherited from Shankly. Toshack, struggling once again for fitness, was undergoing an Achilles tendon operation as the Dalglish deal was being sealed. Though Paisley still considered the Welshman a valuable physical and psychological weapon against European opposition, he omitted him from a 16-man squad announced to the press for the opening European Cup tie of 1977–78 and yet revealed him as a starter 30 minutes before kick-off. Toshack knew his chances of football were limited and did not want to hang around for the occasional game.

Paisley was prepared to offer him an improved two-year deal, just to have him as part of the armoury, but Toshack declined and in January was in the manager's office, hearing from the boss that Norwich and Liverpool had agreed an £80,000 deal. Toshack was more taken by the ambition shown by the owner of Swansea City, Malcolm Struel, in Division Four, and he returned to his native South Wales to manage that side, instead.

Shankly remained a conspicuous figure around the club and its players. He visited Toshack after his Achilles operation. But six of the side which started the 1977–78 season at Middlesbrough were players Paisley had either bought or, in Kennedy's case, very substantially shaped.

Kenny Dalglish saw immediately his new manager's appreciation of the small details which could turn a game. Alan Hansen was sitting next to Dalglish in the dressing-room before the 2–0 home win over Chelsea in early October when Paisley came across and said to Dalglish, 'Watch out for John Phillips straying too far off his line.' Dalglish put his suggestion about the opposition goalkeeper to work 90 seconds into the game from a position 30 yards out and Liverpool were ahead. 'John in a Daze,' reported the *Daily Mirror*.

Another of the early pieces of wisdom Paisley passed on to his new Scottish forward was to allow the ball close into his feet when up against a player who had already been booked, so as to invite a foul. 'Make sure it's in the box as well,' he would tell Dalglish. 'If you're going to get kicked get kicked in the box. It's worth it in there.' Dalglish said he always remembered that. While he might have come to view Paisley as 'Wee Uncle Bob' it was always win at any cost for him.

Paisley was preoccupied with remoulding the team's attacking dimension around Dalglish – a slower but far more imaginative striker than Keegan, who looked to exploit space from a deeper position rather than provide that rapid injection of pace that his predecessor in the number 7 shirt was known for. The 'big man-quick man' combination had gone. Dalglish was not suited to racing after the flick-ons Toshack used to provide for Keegan. What he brought was an ability to hold the ball up, shield it from defenders and bring other players into the game with one pass – as well as react instinctively to goalscoring opportunities himself. 'He has an intuition that enables him to take decisions on behalf of other players,' Paisley said. 'If they are alive to his scheming, if they can tune into his wavelength, he can bring them in bang on cue. He will pull players into the game without them even realising it. He points and they start playing.' Paisley liked to see Dalglish running the team, determining the course of play, demanding and dictating. He did not want players to wait for his instructions.

To accommodate him, he dispensed with Shankly's 4–3–3 and developed a 4–4–2 system with Dalglish one of two mobile strikers, or what in its purest form looked closer to 4–4–1–1, with Dalglish the withdrawn one of the pair. Within a year, Dalglish's role as a creative nexus would begin turning Liverpool's midfielders into heavy goalscorers, who would seize on the flicks and passes into space that he made.

The £200,000 striker David Johnson had good reason to believe that he did not feature in this new formation, even though he had made a name for himself as one of two free-running strikers at Ipswich. He had only scored eight goals in 38 appearances in his 1976–77 debut season and, with no explanation from Paisley, was training with the reserves and initially excluded from a pre-season match at Hamburg – arranged as part of the Keegan deal – in August 1977. Though an injury to Heighway saw him called up for the trip to West Germany after all, Johnson decided to make his unhappiness known to Paisley, so knocked on his office door and handed him a written transfer request. Paisley 'went ballistic', Johnson recalls. 'He was so angry I couldn't understand what he was saying, but he was angry.'

When confronted with such threats and requests to leave over the years, Paisley's reaction differed according to his future plans for the disgruntled player. Johnson felt he was being tested. 'If I had stood there and said nothing they'd have said, "He's a dud, 'im,"' he now reflects. Johnson took his protest further, even travelling to Leicester to meet manager Frank McLintock, who had expressed interest in taking the then 25-year-old off Liverpool's hands. 'I went out of politeness but as soon as I walked through the door I told him, "Frank, I'm not coming. I'm not leaving Liverpool."' He returned to Merseyside to await the time when the Rat might consider him ready.

For all the signs of encouragement that Keegan's departure would not diminish Liverpool, there was a major competitive development on the horizon. Nottingham Forest had been promoted to the First Division the previous season and would immediately present the toughest and most enduring challenge to Paisley.

Forest had not been given a prayer of challenging for the title, not least because Liverpool had won it in three of the previous five seasons, but perhaps there was an omen on the first day of their first weekend back in the First Division. Clough's side won 3–1 at Everton and though Clough was proceeding to rollick the team for what he considered to have been a bad performance, none less than Bill Shankly turned up at their dressing-room door. Clough invited him in and the Scot proceeded to give the Forest players a 15-minute team talk. He told them they could win the league if they played like that and had Clough as their manager: 'Don't just be in the First Division. Win it.'

Liverpool and Forest's common and contrasting strands would emerge in time, as the two became inveterate foes, with Forest emerging as the only club who could be described as serious challengers to Anfield ascendancy. What was immediately apparent was that the clubs shared an ability to spot great players. Clough's assistant Peter Taylor was the one with the gift in that respect, though Forest's specialism was players whom the rest had given up on, including Larry Lloyd, the defender Paisley had considered *persona non grata* and who became a key part of a big domestic threat to Liverpool from 1977.

Individual players rarely troubled Paisley. It was why he claimed not to remember their names. But it's fair to say Forest's John Robertson did consistently worry him. Forest won ten of their first 13 games in their first season back in the First Division, losing only one of them. They had established a credible lead at the top of the table and had just won 4–0 at Old Trafford when Liverpool arrived at the City Ground on Boxing Day 1977 for the first of their many encounters of this era.

In the dressing-room before the game Clough told his players that he had been speaking to Paisley, who had told him that if his side didn't match Forest for energy then they would be beaten. 'It might have been just the way he said it, deliberately to give us a lift,' Forest's John McGovern has reflected. 'But I remember thinking, "My God, are Liverpool really concerned about us now?"'

Liverpool were happy to get a 1–1 draw, because Phil Thompson seemed lucky not to concede a penalty with a challenge on Forest's Tony Woodcock late on in the game and Robertson proved to a handful for Neal. But that left Liverpool fourth, six points adrift of Forest, who still led the table.

Forest were revealing an extreme form of what had brought Liverpool success: a fierce work ethic and defensive resilience, especially away from home, albeit with a deeper-lying defensive line than Paisley's. They were very hard to break down. The Forest challenge emerged precisely when Paisley's professional judgement about the future make-up of his central defence was being put to the test.

Alan Hansen was the new member of it. His arrival demonstrated Paisley's acquiescence to others when it came to signing new players. It was Geoff Twentyman who had watched him, not Paisley – and rejected him as a 15-year-old triallist before concluding that he was worth buying, despite a lingering concern about his languid style and reflexes and whether he might lack speed off the mark.

Though not instrumental in the decision to sign him, Paisley had embarked on the usual little rituals to put the player at ease and get him into Anfield. Being driven in Paisley's car was one of them. Hansen – who had not at all been sure about leaving Scotland – found himself leaving Liverpool's Lime Street station in the back of the Rover, while Paisley and Partick's general manager, Scot Symon, made small talk in the front. Hansen said little but Symon mentioned in conversation that Hansen was a keen golfer. Paisley stiffened. Liverpool didn't encourage that, he said. The suspicion of golf stemmed from the Shankly days. Paisley had no such concern about his players being on a cricket field – that was a sport within his own narrow experience. He viewed golf with scepticism, as a rich man's game.

But this apparent black mark did not prevent the deal being closed. Hansen was uncertain about the possibility of a signing-on fee, though Robinson did not give a moment's thought to agreeing 5 per cent of the £100,000. Symon thought Partick would be paid in instalments but Robinson turned to John Smith and asked, 'Will you sign a cheque?'

It took Hansen some time to assimilate. He was one of life's worriers and initially convinced himself that Paisley was seduced by his laid-back performances in the five-a-sides, where tackling and heading were less important attributes. His expressive style and tricks on the ball, including a favoured drag back, proved particularly disastrous in one game against Manchester United when Jimmy Greenhoff was allowed to steal possession and feed Sammy McIlroy who scored in a 2–0 win. Hansen's failure to deal with a Gordon Hill cross in the October game against United was even more calamitous. Lou Macari nipped in to score.

But it was Paisley's judgement that Hansen was good enough and intelligent enough for the side, and that a quiet word would suffice. The team were about to board a train to London for a match against Arsenal the Wednesday following the Manchester United defeat when he pulled Hansen aside and put an arm on his shoulder. 'Look, lad, I know I'm getting on a bit but I'm still too young to have a heart attack. Just watch it, will you?' The Boot Room also decided that Hansen wasn't strong enough. They saw to it that Hansen put on two stones of weight under what they called the 'Anfield diet'.

There was no more intervention than that. The Boot Room's expectation that a defender 'have a look' at how the team played and intuit the Liverpool method meant that Hansen was not told when to hold the team's defensive line and when to drop back – players were encouraged to think for themselves.

He played half of Liverpool's league games in the 1977–78 season, though another quiet word from the manager formed part of the strategy to ensure that a more experienced central defender – Phil Thompson – was available to ease his introduction into the side. Thompson was badly missed after undergoing a cartilage operation, which had left him in hospital for 13 days. He was beginning his recuperation at home when the telephone rang. It was Paisley – making what Thompson thinks was the only phone call ever to his house. How did he feel? Paisley asked.

'I'll be OK in a week or so,' Thompson told him.

Paisley reminded him he was removing his own fireplace with his leg in plaster after his own cartilage operation. Thompson still remembers Paisley's next words: 'I thought you'd be back in by now.' There was nervousness in the player's laugh because he wasn't sure whether the manager was joking. The telephone conversation lasted a minute or two but that was all it took. Thompson was into his car and at Anfield before the morning was out.

The defensive juggling did not materially damage Liverpool. They would concede 34 goals in the 1977–78 campaign which was around the average for Paisley's nine years at the helm. But Clough's Forest had security at the back that Liverpool could not match. Lloyd was part of an unchanging central defensive partnership with Kenny Burns, backed up by Peter Shilton, which conceded only 24 goals all season.

In the Boot Room, Forest's emergence quickened the need to analyse who in the squad was not cutting it and which young players might be brought through next. Paisley did not consider himself the sole authority. Before Middlesbrough's arrival at Anfield on 2 January, he told Roy Evans that Jimmy Case was unfit and wanted to know which of Sammy Lee or Kevin Kewley, from the reserve team, he should promote to the squad.

'Kewley,' said Evans.

'OK,' said Paisley, unconvinced. 'Will he be the best of the two overall?'

'At this moment in time he looks the better,' replied Evans.

'Will he be the best overall?' repeated Paisley, clearly of the view that Lee was the right choice.

Paisley went with his assistant's recommendation. He gave Kewley his chance the next day and brought him on from the bench. It was the only game Kewley ever played for Liverpool; Lee went on to appear nearly 300 times.

Paisley felt there was something missing, however. He wanted a strong figure at the heart of Liverpool's midfield – and before long his growing belief hardened into certainty about completing a triumvirate of Scottish signings in the space of 12 months. There is no doubt that Paisley's judgement drove the transfer committee's resolve to add Graeme Souness to Hansen and Dalglish as the signings of 1977–78.

Robinson's press contacts were not needed this time. Instead, Paisley used his own informal network, to establish if Souness might be interested. One of the manager's odd assortment of horse racing friends was Bob Rawcliffe, a car dealer who ran a shop at the back of his garage and became known to many of the Liverpool players by selling and servicing cars for them. Among his customers had been Phil Boersma, a Shankly signing sold by Paisley in 1975 to Middlesbrough, for whom Souness played.

Paisley was not the type to consider it beneath himself to use a second-hand car dealer and his contacts to help him in the transfer business. So, just as Robinson had cultivated club secretaries and journalists to find players, Paisley asked Rawcliffe to ring Boersma and encourage Souness to make the move. When Paisley realised that Souness was playing for Middlesbrough at Everton on 10 December 1977 he told Robinson and Saunders to go to Goodison Park together and take one more look. 'If you fancy him we should sign him,' Robinson remembers Paisley saying. But his mind was almost certainly already made up.

Within a month, Souness was meeting Paisley, Robinson and John Smith at the Queens Hotel in Leeds, with Paisley in usual benign player recruitment mode, keeping out of the hard business talk but 'occasionally nodding or smiling', as Souness recalls, and generally creating the sense that Liverpool would be the Scotsman's new family. Liverpool signed him for £352,000.

It was a different story when the player arrived. As so often, there had been no direct instructions from the manager and, such was the expectation Paisley had in him, it was assumed that he would intuitively know what was expected.

Ten minutes into his home debut, against Birmingham City, Souness went deep inside his own half, received the ball from Phil Neal, took it ten yards, played it square to Phil Thompson and, having released it, was surprised to see Joe Fagan and Ronnie Moran screaming at him from the touchline. Only in the dressing-room at half-time, when they laid into him, did he comprehend what the problem had been.

'Do you know what you did out there?' Moran asked Souness, whose shake of the head revealed no notion that he had been guilty of the weakness the Boot Room always felt Alan Hudson displayed. 'You took a ten-yard past off our left-back, who right now happens to be the England captain. And you turned and passed to our centre-back, who right now happens to be a regular player in the England team. Don't you think our left-back, who is England captain, can pass the ball 20 yards to our centre-back, who is a regular player in the England team? We don't do fucking Huddy here, son. We don't take the easy option just to get a touch of the ball. Get the ball in midfield and work, son. We don't do that here.'

Paisley rarely seemed to deliver the criticism, Souness observed. The Scot does not remember a cross word between the two of them. But he became convinced that the manager was as hard as nails too, despite the avuncular image he sometimes exuded, intended to take the edge off him being the boss. By this point Paisley had taken to sometimes wearing slippers around Anfield, and some of the cardigans he tended to sport were lived-in. The slippers provided more comfort for the ankle which always troubled him, but none of the players was fooled by the cardigans. Joey Jones could testify to that after the punishing FA Cup Third Round defeat to Chelsea in January 1978 which revealed that the joking could only go so far and that if you really crossed Paisley you were finished.

The manager was always convinced that Jones could handle fast wingers better than Phil Neal, so he switched the two when he saw the name Clive Walker – the fastest player on Chelsea's books – was on the teamsheet for that tie. But Jones was run into the ground and Paisley left his seat in the stand for the bench, where he threw Jones a tracksuit top when substituting him on 75 minutes. The defender was frustrated, thrust an arm into the sleeve as he put it over his head and struck Paisley in the face. 'There was no malice,' he says, but Jones never played for the first team again.

The Welsh defender sat out the rest of the season, though there seemed to be redemption for him when he started Liverpool's pre-season friendly against Austria Vienna at the start of the 1978–79 campaign. That afternoon turned into a bloodbath, though, with Jones at the centre of a fight. He was removed from the pitch to bring some calm and sold soon afterwards to Wrexham, the club from which he had arrived. He was still only 23 but the Rat had no compunction. Jones fetched £200,000 – nearly double the sum Liverpool laid out for him and a remarkable figure for the second-tier Welsh side to pay. It was Liverpool's capacity to bring money in by selling players before their decline which enabled them to buy the best, despite minimal differential between their profitability and that of other First Division clubs. Their average annual pre-tax profit during Paisley's years at the helm was £67,800, compared with Manchester United's average losses of £78,800, in a period when many clubs were in the red, yet Arsenal were making an average £129,400 a year across the same nine years.

Far from the churn and team-building, it was a more gentle exterior the world saw during a rare venture into Paisley's private world that season when, a mere three years after taking the job he had said he didn't want, he found himself being presented with the big red book which was a measure of success in public life. The series of *This Is Your Life* in which Paisley featured also saw Eamonn Andrews springing surprises on Peter Ustinov, Virginia Wade, Terry Wogan, Arthur English and Barry Sheene. The complex preparations provided an insight into the people and places which mattered in life. Guests were still being contacted when Paisley made a trip back to Hetton-le-Hole with the European Cup. Old friends of his who had been invited to the Thames studios were asked not to meet him, just in case word got out and the surprise was spoiled.

He was deflated when the faces he cherished as much as any were not in Hetton, though that didn't prevent the trip providing one of the images of Paisley which perhaps best captures the quiet man among his own. He was sitting on a bench in the centre of the village flanked by three old friends. With the formality that those of his time knew, all four were wearing jackets and three sported ties. Paisley wore the beaming smile of a man in his natural *milieu*.

Liverpool's fixture list got in the way of the programme. It was arranged around a Tuesday evening game against Queens

Park Rangers, the idea being that he and the players would be accommodated in London overnight, with filming on the Wednesday morning. But adverse weather caused the game to be postponed, so the programme was filmed on a Saturday evening, after the rearranged match at Loftus Road, and broadcast over Christmas. Paisley was peering out into the London rain, from his seat next to chairman John Smith on the team coach, when Andrews emerged from his hiding place near the emergency exit and stepped down the aisle past the players, with his red book.

The manager was lost for words and briefly covered his face with his hands as the grinning Andrews delivered his introduction. 'I thought it was the QPR centre-forward,' he said eventually: a typically gentle piece of Paisley humour which elicited roars of laughter from the players and the broadcaster.

Peter Robinson had convinced Paisley that the camera crew on the bus were working on a documentary for German television and he was under the misapprehension that the team coach's destination was Euston station, for the train north after a 2–0 defeat – only to find himself disembarking at the Thames studios on Euston Road instead.

'It's all your fault, this!' he whispered to Christine when the children walked onto the stage, to be greeted by him and Jessie. By prior agreement the family had spent the day holed up inside with other guests lest word somehow get out. They felt the recognition delighted him, though the recipient of it said considerably less than the surprise guests who stepped out from backstage to shake his hand that night. They included school friend Tom Hope, whom a teacher had feared was seriously injured when the young Paisley used a toy knife – with a blade which retracted into the handle on impact – on him. Hope had played his part in the ruse by falling dramatically to the ground.

Paisley's younger brother Hughie told a story of how they awoke their father Samuel by boxing each other one afternoon when he was sleeping late, after his shift. Hughie's Durham accent was fairly inpenetrable – just as the players sometimes found their manager's to be. Yet though the camera spotlight was also vastly less familiar to him, Hughie seemed the more confident and gregarious of the two brothers as he recounted the story of Samuel arriving in the room and throwing his alarm clock at the pair of them.

An old friend, Alwyn Wade, was filmed in front of a brick toilet block the Liverpool manager had once built in Hetton and George Walker, who had laboured for bricklayer Paisley, stepped out from inside it, to fine comic effect. And then, in what to the Liverpool Football Club contingent must have been a moment of some drama, Bill Shankly stepped onto the stage to acknowledge the successor who, so soon after succeeding him, was basking in the kind of celebrity recognition that the Scot still yearned for.

In elegant grey suit, cherry shirt and striped red tie, Shankly overshadowed Paisley, whose own suit was brown and unflattering. Shankly looked the younger man, though he was six years Paisley's senior. He took a seat on one of the guests' back rows when he had offered a brief tribute to his former assistant – 'a dedicated, loyal man; he was efficient as well and like me he wanted to win' – yet appeared immediately at Paisley's shoulder, centre stage, when the credits rolled. The spotlight drew Shankly like a moth to the flame.

The TV people had suggested that the contingent might retire after the programme to the bar at The Churchill hotel, where many were staying overnight, though the family found a pub around the corner instead. They knew Paisley would want to buy drinks and thought it would be more affordable there, in an environment more modest and to his taste. Frankie Carr, who had flown in from his new base in Hong Kong, was the guest Paisley seemed most pleased to see. 'He's not sent me money back,' Paisley joked, implying he was owed some.

The programme ended with some words from Matt Busby, seemingly delivered from his back garden. 'One might get the impression that Bob is a very quiet person,' Busby said. 'Yes, I would agree with that. But he has this inner steel to motivate his players to great heights and this is a great thing in his favour. He is prepared to give anyone else the limelight, rather than himself. This is a very rare thing these days.'

Such acknowledgement of the then 58-year-old's achievements was a break from what had become an unremitting season – in which there was no escaping Clough's Forest, who had established an unassailable position at the top of the First Division when Liverpool wound up facing them in the League Cup final, too. Only one of the clubs could play in red, so Paisley arranged to drop in to the City Ground, have a drink with Clough and toss a coin for the right. Clough's son, Nigel, span it, Paisley called heads and it dropped tails. 'I can't even win the bloody toss against you lot,' Clough recalled Paisley saying.

Clough had no time for Liverpool's reputation. As he and Paisley led their teams out at Wembley, he stopped to tell his players to wave to the supporters. Paisley didn't notice and had walked on several steps. When he realised, he had to stop and wait for the younger man to catch up.

The Wembley match was drawn 0–0, but four days later at Old Trafford there were the first signs in Paisley's players of what would frustrate them to the core in the years to come against

Forest: an inability to convert their superiority into goals against the most resolute of defences.

The frustration boiled over into some harsh challenges. Forest's Peter Withe and Viv Anderson were booked; Ian Callaghan picked up the first yellow card of a long Liverpool career. A controversial penalty, awarded against Phil Thompson for a foul on John O'Hare who seemed fractionally outside the Liverpool area when he fell, sealed the night.

But with a team containing five reserves, Forest had beaten the champions of Europe and won the first major trophy of their new era. Liverpool had failed to manage a single goal against Clough's teenage goalkeeper Chris Woods in the two matches, the first of which included extra-time. Lloyd might have lacked the finesse that Paisley looked for in central defenders but the fortress was effective. 'The Great Wall', Clough liked to call him.

It was the same story when Liverpool met Forest at Anfield for a First Division game at the end of the season. Liverpool's minds were fixed on European competition by then but Paisley declared the need to 'keep our concentration, maintain our rhythm' which felt like code for not becoming frustrated again. Some of Forest's minds were fixed on awards. Lloyd's central defensive partner Kenny Burns missed the game to collect the Football Writers' Player of the Year Award. That had gone to Emlyn Hughes the previous season. Liverpool finished with 57 points, the same tally that had won them the league in 1977. Forest accumulated a full seven more and became the first side to complete the First Division and League Cup Double.

The European Cup presented an opportunity to salvage the season. The road to the final was not without its surprises and causes for suspicion, as Paisley always knew there would be. Though Liverpool beat Dynamo Dresden 5–1 in the first leg of the second-round tie, they faced such an extraordinary display against the East Germans in the second leg that Paisley and the Boot Room felt that the opposition must have benefited from some kind of stimulant. At least three of the players thought the same. 'Supercharged' was how Ray Kennedy later described the opposition. Liverpool lost 2–1, and Paisley always considered it one of the strongest performances against his side in Europe and another reason to guard against complacency.

The convincing way Liverpool beat the opponents they had met in Rome a season earlier, Borussia Mönchengladbach, was promising. The 3–0 semi-final second-leg win put a grinning Paisley on the front of the *Daily Mirror* with Emlyn Hughes: 'Pride of English.' It was Dalglish who secured the acclaim, scoring in that win and setting up another for Kennedy, who had run the midfield again. Case scored the third with a fierce shot in off the underside of the bar.

The biggest challenge Paisley faced for the final against Club Brugge at Wembley was the usual one that he dreaded: who to leave out and how to avoid their relentless demands to be picked. Steve Heighway had badly bruised a rib three weeks before the Wembley final, felt he had shaken it off by the time the team had trained on the eve of the match, but Paisley had decided he did not want to use him. As the players boarded the coach to their hotel – the Holiday Inn at Swiss Cottage – Paisley approached him and said that he had spoken to Tommy Smith about Heighway's injury. Smith said he had experienced bruised ribs and it had taken a month to shake off. On that basis Heighway would not play, Paisley announced, disappearing back down the bus to join Joe Fagan on their seat at the front.

That Paisley – the master assessor of injuries – would need the medical opinion of Tommy Smith to inform his decision was pure concoction. He just couldn't find the words to tell Heighway, who walked to the back of the bus and literally shed tears of frustration. 'I was flying at that time,' he recalls. 'I absolutely knew I was flying. I don't think he ever understood the torment that caused me. Not because I wanted to play but because I knew I was OK to play.'

Paisley had no compunction about sending Heighway on early – just past the hour – when the final at Wembley against Club Brugge was locked at 0–0. Decisive in dropping him, decisive in fielding him, the substitution turned the game by inducing panic in the Belgian defenders, as Shankly observed on the local radio commentary that night. Heighway had been right – he really was 'flying' – though the Rat would not have admitted it.

The goal which saw Liverpool home also demonstrated the combined benefit of £792,000 of transfer business. Souness, one of the night's most dominant characters, squeezed a pass inside two Club Brugge defenders for Dalglish to run on to and flip the ball over Birgir Jensen, the goalkeeper, to win the final 1–0.

Souness always said that there was an element of fluke about the pass; that he went to block the ball in a tackle, expecting to be kicked, only for the Club Brugge defender to pull out and leave him to guide the ball to Dalglish. For all that, it looked like a sign of shrewd investment from the transfer committee. And it set up Dalglish's 30th goal of the campaign for Liverpool – an extraordinary debut-season tally and one he would not match again in a 13-season Anfield career. Forest's Clough would later marvel at the sums of money at Paisley's disposal (which he did not have), though the value of buying and selling well was revealed in the Anfield financial results for 1978, which showed a profit of £71,000 on a £2.4 million turnover. By the time Paisley's management of Liverpool was done, he had spent £5.5 million on 25 players over nine years and picked up £3.5 million in fees by selling 35 players, putting him a mere £2 million in the red.

That only went to show the value of trusting in others; heading off to the Mallorca sun and relying on Peter Robinson being at the cricket, working his contacts between the overs.

9

RED TREE CHALLENGE

Graeme Souness preferred grilled lobster and Sancerre to the cod and chips which Bob Paisley would instruct John the coach driver to stop off for on the way home from games. They added German Hock to the drinks order of lemonade, lager and orange juice in the end. 'Charlie', they called Souness, short for 'Champagne Charlie'.

He dated Mary Stävin, who was the reigning Miss World when he arrived at Liverpool in 1978, and he led the players out of the Melwood dressing-room to show them his new white BMW 2000 at a time when Phil Thompson's Saab had previously been the high-point of motoring sophistication. The lifestyle made Souness about as far removed as any player could be from Liverpool's homespun philosophies. When he had appointed him captain several years later, Paisley said that he half expected him to toss up with a gold American Express card. But the glamour ended when the game began, from which point Souness ran the team. That's what Paisley loved about him.

In Souness, he found the individual with the force of personality to take Liverpool's philosophy of self-regulation to its ultimate level. Souness could change the system in the midst of a game, according to the course it took. In the dugout Ronnie Moran and Joe Fagan would issue orders, but Souness didn't need them. 'You don't coach Souness,' says Roy Evans, who was in the dugout as reserve-team coach. 'You're just putting ideas in his head and when he gets out there, the game changes. You can say what you've seen and what your scouts have brought in, but when the game starts the players have to work it out for themselves.'

It was from his seat at the front of the team coach one Saturday evening that Paisley was witness to the Souness influence. Liverpool had just lost in the FA Cup but some singing had started at the back. Furious to see that defeat could be taken so lightly, Souness marched down the back of the bus with a face like thunder, ready to throw a punch at the offenders. Roy Evans restrained him. 'I started it,' he told Souness. He had wanted to find a way of lifting the spirits, since there was another game in three days.

Souness was haunted in the early weeks of his first full Liverpool season – 1978–79 – by a defeat which Paisley took harder than any other. Paisley had warned, in the moments after beating Club Brugge in London, that Nottingham Forest, who as English champions would be in the competition with holders Liverpool the following season, posed a major threat to a third consecutive continental triumph. His observation was in black and white, on the back page of the *Daily Mirror* of 11 May 1978, which reported the Club Brugge final. The headline stated: '"Now for the treble," says Paisley', on account of the fact that he told reporters, 'The treble is on.' He would have winced at that. It was unusual of him to have spoken so liberally. Perhaps the Wembley euphoria had got the better of him.

Souness later revealed that Paisley had talked about Forest in the Wembley dressing-room too, though 'No one had taken much notice.' They did when Liverpool drew Brian Clough's side in the first round of the following season's competition.

Forest were hardly delighted by the news either. Their winger John Robertson says his first thought was, 'Oh, Jesus, we're not even going to get a proper trip into Europe here,' and the papers were full of how Forest lacked 'the know-how' to fare well in Europe. But Paisley was the more worried of the two managers. He'd already seen the challenge Forest posed and brought his players back early from their summer holidays for a longer pre-season tour. Since the sides did not meet until 13 September, 25 days after the opening game of the First Division, he was clearly concerned.

His battle with Clough was becoming an increasingly absorbing part of the English football landscape. Clough hailed from Paisley's own north-east – Middlesbrough, 30 miles south of Hetton-le-Hole – and he, like Paisley, had started out on his own journey in August 1974, succeeding Don Revie at Elland Road shortly before Paisley was confirmed as Shankly's successor. It said everything about their respective profiles that Clough's appointment dominated the papers that month, even though it lasted only 44 days.

They were yin and yang, with radically different ideas about winning. One of Clough's tricks, which Liverpool seemed to be on the receiving end of more than most, was casually tripping up opposition players to wind them up. Phil Thompson followed Alan Hansen into the players' tunnel at Anfield on one occasion in 1978 and found Clough behind the young defender, clipping his heels.

Hansen, still too young and gauche to challenge this, kept looking around but Clough carried on. 'What the fuck are you doing?' Thompson asked him. 'Clough didn't flinch,' says Thompson. 'He turned towards their dressing-room and disappeared without even a glance back.'

Jimmy Case got a kick up the backside from Clough as he left the field at half-time during another match. It was evidently retribution for a number of over-the-top challenges. Paisley let this pass. He rarely discussed Clough and had little desire to fraternise with him, with the occasional exception of a Boot Room encounter.

Clough would one day declare in a Granada TV tribute to Paisley that, 'We at Forest learned from Liverpool and they knew it.' But the Forest manager showed a remarkable lack of curiosity on those occasions when he turned up in the Boot Room at 5 p.m. on Saturdays. As with all the managers they invited in, Paisley and his men were surreptitiously seeking intelligence from Clough about his team, but they never heard him ask about Liverpool.

Clough claimed that he appeared at Anfield one day in 1980 to try to buy Terry McDermott, and that Paisley opened his fridge to offer him a beer. 'There was mould inside it, so I said, "Let's have a cup of tea instead."' The honest truth was that Paisley never knew which Clough would turn up. He told a story of getting ready to go home one day when there was a knock on the office door and he found Clough outside, in an old tracksuit holding a bottle of whisky. 'He wanted us to talk football over a drink,' Paisley related. 'I told him I couldn't because I was going home for my tea. Eventually he got up and said he was going to watch Tranmere's match. I think he walked over the river.'

Someone else's battle with drink would find no empathy from Paisley if that individual happened to lead the team which Liverpool found to be their most implacable foe. Clough would later reflect that Paisley 'had a smile as wide as Stockton High Street', alluding to the Teesside town they both knew well. 'He has exorcised the silly myth that nice guys don't win anything.'

But any politeness on Paisley's part was a surface impression. He hated the way Forest were encroaching on Liverpool.

Nevertheless, the outlook for Paisley as the sides prepared to meet in the European Cup first round seemed promising. Liverpool had started the season well – beating Spurs 7–0 only 11 days earlier, while Forest had struggled to rediscover the quality which had won them the previous season's championship. Few commentators doubted that Liverpool would win the Battle of Britain. A poll of the other 20 First Division managers asked them to predict the winner. Just three backed Forest: John Neal of Middlesbrough, Chelsea's Ken Shellito and Alan Dicks at Bristol City. Paisley would have winced at that, too. Such a put-down would certainly have been an incentive for his players. Clough did, indeed, take a leaf out of the Paisley book of psychology by using it. He actually told his players that only one of the managers had backed them.

Forest's players found that Liverpool had gifted them another motivating factor. In his starting line-up for the first leg at Forest's City Ground, Clough was taking a gamble on a young striker, Garry Birtles, who had been a carpet fitter a couple of years or so earlier when he had signed him from a local non-league side for £2,000.

Birtles says of Liverpool that there was 'quite a lot of piss-taking coming in my direction from more than the odd member of their squad'. Paisley's players paid the price when the teams finally got down to business. Highly motivated by the barbs, the 22-year-old left Thompson for dead with a drag back to force a finger-tip save from Clemence, then was on hand to receive from Tony Woodcock to put Forest 1–0 ahead in Nottingham.

It was a scoreline Paisley would always settle for in a European away tie. Liverpool's players were so accustomed to overturning one-goal losing margins in an Anfield second leg that they began reminding their opponents of the fact on the Nottingham turf. Several Forest players claim members of Paisley's team, including Hughes and Thompson, were telling them on the pitch that 'one won't be enough'.

But Paisley would reflect afterwards that his team forgot their usual European principles and were lured into a First Division mind-set against Forest. Liverpool drove forward for an equaliser, where on any football field across the continent they would have been programmed to sit and settle. The consequences were disastrous.

Consecutive clearances from Case and Neal bounced off Forest players and the second fell into the path of Birtles, who escaped Thompson's lunging tackle and delivered a cross which Woodcock headed down for full-back Colin Barrett to volley in. The camera panned to Paisley, visibly cursing in the tight Forest dugout against its whitewashed back wall. 'His comments – I wonder what they are,' speculated commentator Brian Moore. His players didn't need much imagination to know.

Souness was one of those out of position as he drove forward for the equaliser and says he was traumatised by the late goal which he had to take responsibility for. 'The boss, as usual, was right and instead of playing Forest as a European side we played them just as we would have done in a league match and went chasing after goals and a victory,' he reflected later. 'It taught me when to go and when to hold.'

It was Garry Birtles who had the last word. 'Will two be enough, then?' he asked Thompson as Liverpool prepared to kick-off again at 2–0 down. Paisley was treated to the full repertoire of Clough oratory in the 14 days before the return leg. He milked his side's underdog status. 'We are not just battling against

20 players but over 50,000 people: the Liverpool management staff, the secretaries, everyone,' he said. 'I wish I was the manager of Liverpool. I envy Bob Paisley, the manager of the most successful club in the country.'

Paisley did not consider his situation to be enviable at all, as the sides prepared to meet again. 'We've got something to do now,' he said in one of his statements of the obvious. 'It'll be hard to pull back two goals against Forest.'

Bizarrely, Clough's preparations for that night included receiving Shankly on the team coach. He and Clough chatted away as the bus rolled up to Anfield. Clough also ordered his players to walk right in front of the Anfield Kop in their club-issue blue blazers and grey flannels. Birtles thought it was an act of defiance.

Forest played with only one striker in a performance of huge commitment in the second leg, with every one of their players dedicated to the task of keeping Liverpool out. It was a different kind of challenge Liverpool encountered in Birtles that night. 'Phil Thompson and I would be knocking the ball back and forth to each other with Birtles, who had no real chance of winning it, still chasing every pass,' Hansen reflected later. 'Phil and I never ceased to be amazed by his energy and commitment. When the ball had been directed somewhere else I would turn to Phil and say, "Where did they get this guy from?"'

The game ended goalless and Liverpool were eliminated. In 330 minutes of football against Forest since the side's return to the First Division, they had scored just one goal. Paisley's competitive instinct left him loathing this team, though, needless to say, he did not shout the sentiment. He wore the usual phlegmatic look when he spoke to reporters afterwards, his thinly disguised message conveying that Forest wanted only to repel and not to create. 'We've never finished well against Forest,' he said. 'Things go that way in football. They defend well. It's not easy to break down any team which concentrates on that.' Souness put it more bluntly. 'Forest keep us dangling on the end of a string. Whatever the competition, we seem to spend 85 minutes in their half, only to lose.' The challenge was something unique in Paisley's five years of management. Arsenal had been a bogey team, but nothing like this.

The Forest perspective on Liverpool was that too many First Division sides arriving at Anfield were physically intimidated by them, especially when Souness and Case were in the ranks. 'Some teams turned up and were very polite,' says Ian Bowyer, the midfielder who played in both the European ties. 'Souness kicked one or two of them and he didn't worry much. The first goal was effectively the winning goal so many times and half the teams jacked it in if they conceded. In periods of the game they would move the ball very quickly and if they were ahead, they would keep it for long periods of time. Ray Clemence would keep it for an age and you would go five minutes at a time without even feeling the ball. They were very good at keeping possession.We tried to get them to pass the ball to where we wanted them to pass it.'

In the second of the European ties, Forest tried to do some intimidating of their own, by 'looking after' Terry McDermott, as Bowyer describes it. McDermott, considered by Forest to be the weak link physically, was substituted after 70 minutes of that game, having lasted less than an hour of the first leg. 'Terry, not you again is it?' Bowyer shouted across to him as he left the field.

A fractional drop-off in concentration was fatal against Paisley's side, and Birtles believes the self-discipline Clough demanded allowed Forest to challenge them. 'What they were good at was moving teams around and creating space. If you lacked concentration for a moment, you were in trouble. We defended from the front and didn't let them break out.'

Though Paisley was 16 years Clough's senior, they did share some common philosophies. Both were suspicious of injuries incurred by players they needed to be available. 'There was rarely anyone in the treatment room when Cloughie was about,' said Forest's Gary Mills. 'If you were you anywhere near it, they'd tell you, "Get away from there. The boss is around."' There was more than a touch of Shankly and Paisley about that. You needed to be as hard as nails to play for Liverpool or Forest.

Both managers had also identified the value of pragmatic, sometimes defensive football. And both had sought to generate strength through a fierce commitment and refusal to yield. The Liverpool and Forest players would both run through walls to win.

It was where the manager fitted in that the parallels ceased. Liverpool's players always felt that while Forest's team worked for Clough, their own understated manager had them working for Liverpool, as well as him. Forest's players dispute that, though no one could argue that it was the radically different personalities which added most texture to the titanic struggle between the two clubs.

Clough ran Forest with a rod of iron utterly unrecognisable to Paisley's squad. Players who incurred his wrath would find themselves receiving what they called a 'red tree' through their letterbox: a letter bearing the Forest red tree crest informing them of their punishment.

Larry Lloyd found himself on the wrong end of what was described in the press as 'the Great Blazer Row'. As Forest progressed beyond Liverpool to face AEK Athens in Greece in the European Cup second round, Lloyd neglected to don the ubiquitous blue blazer and grey slacks for the coach trip to Athens airport the morning after Forest's win. When Clough ordered him to change immediately he said he could not, as the uniform was in a suitcase which had already been stowed beneath the coach.

The red tree letter summarily fined him £100, which leapt to £200 when Lloyd protested. When Archie Gemmill earned Clough's wrath for the same offence, Tommy Smith reflected that it would never have happened under Paisley's management. 'Clough's methods work to some extent but he gets lost in his own self-importance,' Smith reflected.

Souness felt the same after a match at Aston Villa when six of the Liverpool side travelled to London to take up an invitation to attend a Wings concert at Wembley with the players of other clubs. The Forest group that night – John Robertson, Martin O'Neill, Kenny Burns and Lloyd – clearly risked the wrath of Clough if they stepped out of line.

'I could never have worked for that kind of manager,' says Souness. 'He always talked down to players to my mind and there were double standards about the way he laid down the law. He'd been in the Boot Room having a drink at Anfield but wouldn't let his players go in our lounge for a drink. I suppose it is because I was used to being treated like an adult at Anfield by staff who put themselves on the same level.'

Paisley was unyielding in other ways. His focus was on where the drop-offs in performance lay and where the Boot Room thought there might be a problem. Beyond that, he let the team run itself, and after Souness's arrival it increasingly did.

The First Division campaign did not present a difficulty, once the disappointment of the Forest defeat was put out of mind. Liverpool secured 21 points out of a possible 22 at the start of the season, with two points for a win and both Ipswich Town and Manchester City, two of the division's stronger sides, quickly put away comfortably, 3–0 and 4–1.

Spurs had arrived at a sun-dappled Anfield parading Osvaldo Ardiles and Ricardo Villa, two new arrivals from the Argentina squad who had won that summer's World Cup on home soil. Several players say that Paisley encouraged a mood of disdain among his players for this new-fangled piece of frippery. Liverpool swatted the South Americans out of town to the tune of 7–0. Paisley felt the seventh goal – Johnson raking a 40-yard pass to Heighway, who struck a first-time cross which Terry McDermott raced to meet and head in at the end of 70-yard run – was the best Anfield had ever seen. McDermott's lung capacity frequently allowed him to clear the length of the pitch and still find the technical capacity to finish well, though Paisley would have ridiculed the terminology of a 'box-to-box' player.

There were perceived failings, for all that: Emlyn Hughes was becoming surplus to requirement. He had started to become eclipsed by Hansen the previous season, though maintained a place in the side through his capacity to fill in at full-back. Despite the extraordinary domestic supremacy of that season, it was the defeats that Paisley sieved for evidence. Hughes had been instructed to remain 'tight' on Manchester United's Steve Coppell in the FA Cup semi-final replay at Goodison Park in April 1979 which Liverpool lost 1–0. Though Hansen's positioning was flawed, Hughes had been marooned some 30 yards upfield with Coppell, adhering far too literally to the management's instructions, allowing Jimmy Greenhoff to nick in and score the winner. Hughes never played for Liverpool again. He thought he was being offered a contract extension when Paisley called him at home one day and told him he wanted to talk in his office. But the manager had decided it was time to let him go at the age of 31. Phil Thompson was made captain in his place and Alan Kennedy arrived from Newcastle United for £330,000 at the start of the following season.

There had already been other departures, with Ian Callaghan and Tommy Smith having followed John Toshack to Swansea in the summer of 1978. David Johnson finally formed part of the team, in what was a case of fitting the yeomanry around Dalglish. He was not the most technically able striker and did not command Dalglish's finishing prowess, but the players considered him a workaholic who would always score 9 for effort as he operated across the front line, 'disturbing defences to create space for Dalglish to exploit', as Paisley later put it.

At first, Liverpool supporters wondered why a number 9 would sometimes drift to a position in front of them on the flank. 'You could hear the supporters saying, "What are you doing? You should be down the middle,"' Johnson says. 'They wanted me to be like Keegan – mobile, just operating down the middle.' The reasons for Paisley's refusal of the Johnson transfer request became apparent. He scored 18 times in the 1978–79 season – second to Dalglish's 25. It was the beginning of his emergence as one of the ultimate manifestations of Paisley's collectivism.

Players arrived and players left like ghosts in the night. Paisley moved around so noiselessly that some of them could not remember a single conversation with him, when their own Liverpool days were over.

But the players did not need the manager in their ear, or dispensing letters with club insignia, because they answered to each other – and very often to Graeme Souness. 'It used to scare you stiff, sometimes,' says David Fairclough. 'You were scared you were going to lose the ball because of the bollocking you used to get off the players. I lose it and I'm here and Ray Kennedy is there and it's, "What the fuck are you doing?" The players around you were policing it as much as the staff.'

Souness imparted most fear, though, as the new boy Alan Kennedy could attest. Paisley had always been impressed by Kennedy's pace, which made him one of the few players he cautioned his team about when they went up against him when facing Newcastle. But the new left-back struggled to adjust to the notion of passing the ball out of defence and Souness, for one, did not think Kennedy was good enough.

Souness called for the ball to be played short on the Melwood training pitch one day, but since Dalglish was also asking for it and was not one to take no for an answer, Kennedy played it long.

Souness called for it short again. Kennedy went long again, prompting Souness this time to march up to him.

'I couldn't see you, Graeme,' said Kennedy.

Souness wound back an arm and punched him flat in the face. 'Can you see me now?' he asked.

It was by no means the only fist thrown in that place over the years as the players fought for territory in the ultra-competitive environment that Paisley allowed to form. And it wasn't the last. Once, a fight between Ray Kennedy and Joey Jones had begun on the team coach from Melwood back to Anfield and was still going on when the team arrived there. There was generally minimal intervention from Paisley. He, Fagan and Moran expected such behaviour, viewed it as part of the healthy environment and would simply step forwards and move players onto other activities. No one was censured.

Souness led the team off the field, as well as on it. It was usually he who formed a bridgehead at the bar of one of the pubs they favoured, and it would often be he whom you would find in the players' lounge at 4 p.m. on a weekday afternoon, long after most of the others had gone home. Dalglish was not a figurehead player in the same way.

The players liked drinking at the Sefton Arms pub in West Derby which was handy for Melwood, and the Granton in Anfield. 'Clear away the empties' was the only rule. They were obsessed about that, as if knowing the impression that the evidence would leave. There was plenty of clearing to be done. Phil Thompson, Alan Kennedy, Terry McDermott and Alan Hansen were all banned from the Hen and Chickens pub near Kirkby, the north Liverpool overspill, at one stage because the landlord had had enough of the drinking and swearing games.

The players fought for each other, too. Souness would go to war in protection of teammates when he thought it necessary. He was on a run of games in the reserve team after injury when he saw Derby County's Bruce Rioch dishing out some treatment to the young Liverpool striker Owen Brown. 'Do that again and you're getting it,' he told Rioch.

Alan Bleasdale, who persuaded Souness to appear in an episode of his Liverpool social drama *Boys from the Blackstuff*, which screened on the BBC, quoted a 16-year-old Liverpool apprentice in a piece he wrote about the player. 'He's not just captain of the first team. He's captain of the club,' the apprentice said. 'Even if you're a nobody who cleans the boots and scrapes a game in the youth team, if he thinks you're getting picked on by someone, it doesn't matter who it is, "Charlie" will put them in their place if he thinks they deserve it. And I'll tell you one thing – he only has to do it once.'

Souness's authority created a hierarchy. A reserve-team player would be designated to keep an eye on Miss Stävin for him if he was to be late reaching a favoured Saturday night meeting point – often Ugly's nightclub on Liverpool's Duke Street. But when he and Owen Brown were browsing the *Carson pour Homme* boutique in the city centre one day and Brown was asked to pay £100 for a jacket that had been offered to Souness for only £80, the latter was furious. 'Come on,' Souness said to Brown. 'We'll spend our money where we're appreciated.' They walked out.

And so it was that Paisley left this incredibly small group to form and self-regulate in pubs, clubs, on training pitches and football pitches. The 'Jocks' – leader Souness, superstar Dalglish and cool, sharp-tongued Hansen – liked to think they ruled the roost over the English.

Hansen roomed with Alan Kennedy, who was virtually the valet in the relationship, often bringing Hansen his breakfast. Steve Heighway and Joey Jones formed another unusual rooming partnership and, Jones would admit, not exactly a meeting of intellectual minds. Jimmy Case and Ray Kennedy were another odd couple; almost inseparable and always to be found dining together away from the rest on European trips. The humour was relentless and merciless and you learned to live with it or you perished. Alan Kennedy was vulnerable because he was not always the sharpest. His nicknames included 'Bungalow Billy' (not much upstairs) and the more enduring 'Barney Rubble', after *The Flintstones* character.

Early in the 1978–79 season, Kennedy's teammates lured him into returning a phone call to a supposed 'Mr C. Lyon' on a local Liverpool number, with the promise that this might present a rare promotional opportunity for him. The number Kennedy was told to dial certainly belonged to a place frequented by sea lions. It was not the first time that Liverpool players had used Knowsley Safari Park for their wind-up stunts.

Things were edgier when Ray Kennedy was on the receiving end of the wind-ups. He was combustible and hated finding himself involved in mix-ups with his namesake new signing. So one player would dial the Anfield players' lounge phone from another extension and Kennedy would be told the call was for him, only to find the caller asking: 'Is that Alan?'

Amid the high jinx, Paisley, Moran and Fagan gave the impression of three wise monkeys – 'Allowing us our heads as long as it did not affect what was going on during matches,' as Souness put it.

Paisley was only concerned when he perceived the socialising to be affecting the football. Ray Kennedy spent an afternoon drinking Drambuie and gin with a friend after attending a funeral. A few days later, he was still struggling so much that he put in a tackle on Manchester City's Paul Power which resulted in the defender having to leave the field. Paisley approached Kennedy in a corner of the dressing-room after the match. It 'wasn't the injury' which put Power out of the game, he said quietly.

Kennedy asked what he meant.

'Power must have smelt your breath,' he replied.

Was the Paisley drollness laced with a warning? Kennedy could not be sure and that was what made it unsettling. He would think twice next time.

The manager's Friday morning team meetings were as brief as always. They were always prefaced by groundsman Eli Wass staggering in with the 6-foot-long Subbuteo-size table with balls and magnetic men who would be laid out in two teams of 4–4–2. The players would arrange their chairs in an L-shape around the table before Paisley arrived for a talk, which Souness says did not once entail the use of the actual table in the entire seven years he played for the manager. Often, Tom Saunders's opposition scouting reports would be designed to put the frighteners on the team, but Paisley's message was usually the same: 'You've trained properly and if you're at it this week you are going to be no match for them. You are better players. You win.'

The players' gathering before Paisley's talk was always the main event. Kenny Dalglish had a friend at McVitie's so he would bring the biscuits – chocolate ones, otherwise known as 'the Jock biscuits', for himself, Souness and Hansen; ordinary digestives for 'the riff raff,' as the Scots called the rest. Domestically, no one could touch this tight-knit group. Liverpool were already so dominant by the time they hammered Derby County 5–0 at Anfield in mid-October that they led the table by three points with a goals tally of 33, almost double the number of any other side. Paisley's task was made easier by the supreme confidence that winning bred. They felt that they could beat anyone.

The only real concern that winter was the weather. Paisley began wearing the flat cap which became one of his trademarks – to protect against the cold, his family said – and snow wreaked havoc on the football programme. Liverpool played only two competitive games between Boxing Day and 30 January – a goalless FA Cup third-round tie in 'atrocious conditions' at Southend United's Roots Hall ground, and an Anfield replay which they won. Paisley felt a desperate need for competition and was grateful when Bangor City director Charles Roberts phoned him at Anfield to ask if the club might like a friendly, because there had been 'no snow' up in North Wales.

When Paisley and Roberts walked out onto the pitch an hour before kick-off, on 27 January, flakes began to descend. 'If this isn't snow, then what the fuck is it?' Paisley asked him, though to Roberts' relief it was only a flurry and a full-strength Liverpool won 4–1, with goals from Dalglish, McDermott and Fairclough. 'Unless you were in football he didn't really respect you and if he considered you an outsider, as I was, he could be very abrupt,' Roberts says of Paisley. 'But Liverpool were professional. They brought a full-strength team and several directors and that day set us up financially.'

When the thaw came, goals flowed in the league, too – 6–0 v Norwich; 3–0 v Arsenal; 4–1 v Bolton. But it was the defence which was the most extraordinary aspect of that 1978–79 season. With the personnel now settled – Kennedy (Alan)– Thompson–Hansen–Neal was Paisley's favoured quartet – a mere 16 goals were conceded all season, and two of those were a result of Thompson and Souness putting the ball into their own net. Clemence, who kept 28 clean sheets, had refined the sweeper role that Tommy Lawrence had been ordered into, operating from a high line on the edge of his box. He also introduced the early throw, which became a trademark part of Liverpool's counter-attacking style, based on the idea that 'an opposition team can be at its most vulnerable the moment the ball changes sides', as the goalkeeper once described it.

Paisley and the Boot Room's constant look-out for the whiff of complacency ensured that the slightest drop-off in form could be seized upon with seeming relish, though. When Liverpool lost 3–1 at Aston Villa in April on Easter Monday – the single occasion in the 1978–79 season when the side conceded more than one goal – Thompson's own goal was one of the three. The press room afterwards was treated to one of Paisley's little witticisms: 'They've been reading too many papers, thinking they've won the league already.' But for the dressing-room, the Rat had planned an act of personal humiliation.

'Is the captaincy getting to you?' Paisley asked Thompson in front of the others after the game. 'Is it too much for you?'

Considering this was Liverpool's first defeat in 13 games Thompson was understandably stunned.

'Fuck off,' he replied.

'What, what, what do you mean, "Fuck off"?' stammered Paisley, not expecting Thompson's come-back.

'If you don't think the captaincy is right for me, take it back,' said Thompson.

Terry McDermott was in his element later that evening, doing his Paisley impersonations and re-enacting the scene, amid general mirth among the players. '"Is the captaincy too much for you?" "What do you mean fuck off . . . ?"'

But Thompson knew what Paisley had been doing. 'He had this way of stirring you up,' Thompson says. 'He was looking for a response and he got it. What he said hurt me.'

Alan Kennedy also received a fierce dressing down from Paisley. The day before that game he had been quoted in the papers saying that Liverpool were virtually assured of the title – a reasonable assumption to make since they were six points clear at the time. When Kennedy arrived in the dressing-room with Liverpool 2–0 down, Paisley turned on him, blaming him for the set-back by winding Villa up with his comments. 'It's all your fault. Never, ever say you've won something until you have the medal in your hand.'

The extraordinary level of dressing-room recrimination seems to have been a case of Paisley and staff seizing a rare opportunity to sharpen their team's edge, though the manager may, indeed, have already been forming a notion that Souness would be a better captain than Thompson. He told one trusted journalist as early as 1980 that Souness was the man he wanted to lead the side.

'Champagne Charlie', by then aged 25, occupied a different world to Paisley, yet a friendship developed between them, which was more than could be said about Paisley and any other player. Souness was the only player, for example, whom Paisley regularly met outside of the parameters of Melwood and Anfield. The meeting point was the garage run by Paisley's friend Bob Rawcliffe, the intermediary who had helped lay the foundations for Souness joining Liverpool in the first place. The Scot's house in Sandfield Park was a mile from the garage and also close to Melwood, so, after dropping his children at school, he took to joining Paisley and Rawcliffe in the shop's back office on the way into training.

'Am I OK to . . . ?' Souness would inquire at first, to ensure he was not stepping over the line between manager and player

'Yes, yes,' Paisley would reply, and the three of them would settle down together over a mug of tea. Football rarely, if ever, entered the conversation when Souness was around – racing always dominated it. The encounters seemed to reveal Paisley's ability to compartmentalise his life. Football was work; racing was his passion. 'I can never remember any lengthy conversation about football in the garage,' Souness says. 'That was another part of his life.'

Paisley's residual shyness was obvious to Souness, even on those occasions. 'I don't think he was ever comfortable one-on-one,' Souness says. 'He always had to have a buffer there and if it wasn't Bob Rawcliffe it would be his big friend Ray Peers, or else Tom Saunders.'

That said, the Scot also felt Paisley's wit to be sharper than some players appreciated. 'He was very quick-witted. Often too sharp for those around. Never put on an act. He had a poker player's face.' Paisley seemed to consider himself and Souness akin to each other in some ways. 'He may have thought we were similar types – similar players – looking to lead on the field, making the important tackles and not going in for the fancy stuff,' Souness says. 'It helped me to know how he wanted us to play and I learned more from him than anyone.'

On Paisley's part, there was an unashamed favouritism about this friendship. David Fairclough – who, like Souness, lived at

Sandfield Park between the garage and Melwood – also belonged to Rawcliffe's social network, yet there was no scope for him to pull up a chair on weekday mornings. As he continued to struggle to break into Paisley's starting XI, he resorted to using Rawcliffe as someone who could help persuade Paisley how good he was. 'I'm feeling sharp,' Fairclough would tell Rawcliffe, hoping that the message would get through to Paisley.

'I'm telling him, I'm telling him,' Rawcliffe would reply when pressed, though Fairclough's use of the intermediary had a negative effect on his self-esteem. When the striker called in at Rawcliffe's on one occasion, looking for positive feedback, he was confronted with the size of the challenge he faced. 'He's saying you're not the player you were,' Rawcliffe told Fairclough. 'You've not got that injection of pace you used to have.' This sent Fairclough into the depths of introspection. 'It made you aware of what his doubts were,' he says. 'I always began to look for that in myself. You didn't go around totally oblivious to what he thought. It sharpened up my senses. But it also made me terribly insecure.'

Rawcliffe, whose intentions were good, resorted to trying to generate a sense of self-belief in Fairclough – an approach never adopted by Paisley. A routine developed by which Rawcliffe would bring cars up to Melwood for players and call into Paisley's office for a cup of tea while they watched training, standing in front of the radiator. 'I saw you this morning, smacking that one in,' he would tell the striker the following day.

Fairclough felt that 'chucking-out time' on his Liverpool career was nearing. He dropped completely out of the first-team picture after the 1978 European Cup final, appearing in only four First Division games throughout 1978–79 and, on a Thursday afternoon midway through the season, went to see Paisley. The manager heard him out and the brief exchange was amicable enough, but the player secured no assurances and concluded after the meeting that it was over for him at Anfield.

Three days later, in the Sunday newspapers, Paisley was quoted saying, 'I had a chat with Dave earlier in the week. He's happy here and willing to fight for his place.' Fairclough had said no such thing. Paisley would rather he remain in the ranks than risk watch him scoring for another side and knew the player's deep emotional attachment to the club would make it hard for him to push hard to leave. The Rat had no qualms about feigning a misunderstanding.

Liverpool were soaring – in a way which made the manager's team selection as unimpeachable as ever. By the time the side faced Aston Villa for a second time in that 1978–79 season, three games from the end of the campaign, they were already champions-elect and playing so well that the title was assumed in all the newspaper previews. A win would bring them the league back out of Forest's clutches.

The Villa game took place 40 years to the day since Paisley was first signed by Liverpool, and the match programme depicted a team shot of the side, with Paisley in his customary position in the front row, hands on knees. '40 years on' was the headline.

Liverpool won 3–0, with goals from Alan Kennedy, Dalglish and McDermott. The aftermath featured a chorus in which Paisley's name was chanted – something of rarity over the five years 'Uncle Bob' had been at the helm and perhaps a reflection that Paisley had not sought out the supporters in the way that Shankly had. Cultivating such a relationship was not his style.

But at the end of that night – 8 May 1979 – a rendition of 'We want Paisley' rang out clear and long.

Souness responded – pushing Paisley out towards the Kop. But he walked no more than halfway there, holding his hands aloft before wheeling around and heading back to the tunnel. The images captured him walking quietly amid his players, wearing a garish tie – Paisley pattern – and Liverpool scarf. He cut a very small figure amid the noise and jubilation.

Five minutes later, he arrived in the dressing-room with the championship medals. 'They're in there,' he said. He left the cardboard box in the corner of the dressing-room.

The dominant back page item in the next day's *Liverpool Echo* unintentionally told the story that was preoccupying him as much at the end of this season as it had the last. The piece was ghost-written in the name of Clough, proclaiming Liverpool's recapture of the title. 'We will try somewhere along the line to catch up with them,' Clough wrote. 'We know we are going forward all the time but we hope that for every three steps we take, Liverpool are taking two and half.' Three weeks later, Forest beat Malmö in Munich to take Liverpool's European crown. Clough shouted loud and long about that. It remained to be seen whether the quieter brand of management might actually win out.

10

FRANK'S LONELY ROAD

While Liverpool were taking the title in cruise control in the spring of 1979 St Mirren's Frank McGarvey was heading south over Glasgow's Kingston Bridge to Anfield with nothing more on his mind than what Bob Paisley might be willing to pay him to be their next big-name striker. It was a warm Wednesday morning in the late April of that year and he didn't dwell on why Liverpool were in such a rush to sign him now, when the end of the football season was six weeks away.

The motives behind the club's timing were the same as they had ever been. It was reaching the end of their financial year and they wanted to pay St Mirren in time to reduce their profit by the size of McGarvey's transfer fee – £270,000 – to ease their tax liability.

McGarvey's companion in the car, the St Mirren manager Jim Clunie, mentioned something about this but McGarvey thought nothing of it at the time. When they'd got as far south as Motherwell, McGarvey was speculating over a £10,000 cash signing-on fee on top of £300-a-week basic pay. By Carlisle, he was thinking maybe £40,000 and £500. McGarvey and Clunie met John Smith, Peter Robinson and Paisley at a hotel in Preston and Robinson offered a £12,500 fee straight up and £425 a week. McGarvey, who had been earning £150 a week at St Mirren, didn't need to think twice.

He immediately became Liverpool's fourth most expensive signing, but the club did not seem to be in any rush to get him playing. Paisley was in that avuncular mode which he always assumed during a signing. 'Settle yourself in. Have a little break. Find yourself a house. We won't need you until next season,' his new manager said. McGarvey was a little crestfallen. He didn't want a 'little break', particularly when Liverpool supporters spotted him in the stand a day or two later for a midweek game and started to sing his name.

All seemed to be well when McGarvey joined the players at Melwood at the start of the 1979–80 season. 'You're changing with the first team. You're a first-team player,' Paisley told him.

The 23-year-old was slightly embarrassed. 'I'm not one of them yet,' he replied. Liverpool had paid even more money – £300,000 – to Hereford United for 19-year-old Kevin Sheedy, yet Sheedy was changing with the reserves. But McGarvey was privately satisfied with Paisley's words. When he took up a seat in the first-team dressing-room each morning that autumn – directly opposite Kenny Dalglish – he was convinced his chance would soon come.

It never did. McGarvey would play for Jock Stein's Scotland against Argentina in a friendly that summer, but when he returned to Merseyside he appeared week after week for Roy Evans's reserves, imagining that he was proving his worth. He was the side's top scorer, found the net in 16 consecutive reserves games at one stage, and drew lavish praise from Evans for a particular performance against Nottingham Forest.

But Saturdays came to follow a grimly familiar routine. The reserves travelled in the morning for their 1 p.m. kick-offs and would be back on the coach by late afternoon – just in time to hear which of the first team had scored in a campaign which, though it started slowly, seemed to suggest that Liverpool were well capable of retaining the title in 1980.

McGarvey looked for signs that Paisley could see what he was delivering. But there were none. The early rounds of the League Cup, which brought Chesterfield and Tranmere Rovers to Anfield, seemed to offer opportunities that winter for a young player who had shown ambition, taken the leap and left Scotland. The games came and went. Liverpool remained at full strength every time. Eventually, McGarvey knocked on Paisley's office door, intent on testing out what his prospects were. He asked for a £50 pay rise on account of the number of goals he was scoring for Evans. 'No problem,' Paisley told him. 'I'll arrange it tomorrow.' It would be another £50 a week.

Money never seemed to be a problem for the club where McGarvey was concerned. The player was devastated to find that he would be taxed at 83 per cent on all the proceeds above £400 on his £12,000 signing-on fee, having already committed a big slice of it to a detached house at Formby, the dormitory town north of Liverpool. 'Have you missed out a "1"?' McGarvey asked Peter Robinson, when his first salary cheque arrived.

Liverpool paid McGarvey's expenses for ten trips home to Glasgow, Robinson being aware that McGarvey drove north on those occasions and stayed with his family. 'You must have got the train home this weekend? First class? And you stayed at a good hotel?' he said, manufacturing £900 expenses for the player. His willingness to help him demonstrated Liverpool's philosophy of always looking out for one of their own.

McGarvey's financial problems ran deeper than that, however, and the Liverpool players knew it. He liked the horses and his gambling gravitated into an addiction. After training, he and Emlyn Hughes would venture off to the bookmakers together where Hughes, with his encyclopaedic knowledge of the sport, would take his winnings and leave. McGarvey would stay. He found himself so exposed financially that he persuaded a Liverpool-supporting bank manager he'd encountered to advance him £3,000, concocting a story about needing a house extension.

Most managers would have wanted to know what was going on in their players' private lives. Paisley, always eager to talk racing with anyone who was so inclined, just wanted to impart some tips and knowledge of the turf McGarvey's way. 'By the way, I was talking to Frankie today,' McGarvey remembers Paisley saying, a reference to his friend Frankie Durr. 'And he's got a horse running at Leicester tonight. It'll win. Put something on it . . .

. . . and Frankie was talking to Henry Cecil. He's got two running – one at Chepstow, one at Leicester. He thinks they'll win. And Michael Winner says there's one up in Carlisle that can't get beat tonight . . .'

McGarvey says he bet £10 on every horse the manager suggested and every one of them won. At that stage, Paisley did not seem to have the faintest idea that the man he'd persuaded to come down from Glasgow was drifting into an addiction that would come close to ruining him.

McGarvey rarely encountered Paisley again after that, despite their mutual interest. He did approach him to ask approval to leave Liverpool for a few days to attend the birth of his first child, though Paisley wasn't keen. Instead, McGarvey left for an overnight trip after training one morning, returning to Liverpool 20 hours later after a 450-mile round trip. On his return, Paisley spotted him driving through the Melwood training ground gates half an hour late and reminded him about timekeeping. 'You never know where the Rat will be,' someone observed wryly. There was never sentiment when the next game was up ahead, even if that game happened to be the reserve team's.

An opportunity seemed to arrive on 23 February 1980. David Johnson was injured for the league game against Ipswich and McGarvey was called into the squad. His heart was pounding as Paisley read out the team. 'Up front will be Kenny and Davie Fairclough,' he said. 'McGarvey on the bench.'

The match was combustible, as games against Ipswich tended to be at that time. Fairclough scored after eight minutes, Ipswich's Frans Thijssen threw mud in Terry McDermott's face as he took a penalty, Liverpool drew 1–1 and McGarvey did not get a look in.

He was devastated and decided that it was over for him at Liverpool. Teammates told him to stick it out. But within a few weeks, he asked to leave and Paisley didn't stand in his way. By the following season, he was starting out again at Celtic, having been sold for a £275,000 fee which made him only a £25,000 loss for Liverpool and was further evidence of Paisley's and Robinson's record in commanding high selling prices for their cast-offs. McGarvey would go on play over 150 times for Celtic and score nearly 80 goals for them.

Still, from Paisley's point of view, McGarvey was the only big-money buy of his managerial career who could be described as a failure, though that had nothing to do with the then 60-year-old misjudging what the St Mirren player was capable of. McGarvey bombed for no other reason than the team was so strong that Paisley could not summon any interest in testing him out in it. There were particularly meagre prospects in 1979–80 for those on the fringes: a season when Paisley used only 16 players and, given that four of those 16 started eight games or fewer, was effectively running a 12-man squad.

This system of buying players to reduce profit had a human effect; leaving players who had invested their lives, careers, hopes and dreams in Liverpool out on a limb and forgotten. They were the collateral damage. If they happened to make it at Anfield, then so much the better. If not, then they had at least prevented the taxman walking away with the club's earnings.

The players accepted this because of the success Paisley brought. McGarvey's decision to leave so soon was unusual. David Johnson's agitations for a place included telling the Merseyside press corps he wanted out, as well as handing Paisley his handwritten letter to the same effect, hoping that would trigger a response. McGarvey could have helped his own case by showing more of the same indignation, which the Boot Room always liked to see. Asking for more money before reaching the first team would not have impressed Paisley, though it seems improbable that he didn't badger at least once for a first-team place. In time, the Boot Room would have got wind of McGarvey's gambling addiction, too.

Most players felt the slimmest prospect of being a part of what Liverpool had become was worth persevering with, even if Paisley's awareness of the more marginal players and their lives was breathtakingly vague. His first conversation with Kevin Sheedy – the midfielder who, like McGarvey, barely left the reserve team – concluded with Paisley saying, 'Do your best, Philip.'

Owen Brown was given the professional contract which saw him join Sheedy and McGarvey in the reserves. Paisley told him, 'It's fantastic that you're a high jump champion. That'll be great for us.' Brown had been a long jumper.

The details which Paisley cared about sometimes seemed odd. His curious observation to Brown, when giving him a contract, was to 'take care of your feet. You've got to make sure you always keep on top of your toenails.' There is logic to a manager telling a footballer to protect his key asset, though in this case the advice was baffling.

The strikers were always the ones who complained about not playing because there was always more uncertainty for them than for the midfielders about who might start games. There was only one spot available. It was a question of which of three or four would partner Dalglish. But by the 1979–80 season, Johnson's understanding with Dalglish was beginning to develop. 'You can always give the ball to Kenny and he'll sort something out, while the rest of us are moving off the ball,' Johnson said at the end of that campaign.

Liverpool had had a difficult start to it. They drew Dynamo Tbilisi in the European Cup first round, presenting Paisley with the kind of tough early challenge which had made him bring the players back early when they had drawn Forest the year before. He did so again. They lost again. Without Ray Kennedy and Alan Hansen, who both had thigh injuries, they took only a slim 2–1 lead to Georgia and crashed to a 3–0 defeat in a torrential downpour before a crowd of 80,000 partisan locals.

The struggle extended to the league: the team won only two of their opening seven games and were ninth in late September after yet again succumbing to Nottingham Forest, losing 1–0 at the City Ground where the familiar pattern of failing to break down the Clough defence continued. With his usual awareness of where complacency might exist, Paisley said he felt his players were dining out on the ease of the previous season's title and were showboating. He was perhaps doing a little of that himself, mixing metaphors as he rolled two light sound-bites into as many sentences: 'We're producing six or seven moves in build-ups but then we get carried away with the music of them,' he said. 'But when we get up there, where it counts, we're powder puffs.' Dalglish was not at his sharpest, he added.

That criticism could not be applied for long. Johnson found a level of form and confidence that would make this his most prolific goal-scoring season, finding the net in wins over Ipswich, Manchester City and Everton as the side began to find their stride. They won every game they played in December, ascending ahead of Manchester United to lead the table with a 3–1 win at Aston Villa early in the month.

Johnson did not ascribe his 27 goals in that season to any change in approach. 'I was never a prolific goalscorer so God knows why I got so many,' he says. But, in large, it was about numbers. Johnson started more games because Steve Heighway, who was 31 at the start of the season, dropped right out of the picture, starting only 26 First Division games in 1978–79 and a mere two in 1979–80. Even by Paisley's own sparse standards, his relationship with Heighway was distant and many felt that the striker's academic background did not help. 'He would have seen Steve as a bit of an intellectual,' says Souness. Paisley's suspicion of those unlike himself was not an attractive characteristic and he seemed to avoid conversation with Heighway entirely, as the player's part in the side receded. Johnson – or 'the Doc' as the players knew him, by virtue of the little blue bag of injury remedies he carried around with him – seized his chance. By spring he had earned his first call-up to the England team since 1975.

Through a combination of confidence and growing intuition, the midfielders were beginning to capitalise on the opportunities Dalglish was creating. 1979–80 was also the first season in which Terry McDermott, operating in an advanced midfield position, scored more often. McDermott remained the life and soul of the squad, a player whose capacity to consume copious amounts of

Above: Paisley (front row, second from left) was team captain at Eppleton Senior Mixed school. They won five trophies in 1931 alone.

Right: Paisley in April 1941, during his Second World War service with the Eighth Army which delayed the start of his Liverpool career until 1946.

Below: Home thoughts: an entry from the diary Paisley kept during Liverpool's 1946 USA tour – a rare insight into his interior mind.

MAY 1946

Sunday Sun rises 3.55, sets 7.59
Rogation Sunday
26 TRAVEL BY COACH TO PHILADELPHA. WIN 9-0 HAVE DINNER & DANCE AFTER. IN FACT IT WAS THE BEST NIGHT WE HAVE HAD SO FAR.

Monday Sun rises 3.54, sets 8.1
27 DID NOT ARRIVE BACK FROM PHILADELPIA UNTIL EARLY HOURS OF THE MORNING, RAINING HEAVY BASEBALL CANCELLED

Tuesday Sun rises 3.53, sets 8.2
28 TWO MORE LETTERS FROM JESS I THINK SHE LOVES ME NOW. SPENT AFTERNOON WRITING WENT TO FRIENDS HOUSE FOR SUPPER. BILL LAURIE & I.

Wednesday Sun rises 3.52, sets 8.3
29 SEE OUR FIRST BIG BALL GAME FAIL TO SEE ANYTHING TO AROUSE OUR SPIRITS OVER DODGERS .5. GIANTS .0.

Thursday Sun rises 3.51, sets 8.4
Ascension Day. ● 8.49 p.m.
30 HAVE MY FIRST EXPERIENCE IN PLANE AFTER FOURS HOURS FLYING WE TOUCH DOWN AT DAYTONA TO REFUIL. THEN FLY TO ST LOUIS 6½ HRS FLYING TIME FROM NEW YORK

Friday Sun rises 3.50, sets 8.5
31 JUST LOAF AROUND ST. LOUIS. WE STAY AT FAIRGROUNDS HOTEL. PLAY ST LOUIS BEAT THEM 5-1 BIG PARADE BEFORE GAME. DANCE AFTER DID NOT STAY WROTE LETTERS TO JESS & MA & PA

JUNE Saturday Sun rises 3.49, sets 8.6
1 TRAVEL DOWN TO ST. LOUIS DROME. WEATHER NOT TO GOOD. DELAYED 1 HR. DECIDE TO GO ON. FLY ABOVE CLOUDS ON INSTRUMENTS, HEAVY RAIN ARRIVE SAFELY. VERY GRATFUL.

Week-end

All hands on deck: Paisley and team-mates during the 1946 transatlantic crossing. He was sceptical about the significance of the team's tour success.

Paisley – front row, far left – in a Liverpool team shot from the late 1940s. The diminutive left half was rarely centre stage.

Leading out the Liverpool team in the early 1950s. Paisley was appointed captain in the summer of 1950, months after missing out on the FA Cup final.

Left: Jessie and Bob Paisley were married in 1946. His most steadfast supporter, she was still compiling scrapbooks of his achievements 50 years later.

Below: Paisley during some Liverpool down-time in the 1940s, when the launch of his Liverpool career entailed weekend trips north from the Woolwich Arsenal barracks where he was stationed.

A postcard home from Jerusalem's Wailing Wall. Paisley, a willing participant on Liverpool's money-spinning trips, frequently returned to Israel in retirement and could have managed the national side.

There was usually a doll for
Christine from the overseas trips.
She was spared the Norwegian
troll, which gave Jessie a fright and
migrated to her father's office.

Above: Paisley and Jessie by the fireside
at their South Manor Way house with
Robert, the first of three children they
raised there. Paisley was not keen on
the fireplace and knocked it out while
recovering from cartilage surgery.

Left: Paisley was always a devoted father.
Robert was born in September 1948,
and Graham arrived two years later.

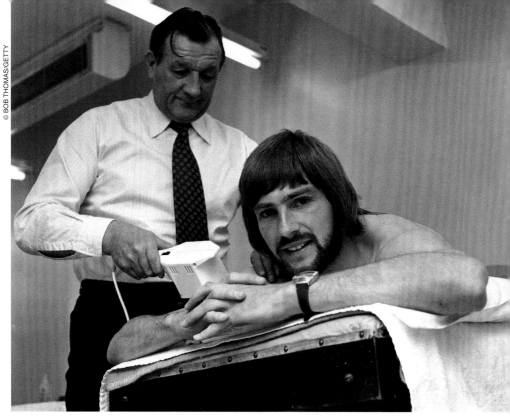

The physio 'Mod': Some of Paisley's physiotherapy work was ahead of its time.
Here, he treats Steve Heighway in May 1974. Two months later Paisley was manager.

Coaching Liverpool schoolchildren – a part of his work during the 15 years
as Bill Shankly's assistant.

Above: Shankly's decision to retain Paisley and Joe Fagan (far right), with Ronnie Moran joining the staff in 1967, was the genesis of the Boot Room collective. They are pictured here in 1968.

Above: Unlikely lads: 'The only thing we had in common was we wanted to win and we were two bad losers,' Paisley said of Shankly.

Right: Shankly did not always give public recognition to his assistant, though Paisley's contribution became increasingly significant in the 1960s.

Above: The tactics board was hauled in for every Friday 10 a.m. team talk but Paisley rarely used it. He considered strategising to be an affectation.

Right: Paisley's dexterity on the 'boxing balls' in the Melwood gym was one of the few sporting attributes of his which impressed his players.

Below: Paisley felt that Emlyn Hughes, his first captain, wanted to be in charge too much but he sought his counsel and benefited from it.

Kevin Keegan felt that Paisley allowed Liverpool's players greater
self-expression. He paid him back unforgettably in the spring of 1977.

Night of their lives: Paisley and his management team celebrate the 1977
European Cup triumph in Rome, with Gola merchandise suitably prominent.
From left: Roy Evans, Joe Fagan, Tom Saunders, Paisley and Ronnie Moran.

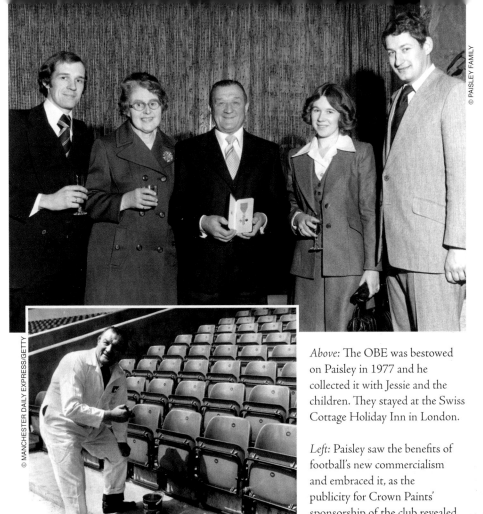

Above: The OBE was bestowed on Paisley in 1977 and he collected it with Jessie and the children. They stayed at the Swiss Cottage Holiday Inn in London.

Left: Paisley saw the benefits of football's new commercialism and embraced it, as the publicity for Crown Paints' sponsorship of the club revealed.

Paisley went to inordinate lengths of subterfuge to sign Kenny Dalglish as Keegan's replacement in 1977. It was his finest piece of transfer business.

Paisley took the European Cup back to Hetton-le-Hole in the summer of 1977. The pleasure the trip brought him was incalculable.

Paisley and Brian Clough walk out before the 1978 League Cup final. Clough stopped to take in applause, forcing Paisley to stop and wait for him.

Kenny Dalglish scores the goal which secured the second of Paisley's back-to-back European Cups, against Club Brugge at Wembley in May 1978.

Nerve centre: Paisley in the windowless Boot Room with (from left) Tom Saunders, Ronnie Moran and Joe Fagan.

With, from left, his closest friend Ray Peers, coach and opposition scout
Reuben Bennett and assistant Joe Fagan on holiday in Mallorca, circa 1980.
The short breaks became a part of Paisley's summers.

Paisley allowed Moran, centre, and Roy Evans, whom he appointed to the
backroom staff in 1974, full input into the Liverpool strategy.

Left: Paisley's ultimate captain Graeme Souness, who was closer to him than any other player, and Terry McDermott who blossomed into one of his best.

Above: Man on the margins: The 1–1 draw in 1981 European Cup semi-final second leg at Bayern Munich revealed Paisley's plotting at its finest.

Right: Paisley in front of the stove at the family home in Hetton-le-Hole, the village he would seize any opportunity to return to.

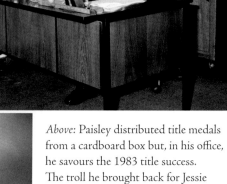

Above: Paisley distributed title medals from a cardboard box but, in his office, he savours the 1983 title success. The troll he brought back for Jessie is on his desk.

Left: Master of his universe: Paisley's in-game management was integral to his tally of 1.5 trophies per season, better than any other English manager's.

Below: The 1983 Milk Cup final win over Manchester United prompted a poignant circling of Wembley with Sir Matt Busby, Paisley's first Liverpool captain.

© PROFESSIONAL SPORT/GETTY

© LIVERPOOL FC/GETTY

© BOB THOMAS/GETTY

Above: Last draft of history: Paisley on the Wembley turf with his 1983 Milk Cup-winning team. It was his 13th – and penultimate – trophy in nine extraordinary years.

Above: 7 May 1983. A 1–1 draw against Aston Villa is Paisley's last game at Anfield as manager. The title secured, there was a rare appearance in front of fans.

Left: Last farewell: Paisley disappears down the Anfield tunnel for the last time. It was his 534th game as manager, with only a visit to Watford to follow.

Above: Paisley and Jessie, devoted grandparents of seven, with Christine's eldest child, Stuart. 'Horse races' on the living-room carpet, the indoor slide and renditions of the Mr Men stories were all in 'Little Granddad's' repertoire.

Right: 'A final photograph. Dearest Bob…' was Jessie's annotation to this last image of her husband listening to music at Arncliffe Nursing Home.

Below: The struggle to replicate Paisley's success has seen him more celebrated now than when at the helm. This banner is unfurled at every home game.

alcohol and be unaffected suggested he had hollow legs, and who reduced the dressing-room to fits of laughter. The source of one running joke was Paisley's propensity to substitute McDermott. He was one of a number of players known as the 'pop-up toasters', a reference to the number of times his number 10 would be dug out of the little wooden box and held up, signalling that he was to be taken off. Sometimes when McDermott's number came up he would run off the pitch backwards, as if being reeled in by a fishing rod. 'Terry Gone Off' they used to call him.

His merciless Paisley imitations continued. It would be the following year, in the League Cup final at Wembley, that McDermott assumed the 'Bob Walk' – slight waddle, arm swinging out wildly – when the players walked out. Three or four players behind him followed suit. 'Bob must have seen that later on TV,' says Souness. 'But as long as he was doing the business he would tolerate it.'

McDermott, the roadrunner midfielder, could get ahead of the crowded middle to threaten a goal and then get back to mop up. He scored 16 goals in 1979–80, a crucial contribution that saw him voted Footballer of the Year by the football writers and his fellow professionals. But despite his comic value, McDermott had a diffidence which made him more akin to Paisley than perhaps either of them realised. He didn't attend one of the two Player of the Year awards ceremonies where Paisley was presenting the prizes, having used the excuse of the train being late and deciding to head off to the Chester Races instead. 'It just wasn't me,' said the self-deprecating McDermott. 'I didn't enjoy them type of things. And I still don't enjoy them now. Very rarely go to one. I'm a pea and pies bloke.'

At the ceremony, Paisley turned the tables and got a laugh at McDermott's expense for once. 'If Terry's gone on one of his blind-side runs, it'll be his last,' he said, drawing one of those pieces of so-called football terminology that made him chuckle.

Paisley had developed a little more confidence in the public realm by the start of the new decade – finding more ways, for example, to plant a false impression through the newspapers. After Alan Kennedy had scored a rather flukey goal in the 3–0 win at home to Leeds United in March 1980 to extend the lead on Manchester United to eight points at the top, Paisley told him to tell reporters he had deliberately curled the shot. The manager's thinking had been, 'Why not make opponents fear a Liverpool goal from out wide?' even if the one in question hadn't been intentional, Kennedy says. It was a little more Paisley 'toffee'. He often tended to be tetchier when a big game loomed. One of the group of Merseyside reporters, the *Liverpool Daily Post*'s Nick Hilton, pushed him for more information about his team selection on one occasion, asking why he had not selected a particular player. 'I've given you the team, haven't I?' snapped the manager.

Paisley's discussions of the press with his players revealed the same old innate suspicion of journalists, though. 'Be careful with them,' Paisley once told Kennedy. He felt that confidences could be breached if the relationships with reporters became too close.

It could take years for a journalist to feel comfortable with Paisley. One four-hour train journey to Southampton demonstrated the challenges of striking up a conversation, for those who did not know him. Local media representatives would often travel on the same train or coach as the team to away matches and the *Liverpool Daily Post*'s photographer Stephen Shakeshaft found himself sitting at a table with Paisley. When some superficial football talk had run its course, Shakeshaft tried asking Paisley about Hetton-le-Hole and his upbringing. Paisley offered a a little insight, but even a subject so close to his heart didn't stretch the conversation for long. The two men soon settled into silence. Shakeshaft would photograph Paisley right into his retirement years and that train journey was the closest they got to what he would call a conversation. Only towards the end of a 15-year working relationship did Paisley feel comfortable enough with the photographer to call him 'Steve'.

There could sometimes be understanding from him towards those he saw each week. An inexperienced Nick Hilton once unintentionally breached the mutual agreement which Paisley had reached with reporters when he was entrusted with making the Sunday telephone call to the manager on the behalf of the press corps. Hilton quoted a section of the conversation in which Paisley criticised Arsenal, intended as an off-the-record observation. Paisley always felt the north London side played negatively but would never have encouraged a controversy by saying so for publication. Hilton's misapprehension saw the *Post* publish a 'Paisley attacks Arsenal' story and he feared the worst when he attended a Robinson's Barley Water Young Player of the Month Award, at which Paisley was present. But in the presence of the older journalists, Paisley said of Hilton: 'He's young. He didn't know the rules.'

He was far less sanguine about Nottingham Forest, who continued to haunt him. As Liverpool slipped out of the European Cup again, Forest sauntered through the first round once more, with a pairing against Swedish side Östers Växjö which rendered Liverpool's Tbilisi clash all the harder to take. Forest won 3–1 on aggregate and Clough was Clough. 'Success hasn't changed Peter and me,' he said of himself and Peter Taylor. 'We were arrogant at the bottom of the league and we are arrogant at the top – and that is consistency.'

There was an opportunity to shut Clough up when Liverpool faced Forest in the semi-final of the League Cup, a competition then sponsored by the Milk Marketing Board. The chance came and went, though. Forest won in Nottingham through a John Robertson penalty and then doubled the advantage when the Scot despatched another at Anfield. Liverpool knocked Forest out the FA Cup, but Paisley's nemesis remained. When the two sides subsequently met at Anfield in the league Robertson taunted the local supporters about his successful League Cup penalties by ambling up to the penalty spot and miming another successful strike, during the warm-up. He even re-enacted the celebration.

'We had to make all the play against difficult tactics,' Paisley said of the League Cup elimination, his competitive streak at its most acute when Clough and his players were in town.

There was another knot of games against Arsenal in the semi-final of the FA Cup: a marathon involving three replays against the north London side. 'The Arsenal series,' as Paisley later described it. It was a sequence which captivated the nation, bringing in more than £162,000 in gate receipts from an aggregate attendance of more than 170,000. The FA had declared that a fourth replay would be settled by penalties when the teams gathered at Highfield Road, Coventry, for the third tie. Both clubs denounced the idea and Liverpool's players were ready to walk off the field in protest if such an eventuality came to pass.

Paisley singled out the threat posed by Arsenal's Brian Talbot before each of the four games, though he kept confusing him with Talbot's former Ipswich teammate Roger Osborne, who had never played for Arsenal. The players kept hearing Paisley discuss 'Osborne coming in at the far post' and then 'the lad Talbot'. The confusion cannot have helped and Paisley was, indeed, right about Talbot, who scored the winner in the last match of the marathon at Coventry. Ray Kennedy accepted responsibility for failing to pick up the midfielder, and suspected his teammates would judge him. 'I've let a lot of people down,' he said.

Despite the abundance of games, it was still profoundly difficult to break into Paisley's team, and David Fairclough remained more desperate about that than most. He scored all-but-one of Liverpool's goals in the 'Arsenal series' and notched 13 that season yet was still down the pecking order. Paisley was pragmatic, wanting to have the player as an impact option and generally unwilling to give him a start. Fairclough's introspection and readiness to take Paisley on created more confrontations than was normal in the Anfield dressing-room.

One weekend, Fairclough was confident that his form had earned him a start against Aston Villa, though Paisley declared before the players dispersed for their usual Friday lunchtime saunter around Liverpool city centre that he was going to have a look at the Villa Park pitch the following day before deciding on the line-up. It was then that Fairclough picked up the early afternoon edition of the *Liverpool Echo* and saw the following day's starting XI – minus his name – complete with the phraseology to suggest Paisley was the source of the information. He jumped into his car and headed straight to Anfield, where he encountered Paisley wandering through the building.

'You said you'd look at the pitch,' screamed Fairclough. Paisley found the attack as discomfiting as usual. He wasn't at his best in this situation. 'Don't be coming here on the bounce,' Fairclough remembers him saying.

'The *Echo*,' Fairclough shot back. 'You've told the *Echo* but not me.'

'Well, sometimes you've got to do what they want an' that,' Paisley blurted out.

215

'Who's "they"?' Fairclough demanded to know.

'Upstairs,' he said, gesturing.

It was one of Paisley's weaker pieces of dissembling. Robinson and Smith would never have had a say on which striker he chose. The habit of saying anything to get out of a tight confrontation never left the European Cup-winning manager.

Steve Heighway's own fight for recognition around that time, and the personal difficulty he had with Paisley, related to what he felt was a similar lack of thought when it came to being dropped.

The curious struggle to be straight on team selection extended to the habit, also employed by Shankly, of using injuries as a good excuse. Terry McDermott travelled to Coventry on one occasion hopeful of playing.

'Terry, you're sub,' Paisley informed him on hearing that the midfielder was 'injured'.

'"Injured"? I've only got a sore thumb,' McDermott replied.

'I'll be the judge of that,' Paisley told him.

And yet if a player was in form and of use to Paisley, it didn't matter how bad the injury he was carrying appeared. 'It was "Are you fit?" and "You're playing" before you could hardly answer,' says Phil Thompson.

The chosen ones in Paisley's squad looked at the frustration of those on the edges and feared the consequences of drifting onto the wrong side of the divide themselves. Injury terrified them because they knew that once they were out of the team they might not get back in – their 'jacket's on a shoogly peg' to borrow an expression coined by Peter Cormack, whom Paisley sold in 1976.

When Fairclough, certainly one of life's worriers, developed a nagging pain behind his knee he was desperate for a solution, knowing that without bursts of pace his game was nothing. 'It might be in your head,' Ronnie Moran told him. Fairclough tried homeopathy, without success, and then visited a specialist who recommended an arthroscopy. 'It involves putting a camera into the knee,' Fairclough explained to Paisley. 'Ah, don't go singing until the tune's played,' said Paisley, innately suspicious. Eventually Fairclough persuaded them to allow the examination to take place. It revealed that a fragment of bone behind the knee was causing the problem, and a section of it was taken off, which resolved matters.

Even Keegan had felt this paranoia. 'At Liverpool the greatest fear was to be sick or injured. However big your name, there was never a guarantee you'd be back in,' he said. Players would go to extraordinary lengths to hide the fact that they were injured.

Joey Jones, who always found praise from Paisley very hard to come by, was accidentally caught by Ian Callaghan's studs in a match at West Ham and was shocked to find, after returning home and taking his trousers off, that the whole of the back of his right leg had gone blue. The rules were that you were to report to Anfield on the Sunday with an injury like that but Jones decided he would try to get away with it and work the injury off. He played the next three games in agony, just convincing himself that it would all go away, provided no one caught him in the same place. Eventually, Moran spotted the swelling and discolouration on his leg. 'What's that,' he asked.

'Oh, I just caught it on the kitchen door,' replied Jones.

He played on until 'one whack too many' on the leg, as he put it, led Paisley to order him to hospital, a full 24 days after the match at Upton Park. The doctors said the bone had calcified; Paisley told Jones he could have snapped his thighbone if he'd received another blow to it. Jones dropped out of the side – though mercifully, from his own perspective, Liverpool then lost one and drew two games and he quickly made it back in.

Yet if Paisley didn't think your injury was genuine then you would be up against it, however justified your presence in the treatment room might be. Kevin Sheedy was one of many players for whom Paisley's much vaunted physiotherapy training never engendered much empathy. He suffered a back injury which the manager and his assistants were suspicious of and later told of being left sitting on a treatment table at Anfield for hours. Sheedy secretly paid for a course of acupuncture at a clinic in Liverpool's Rodney Street – imagining that Paisley would not approve. It solved the problem. By the time he left for Everton in 1982, having rarely broken into the first team, Sheedy felt his reputation had been damaged.

The disparity between available first team places and players desperate to win one of them was illustrated by the extraordinary success of the reserve team. One fixture brought them up against an Aston Villa side filled almost entirely with first team players, who had been dropped as punishment for a bad First Division defeat. Liverpool won 5–0.

But even keeping a reserve-team place was challenging at Anfield. Owen Brown scored a hat-trick in the Villa game but was on the bench for the following fixture. 'The Rat's been on the phone,' Roy Evans told him. 'He says Steve Heighway wants a game.'

Though Paisley had achieved much by the arrival of the new decade – he'd reshaped and modernised the team and collected no fewer than seven trophies in his first five seasons – his track record for developing young players was not good. Case and Fairclough were the two he had brought through by the end of the 1970s, but the Liverpool careers of many young players went by the wayside – and, of course, Fairclough was hardly a first-team fixture. One of the standard jokes when the Merseyside reporters gathered in Paisley's office and asked for Saturday's team was: 'Same as last season.'

Paisley didn't have the slightest idea how the young reserve-team striker Trevor Birch felt when, after the 21-year-old had spent four free-scoring years in the reserves, he called him into his office one day in 1979 and flatly told him Liverpool had accepted an offer from Shrewsbury Town. Birch had come through the Liverpool academy and Paisley was too legendary a figure to challenge. When he was out of the office, and once out of sight, he wept.

The results still talked, though. Europe might have been Forest's domain for a second successive year, with Hamburg defeated 1–0 in the final, but Liverpool put together a decisive unbeaten run of 19 games from October into January.

A 2–1 win over Tottenham in November sent them to the top; a position rarely relinquished. There was some talk about Manchester United's potential to dent their ambitions but it didn't come to much. United's hammering by six goals at Ipswich brought that ambition to an end. It was not until 3 May that Liverpool's title was secured with a 4–1 win over Aston Villa, which coincided with United losing at Leeds.

'The players don't think we've had as good a season as the previous one when we won the league by a record number of points,' Paisley reflected after the title was won. 'But I do. I regard it as a season when we had to battle. When the brain isn't ticking over quickly, when they're drained mentally, careless things keep coming in. They have to run a few extra yards instead of making their brains do the work.'

Such were the injuries that had piled up by the end of the campaign that Paisley's first overseas international signing played against Villa. The Israeli defender Avi Cohen put through his own net to give Ron Saunders' team an equaliser on the title-winning day, then scored in the correct net. He was sold two years later.

Within a month of leaving Liverpool, Frank McGarvey scored the winner for Celtic in an Old Firm derby and was standing in front of Parkhead supporters, arms aloft. Aberdeen manager Alex Ferguson missed out on buying him and was not pleased, having been promised by McGarvey that he would head to Pittodrie if he left Anfield.

The Scottish press wondered what the problem had been at Anfield. But the answer was perhaps there all along, in a conversation McGarvey had with reserve-team coach Evans.

'Try and pass the ball,' Evans suggested, articulating the Liverpool way of pass and move. 'Play a one-two and get the ball back.'

'I'll be more comfortable taking him on there,' McGarvey replied. 'I'm confident I'll beat him, draw a few players and then play the ball in. Draw players to me. That's what I do.'

'Well, just play the one-two and you can get the ball back right away,' Evans insisted.

'No,' said McGarvey, persisting with the idea that he would operate his own way. Evans did not push it. The conversation would have certainly been fed into the Boot Room and turned over there. At Liverpool you rarely had to be told twice about the way the team played and, in any case, Paisley had another striker. Ian Rush was an 18-year-old who'd been signed for £300,000 – another tax-deductible player. If it worked out with him, Liverpool gained; if not, then at least the taxman didn't.

11

HETTON SPIRIT

Bob Paisley had a picture of a litter of piglets on his office wall. 'It isn't easy to stay on top,' stated the accompanying caption. It always amused him. Beside it was a framed copy of Rudyard Kipling's poem 'If' – a gift from Jessie and the children – and a joke clock which went backwards, bestowed upon him by an insurance company.

There was nothing up there quite so emblematic as the image entitled 'Lunch Atop a Skyscraper', the iconic Depression era photograph of 11 men sitting on a girder with their legs dangling over New York, which Alex Ferguson chose for his office 20 years later. Ferguson thought it reflective of the qualities of team spirit, which he drummed into each of his young Manchester United players.

Paisley didn't really go in for emblems. It was straightforward qualities and characters which he looked for, to slot in among his few superstar names: like the donkeys among thoroughbreds at Malton, the North Yorkshire stables where he would spend a week or two each summer with his friend Frank Carr. That was what made Alan Kennedy the player Paisley always swore by. It was significant that when he had finally shrugged off his nervous disposition and convinced himself he could make it at Liverpool, Kennedy tended to be the one who would pop up late and score.

The biggest percentage of his goals for the club came in the last 15 minutes. Kennedy was an individual who ran to the last.

There was always an element of unpredictability about the defender, too, and that did sometimes tend to make Paisley nervous. On the night Kennedy drove from Newcastle to sign for Liverpool, in August 1978, the windscreen wipers on his Triumph TR7 packed up in the sheeting rain, and the visibility was so bad that he had to stop at Leeds. 'I thought because it had a gold stripe along the side it was a good, reliable car,' he said years later. With no way of alerting anyone to this predicament, he arrived several hours late at Burtonwood Services on the Liverpool-bound M62, where he found Paisley reading the racing papers and drinking tea, willing to wait.

It was a metaphor for much that was to follow, but Paisley's belief in his own kin prevailed. Kennedy, 24 when he signed, had been full of insecurity about whether he would ever get a big move from struggling Newcastle. He thought he'd played well enough in the 1974 FA Cup final to demonstrate something to Liverpool, but nothing came of it. On a summer tour of the southern hemisphere with the England 'B' team in 1978, he took to asking squad members from big clubs – Fairclough, Ipswich's Paul Mariner and Manchester United's Gordon Hill – whether their managers might be interested in him. He even took to growing a beard for the Newcastle United team photograph at that time to signal that he was a wild nomad and wanted away. 'Daft idea,' he later concluded.

For Paisley, the chip shop in Hetton-le-Hole was a more significant part of the decision to buy him. Kennedy's mother, Sarah Ann, used to serve Paisley fish suppers there. He knew the boy's people. Kennedy never forgot the look on Paisley's face when he actually ran into that service station, praying he had not lost his chance. 'Glad you got here,' Paisley said, grinning, before they drove to the Liverpool Atlantic Tower Hotel to sign a contract. The manager was happy. A little piece of Hetton spirit for his Liverpool team.

Many shared Graeme Souness's initial scepticism about the new left-back's ability. Ray Kennedy, not always a bundle of joy, expressed frustration with his namesake's lack of awareness. 'He took five years off my career. Whenever I wanted a short ball he'd hit it long. If it should have been long, I'd get a short pass. Alan had no nerves and not much brain, which was why he was lethal at penalties. I didn't dislike him but we didn't gel on the pitch.'

It was a bewildering experience when Kennedy made his debut against Queens Park Rangers at Anfield, at the start of the 1978–79 season. Bill Shankly was standing in his customary spot near the directors' entrance, where he liked to greet the incoming players, and handed him what, at first glance, appeared to be a pill to calm his nerves before the game. It turned out to be a boiled sweet. It did not have the desired effect. There was an inauspicious start when the defender fired a warm-up shot way wide of the net before kick-off and by half-time he had badly miscued several passes. Paisley did not spare the player's sensitivities at half-time. 'Christ,' he said, walking into the dressing-room. 'They shot the wrong Kennedy.'

It was one of Paisley's most memorable lines and evidence, as Souness always insisted, that his wit could occasionally be razor-sharp. 'We were beside ourselves,' says Souness. 'Alan had his head in his hands. He wasn't the most confident.' That's how unsparing the Liverpool dressing-room was.

The Boot Room asked Paisley more than once whether he was sure about Kennedy, but he was convinced that showing persistence and drilling him in the Liverpool way would see the boy through. The manager never felt that Kennedy developed the capacity to pass with the same vision as the best of his players, but that was not the point. 'He's not the type of player who sees a move three or four passes in advance,' Paisley reflected years later. 'He is instinctive, rather than the calculating type, who reacts to situations rather than creates them. He is not a typical Liverpool player.' He was the one player whom Paisley could be indiscreet about in the company of the Merseyside reporters. 'He'd be genuinely exasperated about how unpredictable Kennedy could be,' says Nick Hilton. 'But he'd tell you that with a smile on his face. You could tell how much he liked him. It was as near as Paisley came to giving a sense of affection.'

The rewards of persisting with Kennedy came in the difficult season of 1980–81 – arguably the toughest of them all – when character mattered more than superstar quality. Paisley found himself assailed on all sides by injuries in that campaign and several believe that was when he detected age in the side. Nothing was said, but the players he had relied on to score Liverpool's goals were growing older. Jimmy Case was 28, David Johnson and Terry McDermott were both approaching 29; Dalglish and Ray Kennedy had already turned 29. The average age of the side which started the first game of that season at home to Crystal Palace was 28 years and seven months. The Shankly side that had started the 1960–61 season, 20 years earlier, had averaged 25 years and three months. The side beginning 1970–71 averaged 23 years and nine months.

Liverpool won 3–0 against Palace, with Alan Kennedy scoring seven minutes from time, though gradually the injuries began to hit. This was the season in which Paisley was forced to use far more of his players – 23 in all – and in which only Phil Neal managed the full complement of 42 in the First Division. Kenny Dalglish's run of 147 consecutive appearances, sustained since his arrival from Celtic in the summer of 1977, was finally brought to an end by a damaged right ankle which saw him out of the picture for two games in December and struggle to regain form. David Johnson missed matches with hamstring trouble and David Fairclough required knee surgery but it was the defence which sustained most casualties.

A broken collarbone sustained by Phil Thompson at Crystal Palace in mid-November kept him out for two months, 11 games, and left Paisley going to extreme lengths to preserve Alan Hansen for the side after he jammed his knee in a challenge on Garth Crooks at home to Tottenham in December. With his eye for an injury, Paisley would have known that Hansen had a 'four-weeker' at least. But he kept him going with cortisone injections and Hansen felt he was operating 'virtually on one leg' by the time he played against Wolves just before Christmas. He heard the Molineux manager John Barnwell urge his players: 'Get after the number 6.' It was in the Boxing Day clash with Manchester United at Old Trafford six days later that he finally gave in to injury and was substituted on the hour.

A subsequent medical examination revealed the need to remove a growth on the side of his knee joint. Hansen still missed a mere four matches and was back by February, considerably earlier than advised. There were limited defensive options: untested locals Richard Money and Colin Irwin from the reserves and the Israeli Avi Cohen, who as an Orthodox Jew faced a barrage of criticism that season for playing on a Saturday which was the Jewish holiday of Yom Kippur. When it was put to Paisley that Cohen's religion might not permit him to play on Saturdays, he replied, 'I know a few of mine who don't play on Saturdays.' More evidence that by now the jokes were not always lame. There were consequences for a defence that was chopped and changed, however: the concession of 42 First Division goals, more than in any other of Paisley's championship campaigns.

Two younger options emerged further up the team and Paisley was tempted, though the consensus in the Boot Room was that they were not ready. Ian Rush, signed at the end of the previous season, was tried out in Dalglish's absence at Ipswich, though he went straight back to the reserves the following week.

Irishman Ronnie Whelan was, like Rush, diffident and insecure, struggling to get to grips with the unyielding Liverpool culture. Whelan seemed to worry about how the local trainees viewed him when he arrived from Home Farm for £35,000, a few days before his 18th birthday. Both he and Rush thought they were sneering at them because they were on a higher wage. The Boot Room knew this, though Whelan's struggles went deeper. Even his Irish accent embarrassed him.

In one Boot Room conversation, Paisley said he saw something of Ray Kennedy in the elegance of Whelan's midfield play. His name cropped up half a dozen times that season. Moran told Paisley he wasn't ready and a reserve-team game seems to have convinced Paisley they should, indeed, hold off.

At times, Paisley, Fagan and Moran were like a bunch of crotchety old men as they ran the team together. On Friday evenings before home games, they would be left in each other's company at the Daresbury Hotel once the players had retired – but it only took one of them to say he was turning in early to offend the others. Fagan decided he would pass on the drinks, one night. 'Suit yourself, if that's how you feel,' said Paisley, waddling off. Fagan changed his mind and descended to the bar with

Moran, Evans and Saunders, but there was no sign of Paisley that night. Saunders was usually the peacemaker.

A far more serious dispute added urgency to their perennial talk of change. It occurred during the annual night away at Llangollen's Bryn Howel Hotel that Paisley had instituted. The squad had headed there straight after a derby match, though Ray Kennedy and Case became separated from the rest of the group, who had decided to make a trip into nearby Chester for a night out. The pair had asked to be told when the rest were departing for the evening but no one had remembered to do so. Terry McDermott appears to have been the offender. Several bottles of Chablis had already been consumed with dinner and McDermott's idea of fine dining was never much more than a beef sandwich, so he may not have been up to the role of social secretary. Kennedy and Case were instead driven up to a local Llangollen pub by the Bryn Howel landlord Albert Lloyd, though when the Chester contingent returned at 2 a.m. Kennedy made his displeasure with McDermott known. He appears to have swung for him when Lloyd, trying to prevent a fight, said 'Come on, Alan.'

Being called the wrong Kennedy brought down the usual red mist for the midfielder and within minutes he, Lloyd and Lloyd's son were all involved in a conflagration. Kennedy's version of the story includes him hitting McDermott, picking up a chair and throwing it at the landlord. Case says no chairs were thrown.

It was pandemonium. The police were called and Kennedy and Case were taken into custody. Paisley's sleep was not interrupted: Moran and Fagan dealt with it. A month later, both players pleaded guilty to causing affray and were charged £150 each.

Publicly, Paisley said nothing about this. It was his practice to leave any serious disciplinary incident to Peter Robinson, and the other players witnessed no dressing down of Case. But the manager appears to have been starting to harbour doubts about the midfielder, who had also been convicted of drink-driving. The decision to start young Liverpudlian trainee Sammy Lee in his place, six games into the 1980–81 season, indicated that Case had not been delivering enough on the field to allow the misdemeanours to pass.

Paisley had initiated many of the Boot Room conversations about Lee, having been impressed by him in reserve-team games. He liked his dependability. It was a month after Llangollen that Paisley took Case aside to say that John Toshack's Swansea City had been in touch about buying him.

'I thought it was a bit strange, the way [the Swansea interest] came about, but I put it to the back of my mind and carried on as normal,' said Case. It was the beginning of the process of moving him on.

Behind the scenes, Paisley kept investing faith in the training routine which nourished collectivism and which, they believed, would allow them to shrug off their injury problems. The Melwood ethos was fundamentally the same as Shankly's, designed to create pass and go footballers who would give to the last. The endless five-a-side games, beloved of Shankly, were a microcosm of all the challenges that would be faced the following Saturday. But some said it was a tougher, more unsparing regime than Shankly's. Under the management of Paisley, Fagan and Moran, the five-a-sides were refined so that they would replicate the specific contest that Liverpool were facing next. When the next opposition was known to sit deep, the five-a-side rule would be that everyone must be over the halfway line for a goal to count – encouraging a high defensive line. 'Two-touch' five-a-side games were the Boot Room's favourite, the rule being that if you took a third touch you conceded possession. The players would groan, 'Two-touch again?' when Moran announced them. Sometimes there was the luxury of a 'three-touch'. There were 'pressing' five-a-sides in preparation for the more challenging matches against teams who needed to be closed down. You conceded possession if you didn't press the next man. And there was the 'move' game. If you didn't move when you'd passed the ball, the other side were awarded a free-kick. 'Don't watch the ball. Don't watch it,' Moran would bellow from the sidelines, encouraging immediate movement after a pass was placed.

The footballs would be blown up as hard as concrete and as if that was not enough of a challenge, players would be told individually to leave the match they were involved in to embark on the shuttle runs they called 'doggies' – eight repetitions of 80 metres; four repetitions of 40, if it was a good day – then back to the five-a-side pitch, where the rules might have changed from 'two-touch' to 'press'. 'The man receiving needs time. The man receiving needs time,' they told them over and over again, drilling in the fundamental requirement of a Liverpool footballer: the delivery of a pass which will not force the recipient to be under pressure in possession. That might mean delaying the release of the ball until he has found space or it might mean distributing it fast, before an opponent closes in. Thus, passing the ball was a cognitive process. 'Get your head up.' 'Move it on.' 'Let the ball do the work.' Some players, like Alan Kennedy, took time, but to survive and thrive at Anfield you learned the process by osmosis.

Paisley kept out of the drills, peering out from his office, where he was recognisable to his players behind the unfrosted section of the long window overlooking the training ground, which was protected by wire mesh to stop footballs smashing the glass. There was a telephone on top of the filing cabinet beside the window and Paisley would often be on it as he watched – placing his telephone bets with the bookies, the players always reckoned.

The radiator seemed to be a convenient height for a 5 foot 7 inch manager. 'We always thought he was keeping his balls warm on the radiator,' remembers David Fairclough. Sometimes, on a blisteringly cold day, he would head out to the pitches, clad in hat, padded jacket and big gloves, and approach Joe Fagan. 'Cold today, Joe, isn't it?' he would say, delighting in the austerity of it all, before heading back in for the radiator.

There was deep suspicion harboured in the Boot Room of anything they didn't know about, were not familiar with, or that broke with their little routines. On one occasion David Fairclough found himself reprimanded for doing extra shooting practice with reserve-team goalkeeper Steve Ogrizovic, another who felt he was short of match preparation. Fairclough was 'found out' after he banged his head on a goalpost and had to be taken to Liverpool's Broadgreen Hospital for stitches.

At the end of the training ritual, there would be the part Shankly had lived for: the coaching staff versus trainees' games, which were played when the 'Big 'Eads' had boarded the bus out of Melwood to shower and change at Anfield. Paisley and his staff fixed it to win, just as Shankly always had. If they were losing the game, they just continued until they had taken the lead, with the choice of referee rigged to make sure this happened sooner or later.

A trainee knew he was in form when the staff selected him to be on the coaches' side, as the one to do the running around for them. Roy Evans, the youngest of the coaches by a distance, did much of the leg work. Moran and Fagan controlled the midfield.

Paisley, immobile as ever, took up his position in goal, with the humour residing in the black leather gloves he always wore and his reluctance to catch the ball. He always punched it out theatrically, two-handed.

If you hoped for technical tips or a sign that you were progressing, then you could be waiting a very long time. The assumption remained that if you played for Liverpool, you did not need to be told or coached.

Fairclough, anxious as ever, looked to Moran for advice at Melwood one day.

'You haven't got your old form back,' Moran told him. 'I know what I'd do.'

'What's that?' Fairclough asked.

'Don't ask me, son. Work it out for yourself,' Moran replied.

The barrack-room culture was very often unfair. One trainee was bawled out by Moran for having the impudence to beat him in a challenge. 'You think you're good enough to be a Liverpool player, do you?' Moran asked. 'Let me tell you, you are shit. You will never play for this team . . .' And he didn't.

For all this effort, the domestic struggle was unceasing in 1980–81. There were five games without a win from the end of January to the end of February. Paisley looked for changes in routine which might introduce some intensity. The match-day 'boots under the table' routine was in regular use. He also put a stop to the usual Saturday afternoon practice of Liverpool's equine enthusiasts spending time in the players' lounge watching the horse racing before arriving in the dressing-room at 2.30 p.m. They had to report there by 2 p.m., he said. This was a blow, as the 2.15 was often the big race of the day.

Results coincidentally picked up and the next week Paisley put his head around the door at 2 p.m. 'Let us know who wins the

2.15, will you?' he asked. There was a positive effect on the dressing-room. It was Paisley's way of letting them know they'd weathered the storm.

But by the time Liverpool beat Southampton 2–0 in late February they were eight points adrift of leaders Ipswich. David Johnson withdrew at half-time with a hamstring strain that day, which meant that Colin Irwin – supposedly a defensive deputy for Thompson and Hansen – found himself taking over as an emergency striker.

Dalglish's usual goal tally was being missed. He managed only eight in the First Division that season, comfortably his lowest of the Paisley era. A mere three years after the squad was getting a £50,000 pay-out from a newspaper for breaking through the 84 in a season barrier, only four Liverpool players managed to score more than six in the 1980–81 league campaign. Just one player made it into double figures: Terry McDermott, who scored 13. Just twice between early October and early May did Liverpool win consecutive home games. The record from January read: played 17, won six, drawn five, lost six; 16 for and 15 against. Such statistics don't win titles. Aston Villa claimed the championship instead. It took a couple of late-season wins just for Liverpool to finish fifth in Division One.

It was not much consolation that Nottingham Forest were struggling to maintain their standards too, slipping below Liverpool to finish seventh. Only a point divided the sides domestically and Forest had proved the same obdurate defenders of old. Both league games ended 0–0.

Paisley did have reason to take some quiet satisfaction from what was happening at the Red Tree club, though. Clough and his assistant Peter Taylor were falling out. The obsession over not allowing the side to age too much – something always on Paisley's mind too – saw the European Cup-winning side of 1979 and 1980 dismantled. Garry Birtles went to Manchester United in 1980 and some of Taylor's signings suggested that he might have lost his Midas touch in the transfer market. Justin Fashanu arrived from Norwich for £1 million – in what Clough and Taylor would later admit was possibly the worst deal of their managerial careers together. Ian Wallace, from Coventry, cost another million, and Peter Ward arrived for £450,000 from Brighton. They could not come close to maintaining the standards the European Cup-winning sides had set.

For Liverpool, a release from the domestic purgatory came with a first League Cup win, against West Ham United. The final went to a replay, for which, with Davids Johnson and Fairclough missing, Ian Rush played, causing centre-half Alvin Martin a lot of trouble, curling a shot against the bar and earning praise from Paisley. Rush was '. . . the bonus of the night,' he said. 'His control is good. He is difficult to knock off the ball, and brings people into the game, which is Kenny's asset.'

Amid the First Division struggles, the prospect of conquering the heights of Europe seemed forlorn, though continental competition provided the opportunity The first round obstacle of Finnish side Oulun Palloseura was welcome, after the obstacles of Forest and Dynamo Tbilisi in previous years. A 10–1 win at Anfield sealed the progress.

Then, Paisley encountered an Alex Ferguson team for the first and only time. Ferguson's Aberdeen were fresh from shattering the dominance of Celtic and Rangers in Scotland, and the Scot was displaying the fledgling oratory for which he would become known at Manchester United. 'Come the hour, I will definitely have belief in winning the game,' Ferguson said. 'As long as there's a ball in the park and the human element comes into it, we are in with a chance.

For Liverpool, this is full of imponderables. For Aberdeen, it can only be a night they have never experienced before.'

Paisley's own press conference before the Pittodrie fixture had a more understated aim, though even the most partisan Aberdonians had to agree in the aftermath that, in psychological terms, it had been the more effective.

Liverpool had arrived north of the border to find vast volumes of newsprint devoted to Aberdeen's chances of bloodying Liverpool's nose. 'A 28-page pull-out, 27 pages of which were about what they were going to do to us,' as Alan Hansen later put it. Much of the focus was devoted to Gordon Strachan, the 23-year-old winger who was such a significant part of the Ferguson side which had gone back to the top of the league before this match.

In the circumstances, Paisley decided that he, too, would have something to say about Strachan. 'If Aberdeen ever relent and decide to sell Gordon, he'll become Scotland's first £2 million player,' he observed. 'He impresses me greatly, as do Aberdeen as a team. They don't give much away and, with a few wins under their belt, they'll face us with confidence.'

It was a confidence trick and Paisley's players knew it. Talk up a player and you build the pressure on them – classic Paisley toffee. The manager ensured that the slant of the local coverage was not lost on his players. 'It meant a lot to me to ram those comments back down the throats of people who made them,' Hansen said. 'I never performed with as much fire and aggression as I did in that game.'

Strachan was anonymous and Liverpool won by a Terry McDermott goal at Pittodrie before a 4–0 victory in the return leg. It was the Liverpool style, rather than the Paisley psych-ops, which Ferguson spotted. The discipline, possession-based football and game management attached to playing in Europe were still intact after two years away.

'After that Anfield episode I knew I didn't have to say another bloody word to my players about keeping the ball, particularly in European games,' Ferguson later reflected. 'That was a part of my education and it's always been part of my strategy. Hold onto the ball. Keep passing it. Let the other teams do the chasing.'

There was a 5–1 home leg quarter-final defeat of CSKA Sofia, where the dual absence of Johnson and Fairclough presented 33-year-old Heighway, in his testimonial year, with a chance to reveal that he still had something to offer – and he seized it. His performance, setting up two of Souness's three goals, brought letters to the *Liverpool Echo* demanding to know why he had been overlooked.

Heighway also came on after half-time in the first leg of semi-final against Bayern Munich at Anfield, a 0–0 draw which left Liverpool with a lot of work to do in Germany. This time, Souness was out with a back injury, while Terry McDermott played with a dislocated thumb.

Aware that his Liverpool days were effectively over, Heighway had already signed a two-year contract in the North American Soccer League with the Minnesota Kicks, sold his house and was scheduled to move his family out to the US on the week of the Munich semi-final second leg. Sensing a last opportunity at the club which had been his life, he knocked on Paisley's office door.

'The house is sold and we're leaving next week, Bob,' he said, as reluctant as ever to call his manager 'boss'. 'But if you want me to stay I'll wait and move the family into a hotel. I can do that if you might need me . . .' Paisley said that would help, and without hesitation Heighway moved his wife and children into Liverpool's Adelphi hotel.

Liverpool were playing the following Wednesday night and 24 hours before Liverpool flew out to Germany, Johnson was showing no sign of recovery. Then Heighway was told that Paisley wanted to see him.

'I'm not taking you,' he stated flatly.

'You're joking?' replied Heighway.

'I'm not taking you. I'm taking the boy Gayle instead.'

'But I asked you did you want me to stay. You said: "Yes." We're in a hotel. We cancelled the flights . . .'

The rest of Paisley's explanation was the mumble that tended to accompany these social confrontations. He would never be a match for Heighway in such an encounter so the conversation was over. Heighway exploded. The players heard the commotion at the bottom end of the corridor, in the lounge area adjoining the canteen. Heighway returned to his hotel, where he picked up the phone, organised flights and in a couple of days had gone. And that was the way his 11 years at Liverpool Football club ended.

There had not been much substance on which to base a decision to select Howard Gayle, who had only one previous senior appearance to his name – as a substitute at Manchester City six months earlier – since when he had suffered back trouble.

In the Boot Room, they always wondered about Gayle's temperament. Some of them considered him one of the awkward squad, though he had good reason to be. He was the first black footballer to break into the Liverpool first team and did so at a time when those of ethnic extraction in the city were feeling the profound sense of racial injustice which, on 13 July 1981, would find expression in the Toxteth riots.

There were some distinctly unenlightened attitudes to colour within Anfield at the time. Tommy Smith knew Gayle as the 'white n****r' and did not appreciate that was offensive. It was 'a compliment', Smith suggested several years later, bestowed upon Gayle because the young man had shown he would stand up for himself to him. Perhaps it was no coincidence that those Gayle considers to have been in his corner were all men whom Paisley chose as captains: Emlyn Hughes, Phil Thompson and Graeme Souness.

Some on the coaching staff knew Gayle as 'the Black Prince' and the colour of his skin certainly formed part of the way he was tested. There would be references to his colour at Melwood. When the decathlete Daley Thompson came in to help Liverpool with sprint training at one stage, and Gayle was about to race him, someone shouted: 'Ready, steady, pick up your lips, Go.' The Olympian seemed to accept the casual racism, though Gayle – who had fought it throughout a difficult childhood in a predominantly white district of the city – did not. For that, he always felt he was marked down as a troublemaker. Paisley seems neither to have contributed to nor challenged this prevailing attitude towards colour which existed in his football club's predominantly white community of the time. Gayle's potential to help him beat Bayern Munich was his only consideration in April 1981.

It was again the defence which concerned Paisley most that month. The back four for Munich was makeshift, with both Richard Money and Colin Irwin starting in the Olympiastadion, where only one visiting team had ever avoided defeat in European competition, and where Liverpool needed to avoid one. There was some motivational material, at least. Souness remembers Bayern leaflets promoting package trips to the Paris final, which Paisley got his hands on and waved around in the dressing-room, just as he had used the Scottish newspapers to motivate his players in Aberdeen. Newspaper cuttings also reported the Bayern captain's declaration that Liverpool had shown 'no intelligence' in the first leg. There were also mutterings about Liverpool being past their best. All grist to the Paisley mill.

An encounter the manager had at the Liverpool dressing-room door in the minutes before kick-off proved even more significant, though. The Austrian UEFA match official asked Paisley, as witnesses remember, to 'tell me about this Howard Gayle', the inference being he may not be a legitimate member of the squad.

'He's a registered player of Liverpool Football Club,' Paisley replied, sending the official on his way.

There'd been more worry than usual about the make-up of the team. Ray Kennedy, rooming with Case as usual, heard Paisley, Moran and Fagan arguing loudly over the team selection in the room next door, the night before the game.

With Phil Thompson and Alan Kennedy operating with the untested Irwin and Money in an unrecognisable defence, Paisley, who had taken the extra precaution of personally scouting Bayern with Tom Saunders, worried about the midfielder Paul Breitner, the legendary German international and 1974 World Cup-winning goalscorer. He decided that Sammy Lee must man-mark Breitner. It was the only time in nine years at the helm that he employed such a strategy – though the testimony of Graeme Souness suggests that his decision was so late as to border on an impulse. 'We're lining up and the buzzer goes [to call us out to the pitch] when Bob says, "Sammy, tonight you man-mark Paul Breitner,"' Souness recalls. 'We're saying "What? Well, good luck with that one Sammy."' There was no place in the starting line-up for Case, who knew when he heard Lee being issued with such challenging instructions that his road ahead at Liverpool looked bleak.

Paisley looked a rather helpless figure as he took a seat on one of the benches arranged for the coaching teams (with the stands so far from the pitch there were no dugouts in the

Olympiastadion) – even more so when Dalglish went down under a wild challenge from Karl Del'Haye. With the game only five minutes old Dalglish was off, having suffered serious ankle-ligament damage.

Rush would have been the obvious choice to replace him but the Austrian official's questions about who Gayle was persuaded Paisley to deploy him instead. If the Austrian knew nothing about Gayle then neither would the Germans, he figured. As he put it later, 'The Germans like to do things by the book. The unknown can unnerve them.'

The BBC's commentator Barry Davies captured the size of the gamble. 'Liverpool have lost their most experienced striker and national and international footballer, who has been replaced by a 19-year-old,' he observed. For once, one of England's most distinguished commentators was getting carried away. Gayle was nearly 23.

Nonetheless, it was a Paisley substitution to go alongside Case's deployment at the half-time stage for Toshack against Club Brugge in the 1976 UEFA Cup final, and Heighway's against the same opposition in the 1978 European Cup final. Gayle's pace mesmerised the Germans and repeatedly stretched Bayern's defence, pushing the side back, and consequently relieving the pressure on Liverpool's own makeshift back four. Chasing a long ball from Alan Hansen into the left side of the penalty area, Gayle was brought to ground by Wolfgang Dremmler, whose run straight across the Liverpudlian's path should have brought a penalty.

On 66 minutes, Gayle was booked and Paisley calmly substituted the substitute, concerned that the combustible element in his game could lose Liverpool a man. Case arrived in his place, initially taking up a position in attack and then dropping into midfield. It meant that when Johnson went down injured, with a strained hamstring, Liverpool had used their substitutes and had no further options. He signalled to the bench who waved him on. 'Give us your gun. I'll shoot the bastard!' Evans heard Paisley say.

The Liverpool goal seven minutes from time was the fruit of those months of hard labour at Melwood. Paisley indicated to Kennedy that he should move up the field to assume the role of striker. The struggling Johnson crossed for him to score with his left foot. Lee shut Breitner out of the game. Hansen checked the unexpected diagonal runs of Karl-Heinz Rummenigge by taking two steps into the space which he anticipated the German running into. But above all Liverpool prospered by employing the European style Paisley had developed: slowing play down, passing, keeping possession, waiting for the moment to break.

'Composure, awareness, resilience,' enthused the *Liverpool Echo*. Bayern forward Uli Hoeness reflected on the clashes the two sides had had in 1970, in the Fairs Cup and Cup Winners' Cup. 'Compared with their style then, Liverpool are more like a continental side now,' he said.

Paisley was amused by an encounter in the dressing-room corridor after the match, between Lee and Breitner.

'Well played,' said the German international, who'd just been marked out of the game by someone seven years his junior.

'Thank you, Mr Breitner,' said Lee as he walked past.

Paisley's appreciation of the way Lee had carried out his man-marking role went beyond the parameters of that game. He saw a lot of his own playing style in Lee: they played in similar roles and did similar jobs, and they were both 5 feet 7 inches tall. Lee was one of the few players Paisley talked about at home.

The manner of the victory did not prevent more talk of some of Liverpool's players being too old from forming the backdrop to the final in Paris, where Liverpool would meet Real Madrid.

'They are veterans. We will outrun them,' said the Real coach Vujadin Boškov before the match. Liverpool were also caught up in a wrangle with UEFA over whether they could use sponsors' logos on their kit – something Peter Robinson was trying to resolve in the last hours before the game.

Liverpool limited their exposure to Paris. The team turned the match into a standard European game – flying late to Orly airport, where the familiar Aer Lingus charter was struck by lightning as it approached the runway. The squad checked into the Trianon Palace in Versailles barely 24 hours before kick-off. They left the Trianon at 6.30 on the night of the match – for an 8.15 p.m. kick-off in the Parc des Princes.

At last, it was a final that Jessie could attend. She was as reluctant as ever to fly, so Christine, Robert, Graham and their families all travelled with her across the Channel by hovercraft to France. Jessie was the usual organising force: they all had their own packages of sandwiches for the trip, made by her, each with their names on them.

The difficulties for Bob included young Ian Rush's desire to play. '"You'll definitely be involved,"' Rush says Paisley told him. When the time came to reveal his 16-man squad for Paris, Rush's name was not on it. Kenny Dalglish's ankle had been in plaster but he was out of it in time to play.

Alan Kennedy was also on Paisley's mind. He had broken his wrist in the first leg of the Bayern semi-final, had played on with it through the match, and, inevitably, had to miss the second leg. The arm was tested out with a plaster cast in a league game against Manchester City. Kennedy, too, started in Paris.

The Spaniards had the outstanding player on the pitch: the little midfield architect Juanito. But Liverpool brought to bear what had now been long years of experience of continental competition, playing their collective way. They paced their game carefully, were reluctant not to waste possession with ambitious passes, though they did not hesitate to use the long ball if the situation demanded it. The *Guardian*'s description of Liverpool's game sounded like a mantra straight from one of the Boot Room black bibles. 'They always kept their movements wide and always the man with the ball had good support as colleagues ran intelligently into space.'

With a little of that old inferiority complex, Alan Kennedy was a slightly anxious figure as he walked in at half-time, with the score 0–0. Paisley had told him to keep on his feet against Laurie Cunningham, Real's exciting English winger who, as things turned out, had left him on his backside a couple of times. A 'right rollocking' is what he thought he would get in the interval.

But Paisley said that Liverpool were not pushing up enough, which meant too much of a gap was forming between the defence and midfield. That was why Kennedy was standing where he was standing on 81 minutes when Ray Kennedy sent a throw-in towards him. Considering the midfielder's views on his namesake, he may not have expected much to happen, but Alan Kennedy's surge up the touchline caught Real by surprise. Rafael García Cortés's attempt to thump the ball clear was spectacularly ineffective. If Kennedy had been made of lesser mettle he would have flinched to avoid the Spaniard's hack. Instead he stood firm and was there in the penalty box, finding his momentum carrying him beyond the defender, to swing his left foot through the ball and thrash it into the back of the net. It was a goal that would define him for all of his days.

Years later, Kennedy would describe how the word 'goal' actually formed in his head as he saw the Spanish goalkeeper dive to his left, clear of the shot which he had sent straight at him.

Then he ran with all he had to the Liverpool fans ten yards beyond the goal.

It was a little distance and, for a moment, none of his teammates arrived. He wondered where they all were. Had his effort been disallowed? Was he, at this moment, making a 'complete arse' of himself in front of millions of TV viewers as the match kicked off again behind him? Then Terry McDermott, one of those players who had also lived through the doubts and struggles and exclusions from Paisley's plans, arrived and the fog of momentary doubt lifted. 'You lucky fucking sod!' McDermott said, beaming.

12

TROUBLE

As he watched Alan Kennedy's moment of unconfined ecstasy from the stand, Ian Rush seemed a very long way from making it at Liverpool. He didn't seem to belong to the club that Paisley, Moran, Fagan and Saunders had evolved. Rush was of a different, younger generation, with his preference for the Human League, two-tone bands, skin-tight jeans and white socks. Souness, Dalglish and Hansen were of an ELO and Commodores persuasion – they wore Pierre Cardin trousers and in the dressing-room they destroyed Rush and his fashion statements. 'How many polyesters died to make that shirt,' Souness would ask the self-conscious teenager, who had nothing to hit back with in return. Rush took to wearing a plain t-shirt and pair of jeans to go to training, but the onslaught was unremitting. On account of his pastel clothes and pencil moustache they called him 'Omar', as in Omar Sharif.

There had been the usual Paisley charm offensive to sign him. It helped that Rush's father was a Liverpool fan, and a tour of Anfield helped seal the deal. Like so many before him, Rush was bemused by how this manager had won anything. Paisley, in his cardigan, white shirt and patterned knitted tie and Brylcreemed hair, looked like 'one of the old guys I used to see on the benches around the bowling green in my local park', Rush later reflected.

This avuncular effect helped, though, as walking into Anfield had frightened the life out of Rush. It had been Tom Saunders's Chester contact who had drawn Liverpool's attention to him but Rush was extremely unsure about signing and loved life where he was. He was so comfortable in his own skin in the lower leagues that he imagined a sum of money he thought Liverpool should pay him and then inflated it in the hope they might be put off and leave him alone. £100 should put them off, he concluded. Liverpool would offer three times as much. Rush didn't know that Chester were anxious to bring some money in by selling their prime asset.

His struggle to acclimatise at Anfield was compounded by that acute shyness, which was little less than an inferiority complex in the early days. The Boot Room discussed that at length in 1980.

Rush survived the environment by gravitating towards the quieter ones – Whelan, Lee, McDermott and Case, who despite his propensity to fight didn't give out so much verbal stick. Rush avoided Dalglish – he disliked him and his air of dressing-room superiority. Paisley's inscrutability and lack of communication maddened him too. His debut and the League Cup final replay performance the previous season had seemed like breakthroughs, but he found himself quickly restored to the reserves after each match. The exclusion from the European Cup squad in Paris had been crushing.

The finer points of Rush's game had not been lost on Paisley, though. The qualities he had described seeing in him after the Villa Park replay had notably not included a capacity to score, and the 1980–81 season had ended for him with nine games and no goals. The 1981–82 season brought a significant change in the First Division landscape: there would be three points for a win, draws would be penalised and goals were required more than ever.

After the previous season had seen McDermott top scorer with 13, Paisley could not afford to field a striker who assisted more than he scored, though it took a knock on his door to make him say so. Rush walked in, smarting about Paris and how he was back training with Roy Evans's reserves while David Johnson had been restored to the starting line-up. His irritation emboldened him to ask for a £100 a week pay rise, in line with those given to players who made it into the first team. But he did not discover any warmth in the boss.

'Ten per cent,' Paisley told him, which equated to £30 a week more if he wasn't earning a win bonus by actually playing.

'I think I've done well for you in my first season,' Rush replied. 'Why aren't you offering me more?'

The words he has never forgotten coming back his way were searing. 'Because you're not worth it,' Paisley said.

Rush, like Paisley, was a man of little conversation, though it developed into one of those rare occasions when Rush actually did more of the talking. He remembers all too clearly what Paisley said next: 'Score more goals. You've done OK an' that but you've got to score to get in. Ten per cent. Think it over . . .'

Rush left the room with his ego damaged, damned if he was going to settle for that. Paisley left him to stew back in the reserves, and two weeks later he was back at his door.

'What's happening?' he asked. 'Why have you left me out?'

'Goals,' Paisley told him.

'I keep being told here that football is a team game,' Rush replied.

Paisley said he had watched him in matches and training and that he only wanted to lay passes off to teammates, not try to score. He was afraid to take responsibility. 'When I was your age I was in charge of a tank in the war . . .'

Rush was stung. 'You tell us it's about possession,' he countered. 'They say, "Never give the ball away."'

'Think for yourself, son,' Paisley said. 'Or are you afraid to do that? The great goalscorers are selfish. Lofthouse, Greaves, Law – they were all selfish in front of goal. When you see the goal, be selfish . . .'

'I can score goals,' said Rush, struggling to find anything more to say and increasingly agitated.

'Then bloody well do it,' said Paisley. 'We bought you to score goals. Stop whinging and score some . . .'

'I can bloody well score goals,' said Rush, reduced now to repeating himself as he made for the door.

'Do that or you can go,' Paisley said.

And with that, Rush was back outside the manager's office. 'I felt my legs go to jelly,' he reflected later. 'He was putting me on the transfer list.'

The exchange took five minutes – a very long argument by Paisley's standards, one which would have been beyond him several years earlier and which revealed that Rush fell into the David Johnson and Phil Thompson camp of players the manager considered worth provoking, rather than the Frank McGarvey group of those who were best let go.

Which is not to say that Paisley's parting shot to Rush was an idle threat. Paisley was genuinely uncertain that this conversation would make the slightest difference, as Peter Robinson knew all too well. Crystal Palace had been interested in Rush and Robinson, who still dealt with that side of the business, was sanctioned by Paisley to sell if the club had come up with the asking price. It was by a relatively small financial margin that Rush did not become the 19-year-old property of Selhurst Park in the late summer of 1981.

In one sense, Rush had a point. Paisley's orders did seem to run against the collectivist grain of Liverpool. But the manager saw room for a ruthless, goalscoring individual within the collective. With nothing to lose, the striker set about proving Paisley wrong. He scored as heavily as possible in Evans's reserve team, reasoning that doing so would increase the chances of getting a good move when Paisley sold him. Rush netted twice in a 6–0 win over Blackburn Rovers in the first game of the season, repeated the feat in a 4–1 win over Derby County and scored again in a 1–1 draw against Aston Villa. Within three weeks, Liverpool had drawn Exeter City in the first round of the League Cup, which they were defending, and David Johnson was injured again. Paisley approached Rush as he left the training field the day before the first leg. 'Johnno's out,' he said. 'I'm looking for a selfish bastard to play up front.'

It was a 5–0 win for Liverpool and Rush scored twice. He retained his place to face Leeds United and scored twice more.

'Well done, lads,' Paisley said after that one. Rush tried to catch his eye but got nothing.

He scored another two in the second leg down in Exeter, and a subsequent run of 14 matches brought six more goals. Against his own expectation, Paisley began forming the opinion that the little strategy might have worked. He regularly confided his thoughts on this subject to Souness and Bob Rawcliffe and told Souness that he believed he was getting through to Rush. 'Keep on top of him,' Paisley told Souness. 'Keep telling him he needs to score more.'

Rush, however, was the least of his problems that autumn. Paisley liked to keep the changes incremental but he had been confronted by one which had been unexpected.

Ray Clemence – the vanguard of the Liverpool defence throughout his time as Liverpool manager – announced he wanted to leave for Tottenham. It was his uncompromising response to teammates falling short of the team's standard that many would remember him for. He would let defenders know his opinion if he was unhappy and could do so because of his own consistency – a far cry from those early days, struggling with confidence and his kicking. Paisley reported this to Peter Robinson. He was prepared to offer an improved contract to Clemence, who was then about to turn 33. Yet it was clear that the player's mind was set.

The development was so unexpected that there were rumours that the goalkeeper needed to leave Liverpool after making an enemy of someone in the city. Robinson says he simply felt that Tottenham had been making persuasive overtures behind the scenes. Paisley would have preferred to keep Clemence, but was not a passive bystander in the process. The absence of a meaningful successor for the goalkeeper had been something he wanted addressing. He had followed up a recommendation from Crewe Alexandra to monitor the Zimbabwean goalkeeper Bruce Grobbelaar, who had been on loan to the Cheshire side from Vancouver Whitecaps but had returned to Canada. Saunders and Paisley flew out there together to watch the goalkeeper. They were looking for someone who could operate in the Tommy Lawrence–Ray Clemence 'sweeper keeper' role but Paisley was most taken with seeing one of Grobbelaar's teammates blast a ball at him from the edge of the six-yard box before the warm-up. 'He not only stopped everything but caught it,' the manager later related. 'I could have left before kick-off.' Liverpool made him a 'tax deductible' on 17 March 1981.

Grobbelaar wasn't for hanging around, either. He had joked in training sessions that Clemence was too old and had to 'make way for a younger man'. He then declared through the newspapers that he wanted Clemence's place. Clemence says he felt that after

Paris there were no mountains left to climb with Liverpool. 'I was sitting in the dressing-room and thinking, "We've just beaten Real Madrid. It's not going to get any better than this."' But Paisley felt Clemence was rattled. Years later, he described Clemence asking of Grobbelaar, 'Who does he think he is?'

Paisley liked that. He wanted Clemence on the edge, like everyone else. The legendary indifference to training displayed by 'Nozzle' – as he was known by dint of his large nose – was borne of the lack of competition, and suddenly there was some. Yes, Paisley and the Boot Room were happy with that.

There was a need for defensive addition, too. Colin Irwin and Avi Cohen had failed to convince Paisley the previous season, as the defence had looked far less secure in the absence of Thompson and Hansen. Irwin was sold to Toshack's Swansea; Cohen returned to Maccabi Tel Aviv. The Boot Room had been taken with the Irish defender Mark Lawrenson's performance for Brighton against Dalglish at Anfield two seasons earlier. He was one of the most sought-after players in Britain by the summer of 1981, with an ability to play on either flank, anywhere across the back four, even midfield. It was his tackling that impressed Paisley most, though.

Lawrenson also happened to be available. Liverpool had the profits of the European Cup to spend, and buying him prevented Liverpool's rivals strengthening. Lawrenson, like many players before him, was enamoured with the Paisley signing-on routine. It was a doorman at his Liverpool hotel who informed him that the manager was waiting for him in his car outside. 'When I got in the car I saw that Bob was wearing slippers and a cardigan,' he said. 'I couldn't believe it. They'd just won the European Cup and there was this fellow, who everyone in football thought was an absolute god, driving me to the ground in his slippers! I thought, "You'll do for me!"'

Case, who had been losing a grip on his Liverpool career for the past year, was quietly eased off to Brighton as a makeweight in the Lawrenson deal. Though he would build a career and life beyond his home city of Liverpool, Paisley's decision broke the midfielder's heart.

In footballing terms, the decision to release him was questionable, as Case demonstrated in an eventual six years at Southampton from 1985: there were the same ferocious tackles, supreme passing skills and a vision for patterns of play that saw him blossom with age. Nearly a decade after leaving Anfield he was still regarded as one of the First Division's best midfielders – and a more adventurous one than Lee, who scored half as many goals as Case in more matches for Liverpool than his predecessor. Paisley's side was less flamboyant without Case who, like Joey Jones three years earlier, had become a player whose temperament had breached the limits of Paisley trust – and the manager was unflinching about the sale in such circumstances. 'He didn't sell Jimmy for football reasons,' says Souness. Yet Paisley's doubts about a player could derive from something far less dramatic than a night behind bars.

The manager remained unconvinced by Howard Gayle, despite his heroic role in Munich, and the forward did not help himself by questioning the £30-a-week pay rise Paisley offered him at the start of the 1981–82 season – a smaller lift than fringe players Ronnie Whelan and Kevin Sheedy, whose salaries were brought into line with his own. Gayle took the new contract document away and it was only when Paisley asked if he was going to sign it that he declared to the manager his belief that a European Cup semi-final player deserved more.

A 23-year-old player, giving the impression that he thought he had cracked it: nothing would impress Paisley and the Boot Room less. 'OK, son, go away and have another think about it,' Paisley said and Gayle disappeared back into the reserves, never to surface in the Liverpool first team again. The player had not spoken to Paisley for months before encountering him when boarding the team bus back to a hotel after playing in a pre-season friendly with Malaga in the summer of 1981. Gayle had missed one of the kicks in a penalty shoot-out and was listening to jazz music on one of the Walkman devices which were becoming increasingly fashionable. Paisley leaned forward and in his distinctive strains told Gayle, 'You shouldn't have had them headphones in last night . . .'

'He wasn't smiling and he wasn't joking,' remembers Gayle. 'He was telling me to remove them and I did, without saying anything. I should have signed the contract. Looking back, I think my actions at that time just strengthened Bob's mistrust of me.' Gayle left on loan for Newcastle that winter.

Just six months after that legendary European Cup semi-final win in Munich, a quarter of the side selected had been shipped out of Anfield by the start of the 1981–82 season. The squad for the first game of the new campaign, at Wolves, revealed a manager more concerned about the failings of the previous domestic campaign than the European triumph that had come at the end of it. He fielded three debutants – Grobbelaar, Lawrenson and Craig Johnston, who had been signed from Middlesbrough as Terry McDermott's long-term replacement. The shake-up was so substantial that even the Paris match-winner Alan Kennedy was dropped. There was no explanation from Paisley. 'Of course, I found that very hard to take,' says Kennedy. 'Bob didn't even come up to me to talk about it.'

Despite Ian Rush's goal riot in the League Cup, it was an autumn in which Liverpool's winning quality vanished like never before, and the poor previous season, perhaps papered over by the win in Paris, came to be seen as symptomatic of a deeper malaise. The side lost at Wolves, trailed at home to Middlesbrough before equalising with a penalty, and after a 2–0 defeat at Ipswich in early September had picked up only four out of a possible 12 points. The Ipswich game saw Paisley dispense with his usual gentle humour and deliver a rare public rebuke: 'They have got to be professional, not playboys or fly-by-nights. I am talking about the attitude. The players seem to be saying sorry and think it's over and done with. They will have to change their attitude.'

For a squad infused with the principles of modesty and unpretentiousness, that was about as substantial an insult as any Paisley could level at them in public, and it was intended for that effect. Phil Neal was so piqued by the manager's choice of words that he confronted him and asked which players he had in mind. Paisley, as Neal remembers, '. . . waved his hands in the air, said something incomprehensible and wandered off.'

The words didn't work. By December, Liverpool had won five, drawn six and lost four – an indifferent return which, with money rendered tight by the anti-inflationary industrial policy of Margaret Thatcher's Conservative government and unemployment at a 50-year high of three million by January 1982, left fans voting with their feet. A full 13,000 tickets had remained unsold for the defeat at home to Leeds United on 10 October.

Paisley was uncertain of how extensively to blood Lawrenson, his expensive new defender. He decided it would be a risk to play him at AZ 67 Alkmaar in an early European Cup tie and that the 24-year-old must therefore be on the bench for the visit to Brighton, his previous club, four days earlier. But though he wanted Lawrenson to 'have a look' at how the team worked away in Europe – an expression he liked to use – he seemed uncharacteristically concerned that this would represent loss of face for the Irish international. This may have stemmed from Lawrenson's decision to reject the overtures of Manchester United manager Ron Atkinson and Arsenal's Terry Neill and sign for Liverpool.

'Do you want me to say you're injured?' Paisley asked Lawrenson, before kick-off in Brighton.

'You don't need to do that, boss,' replied Lawrenson, confident enough in his own ability to countenance the demotion.

Liverpool drew 3–3 at Brighton, where an injury to Alan Kennedy saw Lawrenson play at left-back in Alkmaar anyway and acquit himself well in a 2–2 draw.

'I made a mistake. You were ready,' Paisley told Lawrenson after the players left the field in the Netherlands. He did not doubt the defender again.

Grobbelaar was a major problem, though. Signed as a goalkeeper in the Clemence mould, his predecessor's departure to Tottenham removed all the defenders' certainties about where their goalkeeper would be positioned. Souness thought Grobbelaar 'had a nightmare' in those autumn months. The goalkeeper was annihilated in the newspapers – something which, he reflected later, had depressed him. He struggled with the usual Liverpool expectation that players simply sort out their own problems. He knew the former Manchester United goalkeeper Harry Gregg and called him to ask for advice. Gregg said he was busy but could talk him through a few things on the phone. None of which sounded promising.

It was Grobbelaar's predilection for showmanship, rather than his frantic rushes from the goal-line, which bothered Paisley. The handstands he performed during games were not helping. Continuing the thread of suspicion for practical jokers which Joey Jones had known at times, Paisley told Grobbelaar to 'Stop clowning around.' Unpredictability always made him anxious.

It was after a 2–2 draw against Toshack's Swansea at Anfield in October which left Paisley's side 13th that the city of Liverpool was plunged into a period of sorrow and collective memory of the man on whose platform Paisley had built. On 26 September 1981, Bill Shankly suffered a heart attack and was rushed to Liverpool's Broadgreen Hospital. He was a 68-year-old who neither drank nor smoked and who exercised daily. 'When I go, I'm going to be the fittest man ever to die,' he had once said, and there was a desperate irony to the fact this would come to pass, just as those perennial threats to step down as Liverpool manager had, back in July 1974. Three days after his first heart attack, he suffered a second and was dead before the morning of 29 September was out. For Liverpool, a city already in the grip of Thatcherism, it was a huge blow.

The *Liverpool Echo* had published its last interview with him just a few weeks earlier, providing a melancholy reminder of how his decision to retire in 1974 was something he had never come to terms with. The piece was headlined 'The Seven Wistful Years' and revealed the peripheral role he had experienced at Melwood after stepping down, calling in at the training ground occasionally, though only to use the sauna. Paisley knew it had been a different story, of Shankly assuming his usual sentry position inside the players' entrance before home games, standing on the platform when a trophy had been won, and though not a presence on the Liverpool team coach, a passenger on the opposition's more than once. He would never have ventured to say this, though.

'It was a privilege and an honour to have been allowed to work with him,' Paisley reflected two years later. 'People showed what they thought of him when he died. The church was packed for his funeral and then weeks later the Anglican Cathedral was packed for a memorial service.' But genuine though his tribute was, there was an implacable sense in what Paisley said after Shankly's death that he – the man who had stepped out of the shadows – felt the achievements after 1974 warranted recognition. 'To walk out, as he did, and then for things to turn out as they did was enough to make the most placid man envious,' Paisley said. 'He was the man who had started it all off and laid the foundations. He had to take a lot of the credit for what happened at Liverpool afterwards. But, on the other score, there is a bit of credit due to me and the staff because we changed the whole team over. Of the 12 players who created history by becoming the first British club to retain the European Cup with our win over Bruges, only four – Ray Clemence, Emlyn Hughes, Phil Thompson and Steve Heighway – had played in the Liverpool first team under Bill.'

In the aftermath of Shankly's death it was the last of the players the Scot had signed – the complex, brooding Ray Kennedy – who became Paisley's concern. He was missing his friend and soulmate Jimmy Case and was now rooming with Sammy Lee, the young midfielder who had displaced Case. Kennedy felt adrift and melancholy and his complicated mind was not disposed to calm reflection on how to rediscover the form that had bought Liverpool their win in Munich back in April. Frustration set in. He had been sent off twice in three months early in the season and was suspended for the game against Manchester City, which Liverpool went into in tenth.

In the circumstances, Ronnie Whelan felt his own frustrations. He was struggling to get a run in the side but was the retiring sort and not inclined to confront the manager.

A few days before the Manchester City match he finally found the courage to do what Rush had done: put his inhibitions aside and arrive at Paisley's door to ask when, if ever, he would get a decent run in the team. He'd been a part of Liverpool's brightest moment that autumn – the 3–1 win over Everton at Anfield – but, Rush-like, had been consigned right back to the reserves.

Whelan remembers Paisley had the *Racing Post* spread over the table when he stepped inside and spilled his anxieties out. How could he prove himself without playing? When would he get a run? What was the story?

The conversation was shorter than Rush's. Why hadn't Whelan been to see him earlier? Paisley asked. Whelan got the sense that Paisley was actually pleased he had knocked on the door. He fell into that category of player whom Paisley wanted to see doing so and perhaps it was the deference he had shown which provoked a different reaction to the one experienced by Rush. The manager was also more convinced of the Irishman's potential than of Rush's. It was only his strength of character that remained to be tested, and this encounter suggested he might have it. Whelan struggled to muster any kind of reply and the few words Paisley uttered by way of a follow-up were fairly incomprehensible, too. The next minute Whelan was back outside in the manager's secretary's office.

'He was probably waiting to find out from me if I really believed I was ready for the first team,' he reflected later. 'He knew I was a shy lad. He probably knew I wasn't the type to go banging on a manager's door, and the fact that I did go to him maybe convinced him that I was ready.' Whelan played against Manchester City, not knowing as he ran out to play on a crisp Anfield pitch showing evidence of the week's snowfalls that it would represent the low point of Liverpool's winter. The match, in which Liverpool lost 3–1, was a disaster from start to finish. City goalkeeper Joe Corrigan was struck with a glass bottle. City manager John Bond instructed his players to take to the floor when their bus was attacked with missiles as it pulled out of Anfield. And Paisley's team were humbled.

The line-up reflected the side's rapidly changing face. Six of the starting XI – Grobbelaar, Lawrenson, Johnston, Whelan, Lee and Rush – had never collected a league championship medal. But that did not mitigate for the manner of defeat.

Thompson dallied with a clearance near the six-yard box, allowing Asa Hartford to steal the ball and score. Then a poor skied clearance by Thompson, which didn't even leave the penalty area, was dropped by Grobbelaar in no man's land and Thompson had to handle the ensuing shot over the bar for a penalty, which was converted.

Kevin Reeves produced a shot which Thompson should have blocked off before it beat the goalkeeper – 'the sad figure of Grobbelaar', as he was described on the BBC commentary – at the near post. It was Liverpool's third home defeat of the season and it left the side 12th in the First Division.

John Bond did not pass up the chance for sanctimony when he paid a visit to the Boot Room that evening. Liverpool's chances of taking the title had gone, he suggested. Paisley wasn't present that day but he would have adopted the same approach to the comments as Moran, had he been. 'Just wait and see,' Moran told Bond as he left. 'There's half a season to go yet. We'll see who's top in May.' He and Fagan seethed when the City people had gone.

'The Empire is Crumbling' declared an apocalyptic *Daily Mirror* after City's first win at Anfield since 1953. The letters pages of the *Liverpool Echo* were filled with proclamations of how Paisley was sending Liverpool – the reigning European champions for the third time under his guidance – into terminal decline. 'I never thought this would happen,' stated one, penned from the village of Meols in suburban Wirral. 'Liverpool built their reputation by careful planning, wise spending and total dedication at all levels. Above all, the word "pride" was emblazoned into everybody connected with Liverpool and was reflected in the never-say-die attitude. A new word has crept into the vocabulary: "apathy".' Another expressed 'disgust at the attitude of Liverpool towards their supporters'.

'Legend now burden' was the *Liverpool Daily Post*'s headline beneath an assessment which included some melancholic reflections on what had come to pass: 'The public has no stomach for the hero defeated by time. We prefer to hold them in the memory where they remain ageless. Those who knew Dean, Finney and Charlton remember them at their best. Those who followed Liverpool while they became the most successful institution English football has ever known are watching them still and that makes the disappointments that much harder to follow. There are no graceful retirements for football clubs.'

The manner of the Manchester City defeat required something that stripped the paint off the walls and Paisley knew his own limitations. Fagan wanted to speak. On the rare occasions Bob's assistant raised his voice, there was a reaction. So Paisley accepted. 'Say what you want,' he said, and left. His assistant did not hold back. Phil Neal recalls every word of what was said as a furious Fagan picked off the offending players, one by one. Souness first: 'You think you're running midfield? You haven't won a tackle for a month. You're nowhere near anything.' Then Dalglish: 'How many goals have you got so far this season?' Then Grobbelaar: 'You look more like a ballerina. Come and collect the ball like you're supposed to.'

The players had taken to meeting together, to discuss the problems, with Phil Thompson frequently declaring it was all his fault that a certain goal had been conceded. There had clearly been some scepticism in the Boot Room about the notion of the players analysing their problems to death instead of putting things right on the pitch. 'The meetings must stop,' Fagan fumed. 'Now get out of here. We've talked enough.'

Grobbelaar was the one the defenders blamed. He felt some of the side were 'stand-offish' with him in the aftermath of the Manchester City defeat. Superficially at least, Paisley seemed to feel something different. He waited until the squad had gathered at 10 a.m. the following Friday to say his piece, preferring to let the dust settle. He surprised them by declaring that he absolved Grobbelaar from much of the blame by declaring that some of the moves which brought the goals should have been cut off before they reached the goalkeeper. But Paisley did tell Grobbelaar to cut out his handstands.

The strategy was clear. To have condemned the 24-year-old in front of the rest would have shattered his frayed confidence more. There were quieter, more clinical ways of dealing with him if things didn't pick up. Paisley wasn't done yet, though. He was preparing for his own contribution: a quiet and clinically brutal one.

The players were on the coach run down to Melwood, four days later, when Fagan approached Thompson, who was sitting halfway back with his usual partner McDermott. 'The boss wants to see you in his office when we get back,' he said.

Ray Kennedy, sensing something significant, declared that he knew what it would be about.

'Tell me now if you know,' said Thompson, irritated that Kennedy had information that he was happy to use to add to the intrigue.

'I know who the new captain's going to be,' Kennedy replied.

'Are you going to tell me, then?' said Thompson, trying to retain face.

'Graeme Souness,' said Kennedy.

'Now there's a shock,' said Thompson.

Thompson dispensed with any small-talk when he walked into Paisley's office. As Thompson recalls it, Paisley's words to him were: 'I'm taking the captaincy off you for now.' It was Paisley dissembling in the face of personal conflict again – sugar-coating an awkward conversation, because, in truth, he had no intention of ever restoring the captaincy. In the blur of emotion Thompson's vivid memory is of Paisley suggesting he was 'taking too much responsibility on your shoulders'.

'You're wrong. I don't agree with you. But you're the manager so I will have accept it,' the player replied, though he struggled to extend the same magnanimity to the issue of who would be succeeding him. 'It's Graeme fucking Souness, isn't it?'

Paisley mumbled something incomprehensible. 'Aye, aye, just for now, see how it goes n'that,' Thompson remembers him saying. The meeting was over.

Thompson's indignation was something Paisley would have appreciated. 'He was a man's man. You could have a go back. I honestly believe me having a go back took me up a couple of notches. I think he wanted the response,' he says. But there would be no reprieve. Thompson would never lead out his beloved home-town team again.

Paisley was planning changes to the team as well though he communicated the fact in his typically vague fashion. When Mark Lawrenson met the manager in the lift at the team hotel in Swansea – where the team played an FA Cup tie a week later – he was asked, 'Can you play that left-sided one?'

'What do you mean, boss? Left-back? Left-midfield?' Lawrenson asked.

'Aye, aye, that's the one,' Paisley replied.

Lawrenson remained none the wiser and neither was Ronnie Moran. 'Where are you playing?' he asked him ahead of kick-off. It transpired that Paisley had a left-midfield role in mind for Lawrenson, adding some muscularity which had been missing in the combination of Whelan and Sammy Lee against City.

It was Joe Fagan, not Paisley, who looked out for Thompson when Souness led the team out for the first time in the next game – an FA Cup tie against Swansea, with the deposed captain left to work out which was the least humiliating place to put himself in the line-up when the players ran out onto the pitch. (He decided to head out last.)

'You have to make sure you do a great job,' Fagan told Thompson.

'You'll get 100 per cent,' Thompson replied. 'When I'm out there Souness will get my backing but don't ever tell me what to do when I'm off the pitch.' The Swansea cup tie – a 4–0 win for Liverpool – was, by Thompson's judgement, his best game of the season. Lawrenson was among the scorers.

Paisley explained his captaincy calculations to supporters in the match programme for Souness's first home game as captain – against West Ham – and left little doubt that it would be a permanent arrangement.

'Phil told me he didn't believe his job as a captain had bothered him but I believe it has,' he wrote. 'Phil accepted the decision like the true professional he is, saying, "If it's for the best for me and for the team, that is all that matters." I'm firmly convinced that Phil will benefit from the decision. Equally, I'm convinced that Graeme Souness will respond to the added responsibilities. He has the make-up to develop into a top-rate skipper.'

Just to sharpen the sense of loss for Thompson, the image on the front of the programme depicted him lifting the European Cup in Paris.

There was another casualty in the depths of that winter. Ray Kennedy left for Swansea in the January. And results began to turn. Liverpool won five matches in a row and though they then won two and lost two in the next four, a futher run of 11 consecutive wins followed. The two men who had knocked at Paisley's door made very substantial contributions.

Ronnie Whelan was an instant hit. It was he who scored the consolation goal against City and, as the side began to rebuild their league campaign at the turn of the year, he scored in five out of six games. All the players began to feel the difference that he made. Ray Kennedy had never been the fastest of players and by 1981 that was beginning to show. It had meant that Rush had not been receiving the ball as rapidly as he might from Kennedy's field of influence on the left. With Whelan's arrival he, Dalglish and McDermott found themselves receiving possession more rapidly. Whelan's greater mobility also meant that when an attack broke down Souness did not have as much ground to cover.

To Paisley's supreme satisfaction, Rush and Whelan became a pair. They both scored freely after the turn of the year, as Liverpool won 20, drew three and lost two in 25 games – a performance which the three points for each win helped accelerate them to the summit of the league. They called Rush and Whelan 'Tosh and Vitch'. Rush, naturally enough for a Welsh Liverpool striker, took the John Toshack moniker. Though it took him some time to add to his repertoire the headed goals which were a big part of Toshack's game, he was the spear of the faster side that Paisley had built. The Whelan nickname was more complicated. He had a habit of saying 'dust' instead 'just' and so became known as 'Dust' and then 'Dusty'. It was changed, depending on the foreign opposition. When Liverpool played in Eastern Europe Whelan would become

'Dustovich' or, in Holland, 'Dustovan'. 'Dustovich' stuck and he became 'the Vich'. Paisley found it all utterly unfathomable.

But as the newly emerging side worked at close quarters with Paisley that spring, they discovered what he knew. Before the home match against Ipswich in early February, he discussed Frans Thijssen. 'Doin's', as Paisley described him, certainly not the hottest on foreign players' names. '"Thijssen", boss,' Ronnie Moran interjected.

Paisley told them that when he received the ball, he always took it on the inside of his right foot. So whoever picked him up should not let him turn and receive it that way: 'Come across him.' He also told them that midway through the second half, Thijssen would take a rest for ten minutes because he runs out of steam. 'So when you see him coasting, down the middle you go . . .'

And then there was the Ipswich keeper, Paisley added.

'Cooper,' offered Moran.

He was weak when balls were played in from his left between the six-yard line and the penalty spot. But his centre-halves didn't protect him from those balls, so they were worth trying. Liverpool beat Ipswich 4–0 and went third, leaving Ipswich sixth.

The spring was not without its frustrations. Europe brought one of the visits behind the Iron Curtain which made Paisley so deeply suspicious – to CSKA Sofia of Bulgaria, where Liverpool exited controversially. An Ian Rush shot was judged not to have crossed the goal-line when it seemed to have done so, several penalty appeals were dismissed, as was Mark Lawrenson. Raucous Bulgarians were billeted outside the Liverpool hotel, making noise in the early hours. Having taken a slender lead to Sofia, Paisley's players lost 2–0 and went out 2–1 on aggregate.

There was also an FA Cup defeat at Second Division Chelsea, which had Paisley returning home to tell Jessie that he'd had enough and was 'packing it in'. She revealed this years later, but he clearly didn't mean it. Peter Robinson never heard of any such threat.

It was Brian Clough's Forest empire which was crumbling. In 1981–82 the club were on their way to a miserable 12th-place finish – fully 30 points beneath Liverpool – and were knocked out of the FA Cup by Wrexham of the Third Division. At Christmas, while Liverpool were changing captains and issuing verbal gunfire, Clough was taken into hospital with a suspected heart attack and Taylor faced the burden of managing the team alone for three weeks. It almost broke him. Their relationship became a personal feud between two men with competing egos, though the underlying problem was that Forest had overstretched themselves financially. Clough had insisted on a grand new Executive Stand, insisting he wanted his Forest to 'play in a palace'. The repayments on that drained a club which, having slipped off the top, was also having to make do without European gate receipts, Wembley ticket sales and all the TV money that went along with them. In 1982 Forest were £2 million in the red and had to pay off the £2.5 million they had invested in the Executive Stand. It remained there in skeletal form, a 'constant reminder that Forest had to play well to pay for it before the interest charges began to bite', as the writer and former *Nottingham Evening Post* correspondent Duncan Hamilton wrote.

Liverpool's practice of replacing one or two key players a season was something that Clough did not copy. Peter Shilton was one of the last of the great side to leave in 1983 because the club needed hard cash quickly. Peter Taylor left Forest to manage Derby County in 1982.

'We were wrong,' Clough told Hamilton in retrospect. 'In fact we were so wrong I can't believe it. We lost our sense of proportion and paid for it. We were too worried that some players might age too quickly. That was barmy. We never worried about age before. We'd only been concerned about talent. And I suppose we got too big-headed. We believed that everything we did was right.'

At Liverpool, where the term Big 'Ead was deliberately used on the first-team stars to guard against that kind of hubris, Paisley's quiet instructions were the same as they'd been right back in 1974. Young trainee forward Paul Jewell, who would go on to manage in the top flight himself with Wigan Athletic, had just embarked on his task of cleaning a staff area one day, thinking the coaches had all left for the canteen, when he encountered the manager.

'Who needs time on the ball, son?' Paisley asked him.

Jewell was trying to get an answer out when Paisley provided it. 'The one who's going to receive it . . .'

It was the only time Jewell encountered Paisley one-to-one, but the second piece of advice he offered revealed that he and the Boot Room had the precise measure of him and his ability. 'And by the way,' Paisley added. 'Get your shots in quicker.'

Liverpool were benefiting from Rush having taken that very advice. The Rush–Whelan axis took the club to a second successive League Cup win – 3–1 in extra-time against Tottenham Hotspur at Wembley. They both also took the headlines, with Whelan scoring twice and Rush finding the winner. Whelan had scored 14 goals in 10 games and Rush 30 in 17.

When Paisley briefly became the centre of attention on the coach home from a win at Notts County, he seemed momentarily overcome by the sense that this new young team was making it. It was the week of his 63rd birthday, a cake had been arranged, and the players demanded a speech, knowing how much he wouldn't want to deliver one. Paisley picked the cake up and there was a tear in his eye as he spoke. 'If you play like that every day it will be my birthday every day,' he told them.

The only cause of disharmony was the usual one: players not being granted a precious place in Paisley's starting line-up. An episode as the season reached is climax revealed how different the consequences were when the disgruntled individual in question was Souness.

On the May Day Bank Holiday, the team were to play away to Tottenham Hotspur, Souness's first club, against whom he was always desperate to appear and perform. But the captain had missed five consecutive games through injury, all of which Liverpool had won. Paisley himself had missed the last two, suffering from pleurisy – a condition causing stabbing pains to the stomach, which left him recuperating in bed at Bower Road.

Joe Fagan took charge in Paisley's absence and it was he whom Souness approached ahead of the home game with Nottingham Forest on Saturday 1 May, to say he was fit to return. There was no way of accurately judging his match-readiness as Liverpool had not allowed Souness to run out for the reserves, fearing that an opponent would target him. Fagan told the captain he would rather hold him back for the match at White Hart Lane, 48 hours later. Souness duly told his teammates he would be playing in north London during Sunday's journey south, but Fagan arrived at the player's hotel-room door at the Swiss Cottage Holiday Inn, on the day of the match, to inform him – presumably a little tentatively – that he was retaining the same side for the 7.45 p.m. kick-off, with the captain again on the bench.

Souness was incandescent, and told Fagan what he might do with his team before shutting the door in his face, skipping the pre-match meal, showering and heading to the bar, where he promptly downed three gin and tonics and wrote out a transfer request.

It was then that Paisley, who had delayed his departure until the morning of the match owing to his recuperation, sauntered into the hotel lobby and spotted Souness at the bar.

'What's going on?' he asked him.

'You tell me,' replied the captain, relating the morning's events.

'We'll fucking see about that,' Paisley declared, marching off towards Fagan. 'We'll see who's boss.' Two minutes later he returned to tell Souness: 'You're playing.'

'Boss, this is my third gin and tonic,' said Souness.

'How about sub, then?' replied Paisley.

By half-time Liverpool were 2–0 down, and, on the side's arrival in the dressing-room, Paisley told Craig Johnston to 'have a bath'. Souness went on in his place and was integral to Liverpool recovering and drawing 2–2.

'In a way I think it showed that he felt a vulnerability – even then, after all he'd achieved,' says Souness. 'He'd missed a few games and he wanted to stamp his authority.'

Liverpool had reached the top of the table on 2 April with a 1–0 home win over Notts County. They wrapped up the title with a game to go, by beating Tottenham 3–1 at Anfield, in the near immediate Anfield return against Keith Burkinshaw's side. They'd trailed at half-time in that match, too, and Paisley said he was concerned about Lawrenson standing too close to Souness and getting in his way. Lawrenson shifted his position after the break, scored the equaliser and set up Dalglish for Liverpool's second. 'A magic wand' is how Whelan later described Paisley's contribution in that particular interval. 'At half-time Joe and Ronnie would generally do the talking,' Whelan said. 'But if Bob spotted something he would usually pass it on.'

Liverpool took the title by a four-point winning margin. In the space of five months they had reached such ascendancy that they could treat their final match, at Middlesbrough, with extraordinary indifference.

The agreement had been that they would dispense with the overnight stay if they had already won the league, saving the club £300. When the *Daily Mirror*'s Frank McGhee arrived to interview Peter Robinson, moments after Tottenham had been beaten, he found him on the phone to the Middlesbrough hotel, relating the change of plan.

When they set off by coach on the Tuesday morning of the game, it was the quantity of cider stashed on board which surprised the more peripheral members of the entourage. Rooms had been reserved from lunchtime to allow the players to get some sleep for a few hours before the game, against a side which had already been relegated. Paisley, Moran and Fagan sat downstairs in the hotel lounge, drinking tea and talking football. Rush was about to turn in for those few hours when Hansen and Souness arrived at the room he shared with Whelan.

Paisley and his assistants were having 'a good lunch' in the hotel restaurant, Souness informed the pair, so they should both report to the hotel lobby. They did so, finding the entire squad there too, and Souness then suggested that they all might 'go for a walk to a nearby park'. They were heading in that general direction when Souness, with his Middlesbrough knowledge, mentioned a pub tied to the local Cameron brewery. Had they sampled Cameron? No? Then they should. The players broke into groups of four to buy rounds. A quarter of an hour of football discussion ensued before the second arrived. Two hours had elapsed, and substantially more rounds, before Souness suggested they should head back to the hotel, where Moran would be making his rounds of the rooms at 4 p.m. to wake the players up.

Liverpool played dreadfully. David Hodgson was playing up front for Middlesbrough. 'I remember receiving the ball to feet and pretty much running past Alan Hansen like he wasn't there,' he said. 'I'm pretty sure he didn't know what day it was. We still couldn't win, though. They were so far ahead of everyone else they could still get a draw when the whole team was steaming.'

Paisley must have known about the caper, yet he could reflect on the transformation of the season and what he always declared to be the most satisfying of all his domestic titles. 'I'm proudest of this one because there was so much still to do,' he said at the end of the season. 'Our most difficult job is to decide when to introduce new players. Any clown can bring in youngsters, but if you do it at the wrong time you can crucify them. When we were struggling early on, people were shouting for us to get rid of this player and bring in that one. But you can't do it like that. You don't throw out a man who has served you loyally. There has to be some sentiment.'

That was not an entirely honest assessment. There was never room for sentiment. A further five players would be on their way out of Anfield within a few months. But the wisdom of waiting for Rush and Whelan had been borne out. They played when they were good enough to deliver and that was necessary. With their early frayed self-confidence, their paths in 1980 and 1981 could have taken different courses.

The turnaround owed much to the captaincy of Souness – whose demands for intensity and commitment other players feared. Grobbelaar had also heeded Fagan's demand for fewer high jinks – a fact reflected in the defensive record after the turn of the year. By the time Liverpool lost at home to Manchester City they had conceded 19 goals in 17 games. They shipped only 13 more in their remaining 23. But it was the rapid emergence of Rush – the predatory goalscorer Paisley had not possessed since Kevin Keegan had departed – which made the biggest difference.

Liverpool scored 56 goals in 23 games after the City defeat, with other sides surprised by the newfound pace which Paisley's Liverpool had not generally been known for.

Though it was selfishness in front of goal that Paisley had demanded from him, Rush would develop a reputation for working phenomenally hard. He pressed defenders, squeezing possession out of them, and was also extremely unpredictable. Defenders generally knew what they were up against when John Toshack or Steve Heighway were supplying Keegan. Rush brought a surprise component.

Whelan knew what he had seen in the early months of 1982. 'It's not an exact science and never can be because you are dealing with human beings, after all,' he said. 'It's very hard to pinpoint exactly when a player who has given good service is in decline and when a young player is ready to step up – or if he's good enough. I'd imagine that at the start of 1981–82 Bob wasn't sure either. But he would have monitored us closely. He'd have been scrutinising the veterans for sign of age catching up on them. He'd have been picking up clues, because Bob knew players inside out.'

With the old Liverpool qualities restored, Paisley called Rush into his office and told him he decided that the striker had earned the £100 rise he had asked for right back in August. Rush – buoyed by what was unfolding on the pitch and not, as he put it wanting to appear the manager's 'patsy' by accepting – declared that he wasn't sure he wanted a new contract now and would like time to 'think it over'. He returned two days later, suggesting that the £100 rise plus 10 per cent were what he was entitled to.

'Been giving it some thought, have you?' Paisley said. He didn't commit. A few days later, he called Rush back into his office. 'Been doing some thinking,' he said. 'The £100 and 10 per cent it is. Think you're about worth it.'

'Thank you very much,' said Rush.

'An' how'll you justify it?' Paisley asked.

'By scoring goals,' replied Rush.

'I thought you'd already started,' said Paisley, poker-faced. 'That's why I'm giving you the bloody rise.'

Rush told the newspapers all about the secret of his goal-scoring. 'People sometimes ask if I worry when I miss a sitter,' he said. 'But that's pointless, because you don't have the same chance again. You don't think, "I wonder what would happen if I'd missed that goal" so why should you start wondering about the ones that got away? You're on a worldwide stage out there, and to grab one of the goals is something most people never achieve in a lifetime.'

There was no mention of who had first dispensed such wisdom, but Paisley would have been all right with that.

13

END OF THE ROAD

There were moments as the years rolled on when Bob Paisley looked an older man than most other First Division managers. Sometimes he seemed to belong to a different world from those who occupied his stage – Clough, of course, and Manchester United's 'Mr Glitter', Ron Atkinson, who was 20 years younger than him.

Paisley was born when the horrors of World War I were still fresh, had seen the field of conflict through his own eyes, and yet here he now was, working in a place where £1 million would exchange hands for a footballer. Though he still held his players' professional lives in the palm of his hand, and they looked for the slightest clue as to how he viewed them, there were times when he seemed a slight anachronism.

On one flight to Israel in the early 1980s, Terry McDermott decided to lead a few of the senior players in placing food on the top of the head of a passenger sleeping in the seat in front of them. Mash made it onto the said pate, then carrots and peas. When the victim awoke, he was incandescent. Paisley, who was in conversation with Peter Robinson and Souness at the time, heard the commotion, saw what had unfolded and leapt to his feet to give the players a piece of his mind. Souness put a hand on the older man's shoulder and persuaded him that he would intervene to smooth things over. The world had turned since Paisley had boarded that cruise liner to the United States with Liverpool, 37 years earlier, politely playing deck quoits and speaking to the party of GI brides on board.

But the club was still run in a way alien to many others, which felt like a throwback to simpler, quieter days, when one favour earned another. Bob Rawcliffe, the mechanic and second-hand car dealer, had become a part of the club's fixtures and fittings, and so had others. They were unobtrusive, uncomplicated working people who gave freely and willingly of their time and were drawn into the Liverpool FC family. They did not come with a sales proposition. They simply had a role to play – sometimes for the Paisley family, as well as for the club. They all looked after their own. They didn't put food on the heads of sleeping passengers.

Neither did they indulge in some of the other new stunts being practised by Liverpool's class of 1982–83, such as Bruce Grobbelaar's 'fall-down' routine. This entailed the goalkeeper standing, hands behind his back, before falling straight to the floor whereupon he would get his hands out at the last minute to break his fall – except on the occasion when he left the hand movement a little late, smacked his face on the floor and needed six stitches in his chin.

Paisley's was a different world from this, occupied by such individuals as 'Alan the painter' who would sometimes double as a driver to bring out one of Bob Rawcliffe's cars to Christine Paisley when she needed one. There was 'Cyril the insurance' and 'Alf Smith the plumber', who took 11 weeks to install the Paisleys' central heating and, Jessie recounted, recited poetry in his lunch hours. There was 'Godfrey the policeman'; 'Bill and Bob the accountants'. Alf the plumber's daughter had joined the Paisleys on their trip to Paris for their 1981 family holiday. They received a few tickets here, a club dinner or a trip there, either for themselves or those who were close to them. Liverpool and Paisley had the comfort of knowing that when a problem occurred they would be covered. There would be someone they knew who could help.

Intentionally or otherwise, Paisley could be as much a source of the comedy as ever. A boiled sweet was lodged in his Brylcreemed hair in the press room at Queens Park Rangers but no one liked to point it out. Not all journalists appreciated that the quiet man was a wise one, with accomplishment meriting respect. Journalist Paul Newman, of *The Times*, detected after one game at Anfield, where the post-match discussion took place in the back corridor, that a few poked fun at his homespun, rather clichéd way with words. 'Game of two halves, wouldn't you say, Bob?' he was asked, or words to that effect. Paisley either ignored this or was oblivious to it.

By 1982 it had been a little time since he had granted an interview, but to the London listings magazine *Time Out* he explained very effectively that the days of motivating the players with exploits with magnetic figures on the tactics board had long gone. *Time Out* was a curious choice of title for him to speak to, but there was a very Bob Paisley kind of connection. His interviewer, Stan Hey, who would go on to become an accomplished journalist and author, could relate in his letter to the Liverpool manager that his father was a Saturday bet-setter in a betting shop to which Paisley would often adjourn. 'They're too old and wise for me to come in and tell them bedtime stories,' Paisley told Hey. 'Shank would come in, set up the little figures on the tactics board and say, "You're playing against a side with Best, Charlton and Cruyff in the forward line," or whatever, and then he'd sweep the little figures off and put them in his pocket and he'd say, "That's their forward line gone . . ." But you can't do that any more, because the players would just laugh at you. So now I'm glad when someone – the press or another player or manager – has a go at us. I can use that. I'm always picking my brains at home to find something new, searching for the little straws . . .'

The team was on one of the many money-spinning friendlies in the summer of 1982 when Paisley told them that the next season would be his last and he would be calling it a day in a year's time.

A health problem formed part of the decision, he said, soon after stepping down. It occurred on tour and appears to have been a severe infection of the medial, or middle ear. A 'virus' is how Paisley described it. Symptoms of such an infection can include fever, sickness, loss of hearing and loss of balance, and it was the latter which startled Paisley. 'I was just off balance for a few weeks and at the time it was frightening,' he said later.

It was a Granada TV documentary presented by none other than Paisley's old adversary Brian Clough which provided the clearest sense that a health issue might have pushed Paisley towards retiring. 'I thought, well, you know, if you're going to be [having problems] like that . . .' he told the programme's interviewers, initially trailing off. 'If you are ruthless enough to change players, then you've got to look at yourself and say, "Don't go beyond your limits."'

Peter Robinson and the board received no sense from Paisley that health was the motivating factor, though – the pleurisy episode that spring notwithstanding. The manager told Robinson that there were simply other things he wanted to do in his life. A lot of them revolved around horse racing. His achievements had widened his circle of racing friends and, in 1981, he had made his first visit to the Derby with his old accomplice Ray Peers. They travelled by train from Liverpool Lime Street to Epsom station and then walked more than two miles over the Downs to the course together. Paisley was also never happier than at Frankie Carr's place, at Malton.

Robinson tried to persuade him to stay until the end of the 1983–84 season, which would have helped the club groom a successor. Paisley was 64 and Liverpool told him they thought he could have gone on for another two years and enjoyed the success of the new young team he had built. He was not to be persuaded this time, though. 'He was absolutely determined and we could see he was determined,' says Robinson. 'He said he wanted to do other things with his life for a year or two.'

The decision to go was certainly not borne of the self-doubt which had plagued him when he had knocked on Robinson's door back in 1974. The seven-year contract he had signed after weathering that early storm was due to expire at the end of 1982–83 and the board reluctantly accepted his decision not to extend. 'He gave us good notice,' says Robinson, who ensured Paisley had financial advice in place. There was talk in the family home about a sufficient sum of money having been paid into a pension fund.

Paisley received an offer of help with the speech revealing his decision to journalists, which he intended to make at a dinner staged in his honour by the north-east branch of the Football Writers' Association at the Three Tuns Hotel in his native Durham. One of his Liverpool reporters' group, the *Sun*'s Mike Ellis, drove up to Durham with Paisley and said he was willing to deliver a speech of his own about him, thus limiting the time the 63-year-old would need to address the audience. Paisley said that wasn't necessary. When the moment arrived, he got to his feet and spoke for half an hour. This reflected a change Graeme Souness saw in Paisley during his final year at the helm, when the captain would be asked to accompany the manager on speaking engagements.

Paisley was more self-confident and funnier in his delivery, the captain felt. 'Not funny – *very* funny,' Souness says. 'His timing was very good as well. I think that was closer to the true character hidden by the shyness, which could be painful.'

The confident public exterior remained something he had to work at, however. After his death, his family found copies of the speeches he had given, painstakingly prepared in capital letters on the typewriter. A report of the Three Tuns Hotel gathering revealed that Paisley told his audience: 'Another 12 months would see me complete 44 years at Liverpool and then I'll hand it over. We've come through a transitional period and once I'm certain things are running smoothly it will be time to go.'

Wanting to look out for the journalists who had helped him along, Paisley called the *Daily Express*'s John Keith on the morning of the dinner, Sunday 9 May 1982, and told him that he would be making public his decision to finish at the event. He thought Keith and the others may want to write their reports in advance, for the following day's papers. He had travelled a long way in his relations with journalists.

His talk touched on what he had tried to achieve, though it was in the seclusion of his interview with Hey that he best captured his ethos: a game of football based 'on simple things', as he said. 'It's all about control and movement performed at pace and about each player knowing his strengths and those of his teammates. It's all about control of the ball – without that you have no foundation for anything else. After that it's a question of encouraging players to think for themselves and each other. You don't see a Liverpool player give a ball and then stand still . . . Basically we're about good, sound passing and cutting out the chancy ball, which you sometimes have to try, to create something. But we try and do four safe balls for every chancy one. And you can also make things happen by good movement. I can give you a negative pass, but I've then got to have a positive thought by making a positive run, so that you in turn don't have to give a negative pass. If someone's giving a negative pass, you shouldn't look at him but at what the other players are doing. The perfect player hasn't been born, so you have to ensure that you can cover people's weaknesses within the framework of the team.'

Hey interviewed Paisley twice and invited him out to lunch the second time. Paisley turned him down in favour of tea and a plate of biscuits.

He announced to the players that Joe Fagan would succeed him, and Souness was pleased. In an echo of Paisley's own succession from Shankly, the captain believed, 'There would be no wasted time by trying to prove ourselves to a new management.'

The pace of change remained relentless to the very end, with two of the bastions of the team Paisley had first built – David Johnson and Terry McDermott – heading out of Liverpool that summer, as Ian Rush and Craig Johnston eclipsed them. The pair fetched £100,000 each. Paisley again sold his ageing players early enough to collect a very good price. Johnson could have stayed longer. Paisley offered him an improved two-year contract in the summer of 1982 but he was not ready to be a squad player, yet. 'I don't want to waste another two years and be in and out,' he told Paisley. 'If I come back and I'm your fittest player and scoring goals, am I going to be your first choice?'

'No,' Paisley replied. 'But there it is – that's what I'm offering you. Sign it if you want. If you don't, you can go.'

So Johnson went to Everton, where his career had started, and at 30 had another two years of top-flight football to play. He did not take with him the same affection for Paisley that he held for Bobby Robson at Ipswich. That final exchange was 'the first time in my life he was honest with me,' Johnson reflects. The only other conversation with him that he can remember occurred at breakfast during an exhibition trip to Israel, when he and Souness joined him at the table. The location had stimulated Paisley's memories of his Western Desert Campaign days in the war and he talked about that. But Johnson was happy to sacrifice Robson's personableness for the four championships, two League Cups and three European Cups, 204 games and 78 goals that a mere six years at Paisley's Liverpool had brought. 'If you see somebody in slippers and a cardigan with a jovial face like Paisley, you think, "Oh, he must be a lovely fella," don't you?' says Johnson. 'None of it. I just didn't find him that kind of manager. But who am I to criticise Bob Paisley? What a genius. So he didn't give you a cuddle. But if he did, we might not have won what we won. So fair play to Bob Paisley. He did it his way and he was successful.'

McDermott could not say he remembered a single conversation with Paisley either, as he also returned to the club where he began – Newcastle. It had been a curious relationship between the two, with McDermott finding rich comic value in the manager as he oiled the wheels of Liverpool's social machine, and Paisley accepting it as he saw the player overcome his lack of self-confidence and become one of the great technicians of the side.

Also on the way out was Kevin Sheedy, who had lost the battle for a midfield berth with Ronnie Whelan. He was a Frank McGarvey in many ways, except that he had stuck it out for five years and played just five times. For Sheedy, it all ended with a signal from Moran one day that Paisley wanted to see him. The news he received from him was unsparingly bleak. Blackpool, on the lowest rung of the Football League, were interested. When the *Daily Mail*'s Colin Wood, acting as Howard Kendall's emissary, called him to say that Everton were interested too, Sheedy jumped at the chance. He would become a regular player in a side which was hugely successful for Kendall.

David Fairclough clung on a little longer, though the 1980s had not been kind to him, either, with just 21 starts in three years. Those conversations in Bob Rawcliffe's garage should probably have made him aware that he was fighting a losing battle to make it as a regular starter. But it was a call Paisley received from his old racing friend Frankie Carr, from his base in Hong Kong, which set in train the events of a bizarre summer which confirmed the manager's view of him beyond all doubt.

Carr was also working as an agent for a sports agency and he wanted to know if Paisley had any players to send to him in Hong Kong for the summer. Fairclough would be ideal, Paisley said.

'No thanks,' replied Fairclough, when Paisley put that to him, though he did say that the United States might interest him. (Fairclough had struggled with injury throughout the 1981–82 season and felt that a summer playing would get him back to fitness.) Paisley contacted the football agent Dennis Roach, who found Fairclough a place at Toronto in the North American Soccer League, where he spent a good summer. It was when the time came for Fairclough to pursue a place in Paisley's team once more that there was a shock in store. When he called Paisley back at Anfield to tell him things had gone well, he found the manager more interested in telling him that the German side Hanover had 'been on' and wanted to speak to him. When Fairclough insisted that he wanted to come home, Paisley seemed to be prevaricating.

'Well, we'll have to see what suits them,' said Paisley, clearly uncomfortable, not making it entirely clear who 'they' were. Paisley was seemingly looking to extract some transfer market value for Fairclough, who was still only 25.

Fairclough later suspected that Liverpool had sold him to Toronto for £150,000 and promptly had to buy him back when it was clear he did not want to go. No word was ever exchanged on this subject with Paisley when Fairclough arrived back at Melwood. The player simply laced up his boots and started training.

He left the following July, becoming the last player Paisley sold, after nine years in which he had fretted more than any about how to convince the Rat of his ability. On the eve of the last day of the season he awoke to a report in the *Daily Mail*, based on Paisley information, to say that Liverpool were prepared to let him go. When he spoke to Paisley, he was told that the club would offer him a new contract with wages reduced from £600 to £425. After another summer in Toronto, Fairclough wound up in Switzerland with FC Luzern at an age when he had always imagined he would be hitting his Liverpool prime. He was dispensable, though. Paisley had his sights set on a new 22-year-old striker by then – David Hodgson, a third player from the Middlesbrough production line, on whom Liverpool spent most money (£450,000) in the summer of 1982. The conveyor belt never stopped turning.

But it was the earlier acquisition from the Teesside club, South African-born Australian Craig Johnston, whom Paisley struggled with most as his tenure drew to a close. Of all those in the Boot Room, Paisley had been the keenest to sign him. Much like he had asked the club's Phil Boersma to petition Souness to join, Paisley asked Souness to bring his influence to bear on Johnston, another former teammate on Teesside. Johnston says Souness told him, 'Our lot are in for you and I told them you're OK and can play. But they're buying you to replace my mate Terry McDermott, so I can't do you too many favours.'

Brian Clough wanted Johnston for Forest, too, but Paisley was so keen that he called Johnston's house in Middlesbrough. Johnston's girlfriend said that he was too busy to talk. She hadn't realised it was *the* Bob Paisley on the end of the line. Johnston arrived at Anfield to be offered a Liverpool contract. He informed Clough, whom he says offered to double the value of it. Johnston settled for Liverpool, after all, with 5 per cent of the transfer fee for him.

But things began to unravel. While Souness had settled in almost immediately in the winter of 1978, it emerged once the Johnston deal had been done that the Australian midfielder was carrying a serious knee injury and, furthermore, he did not seem to conform to the Liverpool way. There were echoes of the Souness lifestyle about him. He lived in the city centre Holiday Inn and ran around in a Porsche. He wanted to buy a number plate that advertised his Australian roots – ROO 1 – and was struggling to persuade the owner to part with it. So he bought the car too. 'The owner wanted 2,000 quid, but what's money when you've just been signed as Liverpool's latest star?' he later reflected.

Souness more than compensated for his high life on the field of play; Johnston did not. Instead, it was the Liverpool drinking culture he adapted most quickly to. He learned the finer points of what was known the 'full dog day' of drinking, which usually started across at the West Derby Arms. But the Boot Room wondered why he, a player not short on self-confidence, seemed less fixated on the need to get his knee right. Johnston would arrive with his own muesli and nut combination in place of the usual Liverpool breakfast and was seen wearing tracksuit bottoms at Melwood until it was pointed out to him that players were only permitted to train in shorts. The wise old heads wondered whether he really was one of their own.

Paisley called Johnston into his office. He told him that he felt the deal had not worked out. Manchester United were about to sign Bryan Robson from West Bromwich Albion, who would be looking to reinvest some of the transfer fee. He was prepared to let Johnston go.

Did Paisley really mean this? Was he willing to give up a £650,000 record signing without having fielded him once? It was unlikely. Paisley had no idea what West Brom's plans were and he would have been unlikely to hand Johnston to a competitor on a plate. Souness suspects as much. 'I think they were lighting a fire,' he says. 'They wanted him to knuckle down. They would have had no problem selling him if they had to. They could attract any player they wanted.'

Johnston opted to knuckle down. He began to work and his fortunes seemed to change on a bitter December night when Arsenal visited Anfield for a fourth-round League Cup replay. His first goal for the club, five minutes into extra-time, helped secure a quarter-final place.

His work rate soon ceased to be a problem, but it was a focused work rate that Paisley wanted. While Liverpool's supporters were enthused by the midfielder's effort, Paisley, Moran and Fagan all felt that he did not stick to the plan. Johnston, by his own admission, lacked finesse and could sometimes just run around the field 'like a lunatic'.

Never did this seem more the case than in a home game against Sunderland in March 1982, when Johnston was, to Paisley's mind, causing chaos with the intensity of his running. The team had returned from a tough midweek assignment in Sofia, where they had lost 2–0, and they tended to operate in a low-tempo mode on the Saturday after such assignments. Trainee Paul Jewell was in the Anfield stand that day and could see the problems Johnston was causing. 'We all knew the way they managed those games after long European trips, when they might have a touch of jet lag,' he says. 'They'd just see the game out. You could see Craig had too much energy.' Paisley substituted Johnston in the 69th minute, triggering a howl of derision from a section of the Anfield crowd, who loved his commitment. The newspapers reported that supporters shook their fists at Paisley, while cheering Johnston as he made his way down the tunnel.

Paisley was implacable, declaring he would not be swayed by supporters who did not see what he saw. His rationale was that the Liverpool players were all calibrated and operated at the same tempo. 'That would be too intelligent for a few yobbos in the crowd to understand,' he told the newspapers, needled by the negative reaction.

After Johnston's withdrawal, Liverpool maintained the early lead Rush had given them and won 1–0, to stay top of the First Division. Johnston used newspaper interviews to defend Paisley's decision to remove him. But he clearly saw this as a favour to the manager. 'It was all fair and diplomatic but it was the last time I would defend a manager who denied me a first-team place,' he declared years later.

Paisley subsequently qualified his words to smooth things over with supporters. He said that by 'yobbos' he had meant only three or four people. 'They turned on me and I know where they sit and who they are, if they are there next time. I don't want to label everyone with it.' But the supporters were audible. There were many more than three or four.

It was a rare collision between Paisley and the fans, but the episode did hint that Paisley's authority was not what it had been. Such dissent didn't keep him awake at nights. The routines stayed the same as ever and he found ways of fitting the family in, if he could. On away trips to the Midlands, Bob would meet up with

Christine and her new husband Ian McMahon on the night before games. He was relaxed about discussing games and players. McMahon – a football enthusiast – would get the inside track on who was injured. It helped the relationship that Paisley's son-in-law was also keen on racing. Paisley's fierce loyalty to his players was no less evident on those occasions. One conversation with McMahon developed into a gentle questioning of Phil Neal's form. 'Well, he's won three European Cups,' Paisley said.

These remained difficult economic times for the supporters of Liverpool. The British invasion of the Falklands in the spring of 1982 could not paper over the economic realities on Merseyside. Over the course of three seasons there had been a 25 per cent reduction in attendances and it meant that times weren't exactly easy inside Anfield either. This was a full decade before the Premiership launched and the drop in gate receipts meant efforts were redoubled in the area of overseas friendlies, often with farcical results.

On one trip to Marbella, Liverpool were scheduled to play Real Betis and Malaga on consecutive days, with no day's break in the middle as they had been promised. There were also fewer beds at Liverpool's hotel than players. When David Hodgson missed a penalty in the shoot-out which would have extended the squad's stay, he was mobbed by his teammates.

Hodgson had struggled to make an impact. He'd scored nine goals in 37 appearances in his first season and was another in the anxious mould. He'd heard nothing from the management, and the lack of praise was hard to deal with. Once signed, he was left to his own devices.

It was Saunders who approached him after ten games, probably despatched by Paisley. 'Listen, you're the best player of your type here,' Saunders told him. 'Relax and enjoy yourself.' Within two years Hodgson had decided Anfield was not for him and left for Sunderland.

Paisley still looked for new strategies and systems. He was intrigued by the notion of operating with three central defenders – a version of the Italian *catenaccio* sweeper system – with Hansen and Lawrenson covering specific zones in the penalty area and Thompson operating behind them as the 'spare man' or sweeper. Paisley may have been influenced by Jock Stein, who was also interested in the idea and would also employ it for a European Championship qualifying tie in the December of that season.

It was not to be. Lawrenson felt Souness's dislike of the system put a stop to the idea. 'It upset the dynamic in midfield, where he ran the whole game. He hated it,' Lawrenson says. But a thigh injury to Hansen, which kept him out of the first seven league games of the 1982–83 season, also affected the system and even when the three were all operating together it didn't work, chiefly because Hansen struggled to adapt. Under the old flat back four system, he instinctively knew when to move forward into midfield – as the ball-playing defender he had become – and when to hold back and let others advance. The new system left him uncertain of when to stay and when to go.

The new team maintained its domestic predominance despite Paisley's impending departure. Liverpool were joint top when the Goodison Park derby approached in November, and Rush's confidence continued to soar. Rush and Paisley passed each other at Melwood a few days before the game. Paisley casually mentioned that no player had scored a hat-trick in the Merseyside derby for nearly 50 years. Rush scored four.

The intuition between Rush and Dalglish was helping. Rush scored another hat-trick in his next league game, against Coventry City, taking Liverpool to the top spot, which they never surrendered that season. By the time they met Everton again in mid-March, Liverpool were 14 points clear of Watford at the top.

The problems with Craig Johnston gradually abated. He felt he deserved more football than he was getting, having appeared in fewer than half the side's First Division games in 1981–82 and asked Paisley to put him on the transfer list. Paisley did so. There was no attempt to talk him around. The manager's indifference – probably calculated – motivated him, though, just as it had Rush. He appeared in 33 of the club's 42 fixtures the following season, as Liverpool finished 11 points clear of Watford, with 82 points.

Liverpool's supremacy was such that they clinched the title in April, on a day when they actually lost. While they were going down 2–0 at Tottenham, Manchester United could only draw away to Norwich, which ensured that Paisley's players could not be caught. It was their sixth championship in his nine seasons at the helm, won amid more of the late-season high jinks which had characterised their breeze 12 months earlier.

Souness recalls a Middlesbrough-type incident around that time before an away match. The players popped out for a lunchtime glass of wine and were still drinking at 5 p.m. 'There were one or two who would have struggled to pass the breathalyser test when we trotted out that night.'

The complacency was reflected in results. Liverpool did not win any of their last seven games. Paisley may have been in the twilight of his managerial career but he was not thrilled by this. He called his players into a meeting at one team hotel to demand greater intensity, and looked like he meant business when he pulled the curtains closed with a sharp tug on the cord. This brought the entire structure crashing down onto his head. The players could not contain themselves. 'I think even he saw the funny side,' says Souness.

Dalglish had contributed most in that last season, a factor recognised when he was named the Footballers' and Football Writers' Player of the Year. The cover of *Shoot!* magazine on 7 May 1983 featured Johnston, with the subsidiary headlines – 'Man City in turmoil' and 'Clough at the crossroads' – providing a reminder of how the challengers had fallen away.

There would be no fourth European Cup triumph for Paisley, however. Liverpool's campaign was ended by the Polish side Widzew Łódź at the third-round stage. The journey into Poland included the drama of Liverpool's Aer Lingus jet overshooting the short runway and requiring a second descent. That contributed to the old suspicions about continental travel that Paisley took into retirement.

The 2–0 defeat in Poland was followed by a challenging return home leg, which became even more difficult when Kenny Dalglish dropped out so late, through illness, that Paisley was a substitute short. The visitors led 2–1 with ten minutes to play and though there was the usual lack of panic from Liverpool, who played their passing game and won through late goals by Rush and Hodgson, it was too late.

There would be no FA Cup success, either. A Brighton side with Jimmy Case in its ranks put paid to those hopes. The 1977 final against Manchester United would be the closest Paisley ever got to the one prize which always eluded him.

It was the League Cup which afforded Paisley a Wembley valediction. 1982–83 was the competition's second year under the sponsorship of the Milk Marketing Board, and Liverpool and Manchester United contested the final of the Milk Cup. Paisley was by no means overwhelmed by any sentiment attached to his last journey to what chairman John Smith had described as 'Anfield South' over the years. He and Ron Atkinson, the United manager, were linked up for a three-way phone interview with the presenter of BBC Radio's *Sport on Four* at 8 a.m. on the morning of the final.

'Good morning, Bob. How are you feeling at this time of day?' Atkinson inquired.

'I'm OK, Ron,' Paisley replied. 'I've just got out of bed. But I suppose you have just got indoors.'

The game's flashpoint came when Bruce Grobbelaar dashed 35 yards out to halt the advance of United's Gordon McQueen, which upended the centre-half. Grobbelaar's tendency to experience a rush of blood had receded, though United felt he should have been dismissed. He was not and Liverpool won the game the way they had so many Cup ties under Paisley.

Phil Thompson, who missed the game through injury, described Liverpool's passing across the turf as akin to 'water dripping on a stone' and the newspapers saw it that way too. The *Daily Mirror*'s Frank McGhee wrote of 'the patience this team have learned over the years'. Souness, Whelan, Lee and Johnston were 'faultless' he said.

Norman Whiteside scored early for United but Liverpool's patience paid off when the indefatigable Alan Kennedy – as effective as ever in a game's closing stages with the ball at his feet – equalised 15 minutes from time. In extra-time, it was no contest. Ronnie Whelan, who had developed over two years into a player of vision, fine distribution and goals, bent in the winner. Paisley loved the way Whelan could play equally well with both feet.

The scenes on the pitch were much as they always were after Liverpool had won a trophy: euphoric players congratulating each other while Paisley padded around unobtrusively in their midst. An aspect of the celebrations was different this time, though. It would be Paisley's last appearance as manager at a stadium in which he had never climbed the steps to lift a trophy, and Souness quietly suggested to him in the moment that he might wish to lead the team up. 'I didn't need to ask twice,' Souness related much later.

Paisley left his cap behind, so his hair whipped up eccentrically in the wind as he clambered up the staircase, 33 years after watching from the stands as his teammates did so in the 1950 final from which he was excluded. He was perhaps five steps from the top when a scarf was draped across his left shoulder. That was when he laughed. It balanced there precariously as he reached the top, took the trophy and raised it aloft. It was when the players had descended that Souness, rather more familiar with this business, beckoned Paisley to join in the team group.

The image preserves his last triumph in perpetuity. Paisley stands at the edge of the group – top left, just as in those Liverpool team groups in the 1940s – and there could be no doubt now that this team, who had swept all domestic opposition aside since the New Year of 1981, were anything but his own. Only Fairclough – by now a bit-part player, who'd scored twice in a league match against Manchester City and still been on the bench for the next game – remains from the squad he inherited. It is striking how young so many of them in that team picture still look: Rush and Whelan were both 21, Johnston 22, Lee 24 and Grobbelaar 25. All still had so much spooling out ahead of them. Paisley placed a hand on the head of the player crouching in front of him, the one most akin to him – Alan Kennedy, the man still proving that the most important players are not necessarily the most technically proficient. For many, he had been Liverpool's man of the match once again that day. The players were singing a triumphal song, though Paisley did not join in. He just stood there straight-backed, a small man in a grey suit, light brown shirt and diagonal-stripe tie, still clutching the scarf that had been pressed into his hand.

The fans were singing the players' names, so the group parted ways. The players went in their direction. Paisley went in his.

It was on a post-season trip to Tel Aviv, where Liverpool were scheduled to play one of their regular friendlies with the Israeli national team, that Souness handed Paisley a carriage clock engraved with the words 'To Bob, from all the lads', though more chaos preceded the occasion.

The players' El Al flight out of Heathrow was scheduled for the night after the season's last league game, a 2–1 defeat at runners-up Watford, and the drinking started early – not least because Elton John, Watford's owner, encountered some of the squad at the airport and saw to it that they were treated to executive-class hospitality. A heavy drinking session was followed by a free day on the Sunday spent drinking in Tel Aviv's sun-baked main square, ahead of an appointed 5 p.m. rendezvous at the hotel. The players were worse for wear and some were better at handling it than others. A fight ensued between the players which left David Hodgson running to the team hotel for help to break it up and saw Alan Kennedy emerge with a black eye. The next day, Monday 16 May 1983, there was a presentation ceremony for the manager as a prelude to a 4–3 defeat at the Ramat Gan Stadium before 38,000 people which constituted Paisley's last 90 minutes at the helm.

'Have you been fighting?' Paisley asked Kennedy, who did not pretend to deny it.

'Bloody hell,' continued the manager. 'What gets into you?'

It didn't affect a ceremony which was evidently touching in its informality. 'There were tears in his eyes when we handed the clock across and that was unusual for him,' recalls Mark Lawrenson. 'The present we gave him could not have been more predictable but it didn't matter. He seemed to like it more because of that.'

14

AFTERWARDS

It was not easy to let go. The customary way for Bob Paisley to have stepped away would have been to have gathered his possessions – the gold carriage clock; the go-backwards clock; the photographs from his office – and begin to enjoy the life with Jessie that they had never had.

When Liverpool headed off for another gruelling post-season tour to Bangkok in the summer of 1983, it was suddenly Joe Fagan's territory. Fagan was the manager. Yet Paisley went along, too, chewing the fat with Graeme Souness and worrying about some of the financial details which really were none of his business.

The tour included a match sponsored by Seiko, who had put up $50,000 prize money for the winners. Liverpool's opponents were a Seiko XI which included a number of guest celebrity players, including Pat Jennings and Alan Sunderland, who were by then entering the twilight of their careers at Arsenal.

It was Souness, as captain, who collected the cheque and, having left the stadium quickly, found a bank to cash it before giving the players an equal share. Two young players had done well that day. Robbie Savage (no relation to the Welshman of the same name who would pass through Manchester United's academy) scored a volley which flew into the top corner of the net, and Steve Foley had also acquitted himself favourably. Souness wanted to ensure that they both got their winnings, though Paisley spotted him distributing their shares in cash and marched up.

'Where's the cheque?' asked Paisley, whose entire managerial career had involved helping the club on the commercial side. 'That's the club's money?' 'Upstairs' would not be happy.

However good their relationship, Souness was not handing it over. He approached the Seiko representative to ask who the money was for. It was the captain who got the answer he wanted, rather than the former manager. 'The team' came the reply, and that was good enough for everyone to head off and buy presents to take home. Paisley was furious.

As he held onto the club which he once said had been a 'drug' for him, his authority would be increasingly challenged and his apparent value diminish. Paisley was subtler than Shankly in the way he stayed about the place, and no one was unhappy to find him there, yet there are echoes of his predecessor's futile attempt to remain near the centre once he had gone.

It was reported that Brian Clough, Southampton's Lawrie McMenemy and Malcolm Allison, then at Middlesbrough, had all invited Paisley to take a look at their players and systems at close quarters and tell them what he had seen. 'If I spot something different then I'll be at liberty to offer them my opinions. I'll probably take them up on their kind offers,' he said. It was a diplomatic answer. He would never advise those whom Liverpool would be up against.

Fagan was happy to have Paisley still on the scene, and that included his old friend being present in the half-time dressing-room to offer occasional wisdom. Paisley would also be on the team bus for away games, though generally not in the same seat beside Fagan. No one took up the seat next to Paisley on the coach to London for a League Cup third round second replay in November

1983 at Fulham, three months into Fagan's first season. So it fell upon the *Daily Post* reporter Ian Ross – the local paper was still allocated a seat on the team coach for midweek away trips – to sit beside the old boss, as there were no other seats left.

Paisley was wearing odd socks, Ross noticed. With a three-hour journey ahead he decided he would attempt to strike up some conversation. But it was an unsuccessful venture. Paisley was as poor a conversationalist as ever with those he did not know well. To Ross he looked a marginal figure now.

It was only when the bus was pulling away in the direction of home, through the streets of London, that Paisley leapt up and shouted towards the driver. 'John,' he said, gesturing. 'That chippie there. That'll do us.' When the bus had pulled to the side of the road he issued instructions for 24 packets of cod and chips, with Ross included. The occupants of the bus fell silent as it pulled away again and they consumed the contents of their fish wrappers. Ross caught a glimpse of Paisley munching through his own fish supper, looking the soul of contentment.

The old routines were only maintained for a few more years. Though Paisley saw the side collect the 1984 European Cup in Rome, Fagan had gone by the following summer. The players who tuned into English television stations at their hotel in Brussels before the 1985 European Cup final – where Liverpool aimed to join the select group to claim that trophy five times and keep it – heard reports that Fagan would step down after the game. Nothing was mentioned at the training session which ensued. It was at a team meeting Fagan called, following lunch, that he told them, 'After tonight you can call me Joe.'

Fagan was only two years younger than Paisley, though that night at Heysel – one of Liverpool's darkest – aged him visibly. Liverpool fans breached a fence separating rival supporters and charged Juventus supporters, whose retreat towards a retaining wall in the Belgian stadium caused it to collapse, killing 39. The final went ahead anyway, as it was felt that further clashes would occur, and Liverpool lost 1–0.

The images of Fagan being helped across the runway at Liverpool's Speke airport after the team had returned from Brussels revealed a broken man – shattered by the tragedy. Yet the less publicised factor for his disinclination to go on was one that Paisley knew all about: the difficulty of dealing with disgruntled players knocking on his door to ask why they had not been picked. He confided in Robinson the dreadful struggle he was having with that.

Paisley's part in the commemorations that followed Heysel revealed again how far he had travelled. He assuredly read the first lesson at the Metropolitan Cathedral Mass held to mourn those lost – Isaiah 25 verses 6 to 9, 'the prophet's vision of external blessedness'.

There was no new manager stepping up from the Boot Room when Fagan walked away. Kenny Dalglish took over and for a time it seemed that this would presage a more significant role for Paisley again. The Liverpool board, concerned that the responsibility of playing and managing would be onerous for the 34-year-old, asked Paisley to return as 'adviser' to the Scotsman.

It had been two years since he had stepped down and he did not need any persuading to take the role, which seemed to be a significant one. Paisley sat next to Dalglish in the official team photograph for the 1985–86 season, though *Daily Post* photographer Stephen Shakeshaft, who was there that day, said the 66-year-old had been initially reluctant to be in the frame.

Almost from the start Dalglish – not unreasonably – wanted to do things his own way. The assuredness he'd always shown about how Liverpool should play was something Paisley had cherished in him, and that had never changed. It meant that Dalglish didn't much want anyone telling him what he might do.

Initially retaining most of the side Fagan had bequeathed him, Dalglish eclipsed both Shankly and Paisley by winning the First Division and FA Cup Double in 1985–6. The elder statesman continued to watch from the stand. He would see things he felt were wrong and head down to the dugout, as he always had, to point out changes that might be made. But he experienced the sense of what it is to be yesterday's man. His suggestions were not always appreciated in the Saturday afternoon mêlée of trying to ensure the Liverpool team won.

'Bob's appointment made sense,' says Roy Evans, who was on the bench with Dalglish. 'Kenny was inexperienced and Bob had all the knowledge, but there were little teething problems.' On those trips down to the dugout to offer a suggestion or two, Evans remembers, 'He was told to fuck off on more than one occasion. Basically, we'd all be in there trying to sort things out and the last thing we needed was someone else sticking their oar in or telling us what we already knew. We had no problems with him talking things over on the Monday at Melwood or whatever, and Kenny and everyone else had total respect for him. But on match days he needed to take a step back, as that's what this new advisory role was all about.'

There were no sacred cows and that was the way Paisley had always wanted it. Apart from spending the night at the team hotel before games on Fridays, he did not do much. It was Tom Saunders – the man bestowed on Paisley 21 years earlier – whom Dalglish found to be extremely useful, just as Paisley always had. He and Saunders became very close and – with precise echoes of what had evolved in the autumn of 1974 – Dalglish was keen to have Saunders in his own office.

When a journalist expressed surprise to find Saunders there one day, the former head teacher told him that Dalglish wanted him around to answer the telephone, because an empty office with no one to answer the calls might mean a transfer opportunity missed.

But Saunders's part in the transfer side of the business remained more significant than that. He and Dalglish often headed off to watch players together and when Saunders put it to Fagan's successor that the club were missing out on the lower league players they once signed and might perhaps watch some midweek matches together, he agreed. This suggestion saw them venture down the M6 to Crewe Alexandra one night, where they watched the full-back Rob Jones, who was signed in 1987 and became a player of huge promise before injuries curtailed his career.

Saunders, needless to say, rejected the idea he was some kind of adviser. 'No, I never offer any kind of advice,' he said. 'I never say, "Why don't you do this?" because people don't like that. I take messages and [Dalglish] will sometimes say to me, "Oh, what do you think about this?" And I'll say to him, "It's up to you, boss, but you might have seen that maybe he doesn't play well when we're playing away, or he's a bit left-sided." Or, "I think he may have got domestic troubles."' Those were precisely the kind of observations that Paisley would have made.

The games – any games – still absorbed Paisley. His son-in-law Ian McMahon ran the Derby School boys team, and when they played against Manchester Boys Paisley turned up. McMahon saw him before the game began and was naturally looking for any fragments of insight his father-in-law might have to impart. 'Are they your best XI?' Paisley wanted to know. 'Then just let them play.'

Derby were 1-0 up and had won a corner which most of the team advanced upfield for with seconds left, only to leave themselves exposed to a counter-attack at the death, from which Manchester scored. McMahon knew it had been a tactical mistake. 'What do you reckon, then?' Paisley asked the boys in the dressing-room at the end. He let them provide the answer.

There always seemed to be time to give for those he considered his own. One weekend, when McMahon's amateur team played against the Quarry Bank Old Boys, a Liverpool team who played close to the Paisley family home, Paisley gave the players a tour of Anfield and found some antiseptic powder for a knee injury his son-in-law was carrying.

But heaven help outsiders who might question his club. Young *Daily Post* journalist Chris Eakin was despatched to Anfield one day to 'doorstep' the management about claims that a young group of Juventus fans had arrived in an official capacity to see Anfield and remember those who had died in the Heysel Disaster. The fans said they had been afforded no welcome at Anfield and were refused access to the pitch but were treated more graciously when they walked down to Goodison Park.

Paisley was on the steps of a coach which was about to take the team out of Anfield when Eakin spotted him, but the ex-manager snapped at the reporter when approached. 'What do you expect us to do?' he asked Eakin, in an answer devoid of spin or sensitivity.

With his football involvement peripheral, Paisley threw himself into an extraordinary number of public appearances – guided and prompted on many occasions by Jessie. As proud of him as always, she carefully cut out articles chronicling his appearances in the most obscure publications – from the Liverpool's weekly free-sheet *Merseymart* to the *Coal News*. She stuck them into scrapbooks which, ever the teacher, she mounted with yellow paper and sometimes decorated with an image of her husband. *Bob's Scrapbook Number 7* and *Bob's Scrapbook Number*

8 cover these later years: the official opening of a new Liverpool Talking Newspaper studio; the national police 5-a-side football finals; the dedication of local churches; a Boys' Brigade march-past at which Paisley took the salute; the opening of Batley's Wholesale Market, at which Jessie snipped the tape; the Liverpool Prison football tournament. These all featured on the list of appearances.

There was an invitation to a Downing Street reception as guests of 'the Prime Minister and Mr Denis Thatcher'. Paisley was double-booked on that occasion, having already agreed to attend a 'Boxing–Dinner Evening' in his honour at the Piccadilly Hotel in Manchester, hosted by the Anglo-American Sporting Club, which was more his thing. So Margaret Thatcher had to wait.

The couple did eventually attend one of the Thatchers' receptions, though Paisley told Jessie that he didn't know how they had made it onto the guest list. They must have filled a 'space on the end of their list', he assumed. Paisley told Thatcher that she would 'always be welcome at Anfield' if she was visiting Liverpool but did not get the impression she was listening. 'We were standing up all the time and Bob didn't like it,' was Jessie's annotation to the invitation she kept.

They enjoyed far more the Monks Ferry Training Trust's workshop, on the Wirral peninsula, in the company of Prince Charles. 'Bob and I shook hands with the Prince of Wales and he had a conversation with Bob,' Jessie wrote.

Paisley always liked to accept invitations from his beloved north-east. There was the official opening luncheon of the Tyneside Summer Exhibition in July 1983; the North East Show; a Hartlepool United sportsman's dinner followed by official photographs of him with the club's committee men. Jessie kept them all. The suited and booted of Hartlepool look like they can hardly believe whose presence they are in.

It was an eclectic mix of appearances back on home turf. There was a 'Bob Paisley Question Time' in Newcastle upon Tyne, and the re-opening of Hetton-le-Hole's village hall, where Paisley tried his hand at bowls, as well as the unveiling of a plaque on the wall of the old Downs Lane house, in his honour.

The letters of thanks were almost as profuse. One man, who signed his letter 'Kopite', was so overwhelmed to have had a 'snap shot' taken with Paisley at Camp Hill, near the couple's home in Woolton, that he sent Paisley a copy, thanking him for having 'made my day'. The pattern on Paisley's brown cardigan belongs to the 1970s. Jessie faithfully pasted the photograph into the album.

Amid the more formal events – the Indo-British Association; the Royal Association for Disability and Rehabilitation's Men of the Year luncheon at the Savoy – there was the conferment of honours. Paisley became a Freeman of the City of Liverpool and was awarded a BSc in science by Liverpool University. He and Jessie stayed at the Swiss Cottage Holiday Inn – where the team had prepared for so many great occasions including the 1978 European Cup final – before he received the OBE. He was the star attraction on *Songs of Praise* from Liverpool's Catholic Metropolitan Cathedral on 5 January 1986. The *Radio Times* was more interested in host presenter Cliff Michelmore meeting Paisley than the city's bishop and archbishop. Jessie was bursting with pride. She cut out the *Radio Times* listing for the programme and pasted it in.

Paisley had clearly come to love travelling and flying in a way far removed from those wretched weeks in the United States just after the war. Sometimes he would travel abroad under his own steam, seizing invitations to discuss and spread his ideas about football. There was a two-week trip to Indonesia in February 1984, where he arrived on an Indonesian Airways flight at a wet Jakarta airport to be greeted by a guard of honour. He was snapped up for a number of coaching clinics and it was big news for the *Indonesia Times* who pictured him taking them. Paisley cuts a comical, almost colonial figure, in shorts, training top and eccentric black socks, barking out orders and pointing. A press conference followed in Jakarta, at which he suggested there should be another system of coaching in Asia in view of the players' shorter posture.

Within three months Paisley was touching down again in Israel, where he received another celebrity reception. His old defender Avi Cohen was among a large welcoming party at the airport and observing a training session at league leaders Beitar Jerusalem. He met the Israeli president Chaim Herzog, who flatly informed him that Cohen could have developed if Liverpool had only shown more patience. Paisley nodded diplomatically. He was not offended. He always liked Israel. 'They are good people,' he said, and he would have been the international manager there had his wanderlust stretched to that. The Turkish side Galatasaray also sought him out, though that was a proposition he could discount. 'I have discussed the offer with my wife and decided because of the distance and the fact that my wife doesn't like flying, it would not be feasible.'

But it was clearly football that Paisley hankered for. He continued to join Liverpool on their pre-season tours – perhaps aware that these events offered a time among the squad when he might fit in – to Norway, the Basque Country, Denmark and more. Kenny Dalglish occasionally found him a useful complementary figure in the overseas scouting role which Saunders still undertook for them. Paisley travelled with Saunders to Portugal in 1984 to watch Benfica. Liverpool played them four times that calendar year, after being drawn with them in consecutive European Cup competitions.

Paisley could be forgetful, though his old colleagues put that down to Bob being Bob. Before one of the Benfica away games, he and Robinson went to Portugal together to look at the accommodation and ensure preparations had been made. They had gone in separate cars for their flight out from Manchester airport and when they returned Paisley became adamant that his car had gone. 'Are you certain you parked there?' Robinson asked him. Paisley was insistent: 'It's gone,' he told Robinson. They walked around the airport car park maze, couldn't find it and eventually got hold of the Manchester airport security, who offered to drive them around in a further search. Paisley's car materialised in a matter of minutes. He had forgotten which floor he had put it on. It could happen to anyone, especially Paisley, who had always needed reminding when the next meeting was, though his demeanour seemed to have changed and he was certainly a little more withdrawn than before. There was mild concern at Anfield.

A change had certainly become faintly detectable when the only serious prospect of Paisley finding work beyond Liverpool materialised. It was 1986, the year after Dalglish had become manager, and the Football Association of Ireland (FAI) – possibly aware that Paisley's advisory role had turned out to be peripheral – approached him about the now vacant Republic of Ireland manager's job. It seemed like a good fit, because Paisley was becoming increasingly acquainted with the country – Jessie's fear of flying made the ferry trip from Liverpool one of the journeys they could both be comfortable with – and Paisley was well known from the almost annual exhibition matches Liverpool played in the country. He was also an ambassador for the Friendship Cup tournament, contested between Liverpool and Irish children.

The Irish national team were in disarray. A 4–1 home defeat to Denmark in November 1985 was the nadir. Only 15,000 attended the match and many of those were Danes, euphoric about their team's qualification for the 1986 World Cup – the Irish side's hopes had vanished weeks earlier.

Another who caught the Denmark game on television was Jack Charlton, who had been flicking through the channels when he came across the scoreline and wondered how a side with players as good as David O'Leary, Paul McGrath, Frank Stapleton and Mark Lawrenson in its ranks could have fared so poorly. 'I think they had about six centre-backs in the team,' Charlton later reflected.

Time had been lost in a stand-off between manager Eoin Hand, who was determined to stay on until the end of his contract, and the FAI, who had no money and were unwilling to pay the price of sacking him early. The FAI had run up accumulative losses of IR£90,000 for the two previous seasons and were struggling so badly to attract supporters for games that they had resorted to playing away from home. A sum of IR£13,000 had been lost on a friendly match at home to Poland, a 0–0 draw at Dalymount Park in May 1984.

Talk was turning to employing the Republic's first England-based manager, rather than Irish ex-players such as Hand. An advertisement for the post was placed in both the British and Irish press, which did not state whether the job would be full- or part-time, and the FAI's officials Des Casey and Tony O'Neill travelled to England to interview applicants. They met Charlton, who was enjoying his leisure time after walking out on Newcastle United, Johnny Giles, whose spell managing the Vancouver Whitecaps had not worked out, Manchester City's Billy McNeill, the former Arsenal and Northern Ireland manager Terry Neill, former Everton manager Gordon Lee and the one-time Manchester United and Scotland player Pat Crerand.

City chairman Peter Swales refused to release McNeill, Giles dropped out because of negative press reaction about his reputation for square-ball football and both Crerand and Lee were discounted by the FAI, so it became a two-horse race between Charlton and Liam Tuohy, under whose leadership the Irish youth team had prospered.

By the time the FAI's executive committee gathered at 8 p.m. on 7 February 1986 for the potentially decisive meeting, the discussions had become intensely political. Giles had undergone a change of heart and decided he wanted to be considered after all, while camps had coalesced around Charlton and Tuohy, with the latter commanding considerable influence. Then FAI President Des Casey put forward the name of a new candidate, known as the 'Fourth Man'. It was Paisley.

The Irish had approached him the previous year but the story got out into the newspapers, to Paisley's embarrassment. They had tried him again after Hand had resigned but received no further encouragement. But now there was a clear change of heart from Paisley. The FAI executive committee meeting heard that the former Liverpool manager was not worried about the salary but wanted to know who his assistant would be. Most of all, he wanted to avoid any embarrassment of the kind that had been caused when his name had previously been linked to the job. Paisley never liked attention.

Some committee members were hostile to the idea of Paisley, feeling that they were being press-ganged into the appointment by Casey bringing his name to the table so late. Yet Paisley was in a very strong position. An absolute majority of ten or more votes was required to secure selection as manager, with Des Casey having the casting vote. In the first ballot, Paisley secured nine votes while Charlton, Tuohy and Giles received three each. Paisley required just one more vote.

305

Back in Liverpool, there were concerns among some of Paisley's old colleagues that the change in his demeanour might be a cause of difficulty if he were appointed manager of the Irish national team. At least one informal phone call was made from Anfield, cautioning the FAI that Paisley may not be the same manager they thought he was. Yet this did not seem to have made any material difference. His name was added to the shortlist. The committee's discomfort with the way Paisley was brought in so late proved the critical factor, however. Tuohy was eliminated in a second ballot and a third vote still left Paisley one short of the required ten, Charlton on five and Giles eliminated with four. In the straight run-off between Charlton and Paisley, one of those who had initially voted for Paisley now switched, while the Giles support base transferred to Charlton. Paisley had dropped to eight, while Charlton had climbed to the necessary ten. Charlton, who might have beaten Paisley to the Liverpool job in 1974 had Bill Shankly's suggestion been acted upon, reversed things now.

It has never been entirely clear who switched allegiance, though journalist Charlie Stuart, writing in the *Irish Press*, identified Colonel Tom Ryan, who was aide-de-camp to the Irish President Patrick Hillery and officially the Army's representative on the FAI, as the obscure figure who stood between Paisley and the job.

Paisley said he was sure Charlton would do a good job. 'If I could, I would have loved to have helped,' he said a few months later. Charlton was less charitable when the question of Paisley's challenge dominated his own inaugural press conference. He bridled at the line of questioning. 'They [were] going on about Bob Paisley and how he didn't get the job and the way my appointment was made,' Charlton reflected in his autobiography.

'Now, this is all news to me. Apparently, there had been some controversy in Ireland about the way the thing had been handled but when Bob Paisley's name was introduced that evening, it was genuinely the first occasion that I was made aware that he'd been a candidate. And I wasn't particularly interested anyway. So when this guy is rabbiting on, I stop and tell him some basic facts. I don't give a damn how I got the job. The pertinent thing is that now I have it – and, for better or worse, he'd better get used to the idea.'

The decision marked the end of any prospect of Paisley taking up another managerial position. The Welsh FA secretary Alun Evans used Liverpool chairman John Smith as an intermediary when he wanted to approach Paisley about the vacant Wales manager's job early in 1988, following Mike England's sacking after eight years in the role. Evans had been 'badgering' Smith about Paisley at a lunch, and it was not the first time Wales had expressed an interest, Smith said. 'I told him to put it in writing.'

There were good reasons for Smith to stall. The changes in Paisley had become more manifest. He still wanted to come to games, though his response to the many people who would press themselves upon him tended to entail him just smiling at them. People took that as him agreeing with them, though it became increasingly clear to those he knew that he was not as he was. He was making no contribution at meetings.

Jessie may also have realised that managing Wales could have bad consequences when her husband's mind was not maintaining the threads. There was talk in the family of how she had put a stop to him taking that job.

Paisley was one of a number of candidates to be interviewed by the Welsh before the position was given to Terry Yorath. Paisley's return to the helm of a side came only in a one-off commemorative game. He took charge of a combined Liverpool and Juventus side to face a Northern League XI for a game to mark the centenary of Newcastle United.

Paisley's role at Anfield became even more marginal. He no longer took a seat on the coach to away games, as Dalglish had decided that he wanted that to be the preserve of a tighter group of players. Bob undertook duties where he could at Melwood, but his light training session with some of the club's injured young players in October 1986 left him suffering a broken ankle. He'd only realised there was a problem when he got to his feet to answer a telephone after lunch, he said. A few months later, Paisley's two-year contract as adviser to Dalglish was not extended. The Glaswegian Paisley had signed in the summer of 1977 was his own man now.

Paisley was not. Four years from his departure, he had taken to making outspoken public pronouncements. This was not the individual they had known. In November 1986 Phil Neal incurred his wrath in the *Daily Mirror*. Neal's departure from Anfield for Bolton Wanderers in 1985 had been acrimonious on his part because he was convinced that he, not Dalglish, would and should have succeeded Fagan. Neal's second ghostwritten autobiography, *Life at the Kop*, was more critical of Liverpool than any other written by a Shankly or Paisley player.

Paisley said that Neal, as well as Chris Lawler and Geoff Twentyman, with whom Dalglish had also parted company, should 'stop bellyaching and biting the hand which fed [them] for so long.' If Liverpool 'was such a bad club, why had they stayed for so long?' he asked. Neal and the others had let the fans down, he said. 'Football is their only escape from the poverty and deprivation in an area of massive unemployment.' This was written up by the *Mirror*'s Chris James – one of the five Merseyside reporters Paisley trusted and who knew what was on and off limits. James seemed to believe that the public attack on Neal and others was intentional.

A little over a year later there was another broadside railing at the poor standard of First Division football. Paisley was invited to speak at a young player of the month award ceremony on Merseyside at a time when the team were 15 points clear at the top of the First Division, yet he chose to say that Dalglish's side were 'aided and abetted by the poorest First Division I have seen in my years in the game'.

John Aldridge, who was signed by Dalglish in 1987, incurred Paisley's criticism in another piece. Paisley complained that 'there isn't a great deal of talent around' and that clubs no longer did enough scouting. Paisley appeared to have become bitter. Aldridge felt a particular distress, which Liverpool tried to smooth over. In 1988, the two met up and the club ensured there was a photographer on hand in the dressing-room to capture the moment. That encounter troubled Aldridge, though. Paisley's train of thought seemed confused and he was repeating himself. Paisley's attempts to explain himself didn't much help. 'It's completely stupid because all I did was give my honest opinion about Aldridge's playing ability,' Paisley said, as if that put it right. 'I merely said I wouldn't have bought Aldridge and expressed the view that although he is a good goalscorer he has his limitations.'

A far bigger controversy lay around the corner. On 28 February 1989, the *Daily Mirror*'s sports pages were dominated by what it described as the first of a two-part revelatory interview with Paisley. He had been speaking loosely and expansively again, though this time in a far more damaging way, which threatened his entire relationship with Liverpool. Contacted by the journalist Ted Macauley, he gave a withering assessment of the Liverpool side which was fifth in the table and nine points adrift of leaders

Arsenal at the time. It was all profoundly embarrassing. The *Mirror* sought to demonstrate that it had acted professionally, quoting its chief sports photographer Albert Cooper, who was a witness to the interview. 'It seemed he had something to get off his chest,' Cooper said of Paisley.

It was painful for Robinson to see what had happened to Paisley, the manager he had hired, helped and whom he could call an old friend. On reflection, he suspected that the Macauley call had been received by the Liverpool switchboard, who were asked for Paisley's number and that direct contact had thus been established. 'You've got to be very careful and let us know if anybody else approaches you,' Robinson told Paisley. He encouraged him to let Tom Saunders know if other requests for interviews were made. 'Yes,' Paisley replied.

Paisley was asked to attend an Anfield board meeting, at which he was told he must not give any interviews in the future. He apologised and offered his resignation. The board said that was not necessary.

The embarrassment was compounded by the fact that a second part of the *Mirror* interview was published on the day of the board meeting, which stretched to three and a half hours. The second piece, headlined: 'Be Ruthless, Kenny', had Paisley saying that Liverpool were 'not the team they were', 'not good enough', and that it would take major investment to put them back. It was the personal nature of the attacks which ran against the grain. Paisley identified Alan Hansen and his last signing as manager, Jim Beglin, as players whose long-standing injuries means that Dalglish should sell them now, as there was 'no room for sentiment' and Kenny couldn't 'afford to let his heart rule his head'. The running style of Beglin was a problem, he believed, while 'Hansen is 33 and time is against him', Paisley continued. 'He was down to play a few days ago but cried off because he was not up to it. Alan's brother quit at 25 with a back injury and it was always in the back of his mind that it was a problem that ran in the family. I couldn't get the fear out of his head and we sent him to specialists all over the country to put his mind at rest but [that] didn't seem to make a difference.'

There were also personal critiques of three others he thought were not good enough: Gary Gillespie, Barry Venison and Kevin MacDonald, who had all been signed by Dalglish.

Some of the observations were valid. Hansen also felt that MacDonald was not up to the level. Beglin's career was, indeed, over, and he did not come back from injury. Venison was in and out of the team and not of the old Liverpool standard. But Paisley's comments were wild and factually wrong. It was knee trouble, not back problems, which were plaguing Hansen at the time and had prematurely ended the career of his brother, John. Hansen recovered from the problem to play a significant role in the 1989–90 season, when Liverpool won the First Division by nine points, and Gillespie remained a significant player.

Dalglish made it clear that he could not accept what Paisley had said. 'He was instrumental in bringing me here,' he told journalists at the time. 'Anyone connected with [the club] must respect his achievements, but at the same time I could not condone the articles that appeared in the newspaper.'

Paisley's mind was failing, though. When the replicas of the three European Cups he had won were taken out for him to be photographed with by a local photographer, to accompany an article for the Anfield match programme, he couldn't identify their significance. 'What are these?' he asked.

The *Mirror* episode effectively brought to an excruciating and ignominious end Paisley's relationship with the club he had devoted precisely 50 years of his life to. The family's first clear realisation that his mind was beginning to fray came two months after the *Mirror* articles, at the time of the birth of a grandchild – Christine's daughter Kirsty – in Derby.

Paisley drove Jessie to the Midlands, though on the way home he stopped the car and asked her which way he should go. Jessie was concerned. He had made the journey scores of times when Christine had been at college in Derby and could not understand why he had forgotten now.

The next trip across to Derby was for Kirsty's christening. It was arranged that old friends of the Paisleys, Jim and Edith, would drive so that he would not have to. Jim hurt his hand before they set off, so Paisley had to drive after all, though his friend sat in the passenger seat, quietly ensuring they reached their destination.

All this brought about a greater retreat into family life, where Paisley discovered, as a grandfather, all that he had missed out on as a father by spending so much time away.

There was an indoor slide at the Bower Road house which Paisley kept for the children to jump onto, and a rocking horse, though it was the impromptu 'horse races' that his seven grandchildren – Jane, Julie, Carol, Helen, Rachael, Stuart and Kirsty – also remember well. Paisley and sons Graham and Robert would get down on all fours and a child would jump on each of their backs for the race across the floral carpet, with the pair on the left needing to avoid a collision with the stool of Jessie's piano.

There were *Mr Men* books to be read to the grandchildren as they sat on Paisley's knee – 'Little Granddad', they called him. Jessie had a big chess set with brass pieces that would be fetched out. There was snakes and ladders, with Paisley making them laugh by counting in Spanish, and sessions on Jessie's electric organ, with Paisley attempting to teach the grandchildren his party piece – 'Amazing Grace'.

Paisley's routines also entailed picking up Graham's younger daughter, Rachael, from nursery. There was some hilarity when he pushed Christine and Ian's son Stuart through the park in Derby and was recognised by a passing stranger. 'I know you,' she said. 'Aren't you the butcher from Mansfield?' Paisley was tickled. And there would be times, on Sunday afternoons, when Paisley, Graham and Robert would disappear to the snooker table that was upstairs.

Paisley also returned to some of their old routines from after the war. He was once again a regular figure with Jessie at Woolton parish church. They spent time with old friends. A German schoolteacher whom Jessie had met years ago, Wolfgang, often corresponded, and though more Jessie's friend than his, Paisley had always found him companionable. Germany interested him because he had always found something appealing about their football methodology. Wolfgang and his wife Christa visited.

His recollections and memory were fading, though, to the point that Jessie and the children worried deeply. The reality struck Christine when he and Jessie came to stay with her in Derby, while her husband was away in America. 'Will there be a time when he doesn't remember me?' Christine asked her mother. That moment came with an enormous inevitability.

In 1993, the journalist Stan Hey, through whom Paisley had articulated so eloquently his methods and philosophy, wrote to Paisley, hoping for contributions to a piece he was writing for the *Observer* to mark the end of the standing terrace at Anfield's famous old Kop. Jessie wrote back to confirm that Alzheimer's disease had, sadly, wiped away all memory of his achievements.

Dealing with the erratic and chaotic consequences of Alzheimer's became very difficult and the couple's lives became unrecognisable from those they had enjoyed in Paisley's comparatively brief retirement.

In early 1996, the challenge for Jessie of caring for her husband became too great and Paisley took up residence in the Arncliffe Court Nursing Home, two miles from their home. She visited every day, sometimes collected from the Bower Road house by Dick Harper, a friend of the club who had taken up the Bob Rawcliffe role of supplying cars, and the children attended almost as often. Their husband and father was almost entirely lost to them, though. While some struck down by this affliction are confused and deprived of short-term memory, Paisley's powers of speech had gone entirely, and that made visiting a difficult and awkward experience for some. Few players, if any, visited, which was a source of occasional sadness to Jessie, though there was an understanding that it would be uncomfortable for all but the close family.

Jessie had a photograph of him with the First Division trophy placed on the wall of her husband's airy room there. One day early in 1996 she took a photograph, which captures him listening to music from a cassette recorder, stooped in his seat and unrecognisable from the man his many players remembered. He was smart, his hair slicked back as always. 'A final photograph. Dearest Bob, listening to music at Arncliffe Court Nursing Home,' Jessie wrote in her annotation. He died at 9.30 a.m. on 14 February 1996.

A letter from the Bishop of Liverpool, the Rt Rev. David Sheppard, acknowledged more than any the desperate sadness of what had been an incremental loss. 'I know that Bob has been so ill for a long time and, in a sense, you had lost him already,' he wrote to Jessie. 'But death makes you realise what a gap there now is. I know how patiently and caringly you have supported Bob.'

There were perhaps 500 letters to Jessie – very many of them handwritten, hundreds from supporters, dozens more from those who followed other clubs, and some from those who saw Paisley as representative of a football era devoid of the noise and ego which had increasingly engulfed it. One arrived from the nephew of a British missionary priest, explaining an encounter with Paisley years earlier, when he had been making his way as manager. The priest, in his seventies, had made Mauritius his home and place of work and had briefly returned to Liverpool in the 1970s, prompting his nephew to write to the club, enclosing a cheque in a letter addressed to Paisley, explaining the circumstances and asking that tickets for the team's forthcoming match against West Bromwich Albion might be found for the two of them.

Two months later and a week before the game in question, the cheque was returned by the club's ticket office with a standard letter explaining the match was sold out. The nephew was angry and had fired off another letter to Paisley. Two days later, Paisley called the correspondent directly, explaining that the original letter had not reached him, had probably been forwarded straight to the Liverpool ticket office and that he had secured two tickets for the game if they were still wanted. The correspondent insisted on paying. Paisley refused. So they settled on the money being paid to charity instead.

The day after the game, the clergyman decided to deliver a letter of thanks in person to Paisley, and precisely as he reached the club car park, the Liverpool manager emerged from the main entrance. The man approached, handed over the letter with brief thanks, and turned to go. 'You must be the priest from Mauritius,' Paisley said, to his overwhelming surprise. He invited him into his office for a cup of tea, where they talked about the Liverpool of old, football and (the nephew thought) World War II tanks. When a stranger's interests conformed with Paisley's he could put his shyness aside and the warmth came through.

The old man returned to Mauritius the following week and died before the next football season began. The letter described the same Paisley that managers and coaches had known down the decades – instinctively reserved and sometimes awkward, yet modest and self-effacing and ready to hear, converse and collect knowledge with those to whom he could relate. In that sense, Paisley was a conversationalist, though most of his players would laugh at such a notion.

The letters to Jessie from the football community filled two scrapbooks and spilled into a third, and these were the ones which told the story of Paisley known to the world he had occupied. They came from almost all of those rival clubs who must have cursed him and his methods across the course of his nine years at the top of the game. If Nottingham Forest sent one, then it missed Jessie's system, but there were letters from the two Manchester clubs, Everton, Leeds, Arsenal, Leicester and Coventry – and their collective sentiment provides the most powerful epitaph to Britain's most successful football manager. 'The most modest person I think I have ever met,' wrote Arsenal's managing director. Leicester's secretary told of the 'good humour' they loved and of the Bob Paisley 'smile' amid the inestimable success. 'His loss will be felt,' said Leicester. 'A great ambassador for your famous club and for us all,' said Stoke City.

The football community respected, acknowledged and marvelled at Paisley's success, but it was the modesty and humility in the midst of that – proof that the quiet man can win through – which astonished them all. That's what they wanted to say.

EPILOGUE

They gathered outside the church under a leaden winter sky, 15 years on from the days when they had thought themselves invincible. Unconsciously, they eased back into some of those old groups that they'd once established at the training ground and stadium, five miles north across the city.

The 'Jocks' – Alan Hansen, Kenny Dalglish and Graeme Souness – seemed to form the same tight knot as ever. Tommy Smith and Joe Fagan – who'd first laughed and argued together in the Shankly days – walked through the churchyard in conversation. They were there to see Bob Paisley laid to rest, though not all of the old squad were present. The most prominent faces in the images and press cuttings of the day that Jessie Paisley kept were the ones he had picked for his teams again and again.

That was no coincidence. They were the individuals who could say they felt warmth and affection for Paisley, but not so all of those who played for him down the years. The outside world remembered the modesty, humility and humour, which were all certainly abundant in Paisley. But on the inside – the place where it matters and where the winning was planned – Paisley was hard: unflinchingly, ruthlessly hard. An individual so uncompromising when it came to football that, with little or no explanation, he would drop players, or sell them or leave them looking for encouragement that never came. That's why he remained 'the Rat' to many of them and why some struggled to say that they liked him.

Attempting to piece together the story of this life has revealed those mixed feelings. In the early stages of research for this book, word came back from those who know Liverpool inside out that some people didn't care much for Bob Paisley. Not all would want to talk. It proved to be so.

It didn't help his popularity that Paisley's way with players was inconsistent, according to how well they played football. Those in whom he put most faith, like Souness, Dalglish and Hansen, could do no wrong. Others would step in when they were injured and do a good job but as soon as there was a hint that the absent player's affliction was dealt with they would be back out in the cold again. A half-fit Souness, Dalglish or Hansen was preferable to a fully fit anyone else.

The thread running through every selection decision was the question of whether a player was more likely to make his team win. The cap, the cardigan and the slippers were surface details. The quiet and undemonstrative exterior obscured a fiercely analytic interior mind, furiously computing how to win.

Lawrie McMenemy, the former Southampton manager, was as enthusiastic as anyone in response to the request for a discussion on Paisley for this book. He loved Paisley's lack of pretention and absorption in the game and his good grace when battle was done. He found a glass of Scotch and conversation awaiting him when he stepped into the Boot Room. But the most telling part of his testimony relates to the game at Anfield which Southampton won 1–0 during that hard autumn of 1981. The Liverpool bench gave him dog's abuse. 'I always thought they were the worst losers,' he said. 'We had the temerity to go there and win . . . and the abuse I got was unbelievable. I remember asking a policeman to go and tell them to calm down. And as soon as the game was over they shook hands. It was as if it had never happened. They congratulated me, praised the side and so on. Amazing. They couldn't have been more friendly.'

Brian Clough saw all this, too. Decent, modest, warm when the moment was right – Paisley was all of those things. 'But he knows how to be hard without being too loud,' Clough said, just after his adversary had retired. 'He's as hard as nails and as canny as they come.'

It takes courage to be tough in the way that Paisley was tough because it does not invite the embrace of players, who will then cut you very little slack if things go wrong. There is little margin for error. You must get the decisions right. Jamie Carragher, the former Liverpool defender and one of the shrewdest assessors of the club, sees Paisley's success through this prism. 'You always try to get to the bottom of the secrets of success and you look at this quiet man and how's he done this,' Carragher says. 'You look at how ruthless he was, making those big decisions. It's OK making big decisions for as long as you keep getting them right.'

Paisley got them right because he spoke less and listened more. None of the greats of management incorporated the views and intelligence of others quite as he did. Boot Room companions, opponents, players, players' teachers – if there was someone he thought might offer an angle, then Paisley wanted to hear it. It meant that he could strip away everything and look for the tactical patterns of football, the players and combinations which could best deliver success, and pinpoint weaknesses in opponents.

He got more of the decisions right than Bill Shankly, yet because Shankly built the platform from which everything rose, he was the one they remembered. It was in early 1997, nearly a year on from Paisley's death, that Carragher made his own Liverpool debut and even then – only 13 years after the last of Paisley's six titles – Shankly's was the name you tended to hear around the place. 'You very rarely heard anyone mention Bob Paisley,' Carragher says. 'A lot of it was "Shanks". It was maybe every few weeks it would come up: a laugh or a joke and maybe someone saying, "That's what Shanks said." You felt a lot of everything we were doing was the imprint of Bill Shankly.'

When Brendan Rodgers became manager in 2012, it was Shankly's work he studied and whose memory he invoked. When charismatic Jurgen Klopp arrived to take up the same seat in 2015, comparisons with Shankly almost inevitably abounded once more.

This had something to do with the way Paisley retained what Shankly put in place. That requires modesty. Ego tells you to strip it all away and build some acclaim. Carragher found so many of the Shankly ways, though: still the five-a-sides; still the 'no one bigger than the team' mantra . . . the pass and move . . . the ban on bread rolls.

It was Paisley's modification of the team for Europe which Carragher finds most tactically interesting. He 'narrowed' the team, removing the wingers and populating central areas with midfielders who could be relied on to get the job done in distant corners of Europe. It sounds like the most incidental of changes but the results it began delivering were seismic and almost instantaneous. The success that followed in the 1980s has almost obscured how many trophies Paisley actually won in his first five years. 'I remember first looking at what they did between 1976 and 1978,' says Carragher. 'The league and UEFA Cup in '76; the league and the European Cup in '77; and the European Cup in '78 – three European trophies and two league titles in three years. It takes some beating, that . . .'

Paisley had certainly built a side to flourish beyond his time at the helm and would surely have reattained the giddy heights of 1977 had he heeded Peter Robinson's plea and stayed on for another year. The team, managed by Joe Fagan, which won a fourth European Cup against Roma on their Italian home soil in May 1984 was entirely of Paisley's making and, with the exception of Michael Robinson's addition to the goal-scoring ranks, it was entirely Paisley's team that won the league that season, too. With the system so engrained, it felt like Liverpool could go on for another generation.

It was telling what Fagan struggled with most: how to deal with disgruntled players, knocking on his door to ask why they had not been picked. The strategy Paisley had adopted – ignore them and they will hopefully go away – might not have been popular but it allowed him to sleep at night.

But the seamless process of replacing a manager from within could not go on forever. Kenny Dalglish continued the tradition, even as the collectivist principles were beginning to fray. The demolition of the Boot Room during Graeme Souness's reign was more symbolic than significant, but by seeking to impose more continental methods, Souness alienated players and supporters. Roy Evans was brought in to provide a link back to the past, yet he did not have what Paisley had. Carragher feels it was impossible for Evans to change the image he had among the older professionals as a 'nice guy'. 'Between 1994 and 1998, Liverpool were respected and "nice" to watch, but they didn't have the steel needed to take the step to a higher level. The philosophy that had made the club so strong and proud took a pounding. A new wave of "celebrity" footballers plagued the club, threatening the most important bond of all – the respect between players and fans.'

Some of the ideas the Frenchman Gérard Houllier brought in 1998 – massages; meals at Anfield after the game to nurture a sense of togetherness – created an element of scepticism among the old guard, though the Houllier culture was not so different, especially when it came to playing in Europe. 'Togetherness, being difficult to beat, playing when we had to. A lot of the things that were always said were then being said in a different voice,' says Carragher.

Fundamental change was inevitable, though. The salaries were becoming huge, the squads international – populated with continental players who trained differently and simply could not be fed the old diet of British working-class football socialism. 'It's like everything in life: it comes to a certain point where you have to move on and that's what Liverpool had to do, really,' says Carragher.

It was Paisley's attention to small detail which struck Rick Parry, who arrived at the club as chief executive in 1998, by which time Manchester United had established a financial advantage over the club and won four Premier League titles. 'It was all about doing the little things well, while splashing out the odd million here or there, with the financial differential between Liverpool and the rest being comparatively minuscule,' Parry says. 'Paisley saw the need to empower people and how, if you've got great players, there's a lot to be said for letting them get on with it and keeping it simple.'

Relatively few managers appear to have seen this light. Parry cites Claudio Ranieri's accession to the Leicester City management seat, where the Italian was comfortable enough in his own skin to make relatively few changes, and Vicente del Bosque, whose Spanish side ascended to a 2010 World Cup and 2012 European Championship with a light touch. Carlo Ancelotti – the only manager to have clinched three European Cups as Paisley has – is another. 'Football is the most important of the less important things,' he has said. 'It's important that the manager sometimes *doesn't* speak about certain things and isn't responsible for every detail.'

To the end Jessie was Paisley's greatest and most indefatigable enthusiast. She maintained her chronicle of his achievements, compiling six scrapbooks containing 'Memories of Bob'. A brochure published for the Liverpool shareholders' annual general meeting in 1996, the year Paisley died, included a list of the club's honours. Jessie underlined and marked those which her husband had delivered and annotated it: 'Bob's achievements marked with a tick.' The *Independent*'s obituary that month included a typographical error and the suggestion that Paisley had been afflicted with Parkinson's disease, not Alzheimer's. She amended both mistakes in ink.

Some of Paisley's players tried their hand at management but more struggled than succeeded. Phil Neal, convinced he would succeed Fagan in 1985 and devastated when he didn't, had a shot with Bolton Wanderers and Coventry City but it came to nothing. There were brief and unsuccessful spells at Oxford United and Peterborough United for Mark Lawrenson. Sammy Lee also had an unhappy time at Bolton. Souness did see Liverpool to the 1992 FA Cup, though it was at Blackburn Rovers, whom he restored to the First Division and brought a League Cup, where his management has been best remembered. Of Paisley's players only Kenny Dalglish, keeper of the Liverpool managerial flame, and Kevin Keegan, a saviour at Newcastle, could be genuinely called a success.

When Souness became manager, acceding to the role he first learned about from Paisley in Bob Rawcliffe's garage back in the early 1980s, he stood at the frosted window in his office, in front of the radiator where they had always joked about their boss warming his balls. There was hardly a day when Paisley and his methods did not come back to mind and when he wondered how on earth the old man had done it. One day, in the depths of the losing battle Souness faced in rediscovering the success that Paisley had delivered, Tom Saunders wandered in.

'Did Duggie ever realise what he had with that group of players of ours?' Souness asked him.

There was a moment's thought before the answer came. 'He was never happy,' Saunders said. 'He always wanted to improve on what was there.' It seems significant that Souness – Paisley's captain and sometime confidant – needed to search for an understanding of why he had so thrived. Paisley barely spoke of his methods, let alone shouted about them. He moved almost invisibly, absorbed by the only task that really mattered: picking a winning team.

'Football is a simple game, messed up by managers and players,' he once told his players, in a characteristically brief team meeting which his striker David Johnson always remembered vividly. 'Get the ball. Pass the ball. Keep the ball. But if you overcomplicate it you are going to meet yourself coming back.' At the end of it all, the secret of football's quiet genius and his most extraordinary success was no more and no less than that.

BIBLIOGRAPHY

Bowler, Dave, *Shanks: the Authorised Biography of Bill Shankly* (Orion, 1996)

Cain, Susan, *Quiet: the Power of Introverts in a World That Can't Stop Talking* (Penguin, 2012)

Callaghan, Ian, *Cally on the Ball* (Sport Media, 2014)

Carragher, Jamie, *My Autobiography* (Bantam Press, 2008)

Case, Jimmy, *Jimmy Case, My Autobiography* (John Blake, 2015)

Charlton, Jack, *The Autobiography* (Partridge, 1996)

Clemence, Ray, *Clemence on Goalkeeping* (Lutterworth/Richard Smart, 1977)

Cormack, Peter, *From the Cowshed to the Kop, My Autobiography* (Black &White Publishing, 2012)

Dalglish, Kenny, *Dalglish, My Autobiography* (Hodder & Stoughton, 1996)

Docherty, Tommy, *The Doc, Hallowed be Thy Game, My Story* (Headline, 2006)

Dohren, Derek, *Ghost on the Wall: the Authorised Biography of Roy Evans* (Mainstream, 2004)

Fagan, Andrew and Platt, Mark, *Joe Fagan, Reluctant Champion: the Authorised Biography* (Aurum, 2012)

Fairclough, David, *Supersub: the Story of Football's Most Famous Number 12* (De Coubertin, 2015)

Ferguson, Alex, *Managing My Life, My Autobiography* (Coronet, 2000)

Gayle, Howard, *61 Minutes in Munich: the Story of Liverpool FC's First Black Footballer* (De Coubertin, 2016)

Goldblatt, David, *The Ball is Round: a Global History of Football* (Viking, 2006)

Grobbelaar, Bruce, *More than Somewhat* (Willow, 1996)

Hansen, Alan, *A Matter of Opinion* (Partridge, 1999)

Hamilton, Duncan, *Provided You Don't Kiss Me: 20 Years with Brian Clough* (HarperCollins, 2007)

Hey, Stan, *A Golden Sky: the Liverpool Dream Team* (Mainstream, 1997)

Hughes, Emlyn, *Crazy Horse* (Arthur Barker, 1980)

Hughes, Simon, *Geoff Twentyman: Secret Diary of a Liverpool Scout* (Sport Media, 2009)

Hughes, Simon, *Red Machine: Liverpool FC in the 1980s, the Players' Stories* (Mainstream, 2003)

Johnston Craig with Jameson, Neil, *Walk Alone: the Craig Johnston Story* (William Collins, 1989)

Jones, Joey, *Oh Joey, Joey: My Life in Football* (John Blake, 2005)

Kay, Oliver, *Forever Young: the Story of Adrian Doherty, Football's Lost Genius* (Quercus, 2016)

Keegan, Kevin, *Kevin Keegan* (Arthur Barker, 1977)

Keegan, Kevin, *Kevin Keegan, My Autobiography* (Warner, 1997)

Keith, John, *Bob Paisley: Manager of the Millennium* (Robson, 1999)

Kelly, Stephen, *The Boot Room Boys: Inside the Anfield Boot Room* (Collins Willow, 1999)

Kennedy, Alan and Williams, John, *Kennedy's Way: Inside Bob Paisley's Liverpool* (Mainstream, 2005)

Lees, Dr Andrew and Kennedy, Ray, *Ray of Hope: the Ray Kennedy Story* (Pelham, 1993)

Lloyd, Larry, *Hard Man, Hard Game* (John Blake, 2008)

Macpherson, Archie, *Jock Stein: the Definitive Biography* (Highdown, 2004)

McGarvey, Frank, *Totally Frank: the Frank McGarvey Story* (Mainstream, 2008)

Neal, Phil, *Attack from the Back* (Arthur Barker, 1981)

Neal, Phil, *Life at the Kop* (Queen Anne/Futura, 1986)

Paisley, Bob, *An Autobiography* (Arthur Barker, 1983)

Paisley, Bob, *My 50 Golden Reds* (Front Page, 1990)

Paisley Family, the, *The Real Bob Paisley* (Sport Media, 2007)

Platt, Mark, *Liverpool: Cup Kings 1977* (Bluecoat, 2003)

Robson, Bobby, *Farewell But Not Goodbye, My Autobiography* (Hodder & Stoughton, 2005)

Rowan, Paul, *The Team That Jack Built* (Mainstream, 1994)

Rush, Ian, *Rush, the Autobiography* (Ebury, 2008)

Sandbrook, Dominic, *Seasons in the Sun: the Battle for Britain, 1974–1979* (Penguin, 2012)

Shankly, Bill, *My Story, the Autobiography* (Arthur Barker, 1976)

Sheedy, Kevin, *So Good I Did it Twice: My Life from Left Field* (Sport Media, 2014)

Smith, Rory, *Mister: the Men who Taught the World How to Beat England at their Own Game* (Simon & Schuster, 2016)

Smith, Tommy, *I Did It the Hard Way* (Arthur Barker, 1980)

Smith, Tommy, *Anfield Iron, the Autobiography* (Bantam, 2008)

Souness, Graeme, *No Half Measures* (Grafton, 1985)

St John, Ian, *The Saint, My Autobiography* (Hodder & Stoughton, 2005)

St John, Ian, *Room at the Kop* (Pelham, 1966)

Szymanski, Stefan and Kuypers, Tim, *Winners & Losers: the Business Strategy of Football* (Viking, 1999)

Taylor, Daniel, *I Believe in Miracles: the Remarkable Story of Brian Clough's European Cup Winning Team* (Headline, 2015)

Taylor, Rogan and Ward, Andrew, *Kicking & Screaming: an Oral History of Football in England* (Robson, 1995)

Thompson, Phil, *Stand Up Pinocchio: My Life Inside Anfield* (Sport Media, 2005)

Toshack, John, *Tosh, an Autobiography* (Arthur Barker, 1982)

Walker, Michael, *Up There: the North-East Football Boom & Bust* (De Coubertin, 2014)

Whelan, Ronnie, *Walk On: My Life in Red* (Simon & Schuster, 2011)

Williams, John, *Red Men: Liverpool Football Club, the Biography* (Mainstream, 2010)

Wilson, Jonathan, *The Outsider: a History of the Goalkeeper* (Orion, 2012)

Wilson, Jonathan with Murray, Scott, *The Anatomy of Liverpool: a History in Ten Matches* (Orion, 2013)

Wilson, Jonathan, *Inverting the Pyramid: a History of Football Tactics* (Orion, 2008)

ACKNOWLEDGEMENTS

I am privileged to count three of the outstanding sportswriters of these times as friends and I thank them – Simon Hughes, Ian Ladyman and Michael Walker – for their immense wisdom and patient counsel. Jamie Carragher's help in providing historical perspective and tactical interpretation was more valuable than he may know. John Keith knew Bob like none other and his willingness to share his own vast knowledge has helped this book hugely along its way. It has been a privilege to have my former *Independent* colleague Phil Shaw, one of the very best football writers and historian, casting his steely eye over the proofs.

Others from the same great community of reporters who dig, inquire, find out and do journalism's hard yards have offered their insight freely. So, thank you, Jonathan Wilson, Oliver Kay, Daniel Taylor, Mark Platt, Rory Smith, Simon Hart, Miguel Delaney, Jonathan Northcroft, Patrick Barclay, Tim Rich, Paul Newman, Simon O'Hagan, Raphael Honigstein, Pete Jenson, Robin Scott-Elliot, Rob Harris, Mark Ogden and Chris Wathan. The reporters who covered Bob's life and work knew him like none other – John Roberts, Ian Ross, Mike Ellis, Nick Hilton have also shared their memories so generously and I am indebted to them all for that.

It has been a privilege to come to know Bob Paisley's wonderful family, without whom this book would be a shadow of its final form. Thank you, Graham, Christine, Robert and Ian, for your kindness, patience, steadfastness and generous hospitality.

There has been no greater inspiration in this past year than times spent with my dear friends Nick and Helen Harris. They are a source of strength to me every day.

So many of Bob's players and colleagues have given their time, too – raking through the memories and putting up with obscure questions about events half a lifetime ago. An afternoon discussing those times in the company of Peter Robinson, a kind, shrewd and gracious man, was a most precious experience. Thanks to so many players: Graeme Souness, Owen Brown, John Toshack, Roy Evans, David Fairclough, Steve Heighway, Phil Thompson, Phil Neal, Howard Gayle, Joey Jones, David Johnson, Alan Kennedy, Ian St John, Jimmy Case, Ian Callaghan, Mark Lawrenson, Peter Cormack, David Hodgson, Chris Lawler, Steve Ogrizovic, Paul Jewell, Trevor Birch, as well as Nottingham Forest's Ian Bowyer and Garry Birtles. And so many others: Alan Brown, Professor Phil Scraton, Steve Hothersall, Ron Atkinson, Lawrie McMenemy, Jimmy Armfield, Professor Rogan Taylor, Ian St John Jr, Cameron Toshack, Steve Shakeshaft, Alastair Machray, Chris Eakin, John Toker, Stephen Done, Tony Pastor, Stephen Feber, Charles Hughes, Alf Bennett and Clive Tyldesley.

To have spent most of a journalistic lifetime on the *Independent* is a privilege I did not dream of when I started out, and I have my colleagues to thank for allowing me to disappear to write this book. Thanks to Matt Gatward, my superb Sports Editor, and Dan Gledhill, whose own football affinities perhaps provided an ulterior motive. I could mention so many of the colleagues I have worked with on our great paper, but nearly ten years ago Matt Tench gave me a chance to write about sport, for which I will always be grateful. His river of ideas remains an inspiration. Thanks, too, Neil Robinson, for some great times. The changing world for the publication which we have all loved has made some of these working relationships far too brief.

Thank you to David Luxton – agent, friend, patient guide – for the phone call which elicited the hour or so of talk, which elicited the book. Thank you to Bloomsbury, who have opened my eyes to their world of energy, creativity, innovation and grace – especially my wonderful editor, Charlotte Atyeo, who with wisdom, patience and great tact helped me to bring to life my depiction of Bob when it was not always there. I am indebted to Ian Preece, the most superb copy-editor, and Holly Jarrald, managing editor and another great member of Bloomsbury's team.

The books, newspapers and magazines consumed during the journey have seemed infinite but the Liverpool Football Club statistical website www.lfchistory.net has been more valuable than any and is a treasure trove of information. Thank you, Arnie Baldursson and Gudmundur Magnusson for building and maintaining this wonderful structure. Thank you to the staff of the British Library and Liverpool Central Library for always being so willing to help. The National Football Museum's Collection Officer, Alex Jackson, was a mine of information as always, navigating me through the museum's archive at Preston.

Last, but obviously not least, thanks go to my family: my brother Pete, with whom I've shared all the football adventures worth having, and my mum and dad, Colin and Jean, for furnishing us both with all the chances to enjoy them. Thanks to Ben for your encouragement and for the inspiration your own superb journalism brings me. To Emily and George for your jokes, tea and brilliant company. And to Alice, for your critical eye, your sense, your love and your unending tolerance.

Styal, Cheshire. November 2016

INDEX

INDEX